My **TV**
for Seniors

Michael Miller

que®

My TV for Seniors

ISBN-13: 978-0-1355-9155-0
ISBN-10: 0-1355-9155-4

Library of Congress Control Number: 2019931696

2 2019

Editor-in-Chief
Mark Taub

Executive Editor
Laura Norman

Marketing
Stephane Nakib

Director, AARP Books
Jodi Lipson

Development Editor
Wordsmithery, LLC

Technical Editor
Jeri Usbay

Managing Editor
Sandra Schroeder

Project Editor
Lori Lyons

Indexer
Ken Johnson

Proofreader
Debbie Williams

Editorial Assistant
Cindy Teeters

Designer
Chuti Prasertsith

Compositor
Bronkella Publishing

Contents at a Glance

Table of Contents

3 **Getting Local and Broadcast Television Over the Air**   **55**

7   **Watching the Big Three Streaming Services: Amazon Prime Video, Hulu, and Netflix**   **171**

11   Watching Streaming Sports—Live!   **265**

12 **Watching Streaming TV on Your Phone, Tablet, or Computer** **285**

About the Author

Michael Miller is a popular and prolific writer of more than 200 non-fiction books, known for his ability to explain complex topics to everyday readers. He writes about a variety of topics, including technology, business, and music. His best-selling books for Que include *My Facebook for Seniors*, *My Social Media for Seniors*, *My Internet for Seniors*, *My Smart Home for Seniors*, *My iPad for Seniors*, *My Samsung Galaxy S7 for Seniors*, *My Windows 10 Computer for Seniors*, *Easy Computer Basics*, and *Computer Basics: Absolute Beginner's Guide*. Worldwide, his books have sold more than 1.5 million copies.

Find out more at the author's website: www.millerwriter.com

Follow the author on Twitter: molehillgroup

Dedication

To my father, who always brought home the latest and greatest televisions from his TV and appliance store when I was a kid.

Acknowledgments

Thanks to all the folks at Que/Pearson who helped make this book a reality, including but not limited to Laura Norman, Charlotte Kughen, Chhavi Vig, Lori Lyons, and Tricia Bronkella. Thanks also to technical editor Jeri Usbay, who verified all the technical details in the book. Special thanks to Jodi Lipson at AARP for conceiving the idea for the book and helping to make it take shape. Thanks also to my neighbor, Kim Glatt, for letting me use and take photos of her DirecTV system; and to my oldest stepdaughter, Kristi Lee, for letting me use her Apple TV device, and to my youngest stepdaughter, Amy Rogneby, for letting me take pictures of her Samsung TV menus. Additional thanks to those folks and companies who provided access to the streaming services and hardware discussed in this book: Chad Campbell (Acorn TV), Travis DeLingua (DC Universe/Spark PR), Felicia Pollack (CBS Interactive), Jennifer Press (fuboTV), Olivia Proffit (Google), Deborah Schonfeld (BritBox/BBC), Eileen Tanner (Philo/Zebra Partners), and Emily Weichert (HBO).

About AARP

AARP is a nonprofit, nonpartisan organization, with a membership of nearly 38 million, that helps people turn their goals and dreams into *real possibilities*™, strengthens communities, and fights for the issues that matter most to families such as healthcare, employment and income security, retirement planning, affordable utilities, and protection from financial abuse. Learn more at aarp.org.

This book is part of AARP's TV for Grownups initiative.

We Want to Hear from You!

As the reader of this book, *you* are our most important critic and commentator. We value your opinion and want to know what we're doing right, what we could do better, what areas you'd like to see us publish in, and any other words of wisdom you're willing to pass our way.

We welcome your comments. You can email or write to let us know what you did or didn't like about this book—as well as what we can do to make our books better.

Please note that we cannot help you with technical problems related to the topic of this book.

When you write, please be sure to include this book's title and author as well as your name and email address. We will carefully review your comments and share them with the author and editors who worked on the book.

Email: community@informit.com

Reader Services

Register your copy of *My TV for Seniors* at informit.com for convenient access to downloads, updates, and corrections as they become available. To start the registration process, go to www.informit.com/register and log in or create an account*. Enter the product ISBN, 9780135591550, and click Submit. Once the process is complete, you will find any available bonus content under Registered Products.

*Be sure to check the box that you would like to hear from us in order to receive exclusive discounts on future editions of this product.

In this chapter, you learn all about the latest video technologies and how to choose the right television for your viewing needs.

→ Bigger, Better, and Sharper: High-Definition TV
→ Different Types of Screens
→ Screens of All Shapes and Sizes
→ Getting Smart About Smart TVs
→ Shopping for a New TV: A Checklist
→ Adjusting Your Set for the Best Picture

Choosing the Right TV

TV has changed a lot since we had just three networks (and maybe a local independent station) to choose from. Today you can find great programming—classics and new shows, dramas, sitcoms, sports, movies, documentaries, and so much more—available on hundreds of broadcast, cable, satellite, and streaming channels and services.

The technology we use to view this programming has changed a lot, too. When I was growing up in the 1960s we watched whatever we could watch on a huge piece of furniture (that took up a lot of space in the living room) with a small black-and-white screen. The television sets of my youth used ancient cathode ray tube (CRT) technology to display their fuzzy pictures; inside the massive wood cabinet was an equally massive chassis into which a dozen or more heat-producing vacuum tubes were plugged. These television sets of old were big and heavy and needed servicing a few times a year. They didn't even have remote controls.

Today's TVs are much improved. Everything has been transistorized and computerized so it all fits into a very thin unit. All the sets feature flat-screen displays with high-definition resolution—the screens are bigger and wider and a heck of a lot sharper than what we used to have in our living rooms. And they all have fancy, albeit somewhat complicated, remote controls.

If you still have an older CRT-type television, you need to ditch that beloved monstrosity and buy a new flat-screen TV. Heck, even if you have an older flat-screen TV you might want to look into the latest and greatest models; there's been a lot of technological advancement in the past few years, all in the interest of delivering a better picture at a lower cost. All the new programming you like will look better on a newer flat-screen TV!

Bigger, Better, and Sharper: High-Definition TV

High-definition (HD) television provides a sharper, more life-like widescreen picture than anything you've seen before. It's perfect for movies, sporting events, and just about anything else. And because the picture is sharper, it can also be bigger; you can sit closer to a bigger HD screen than you can an older, standard-definition one.

Understanding HD

It's hard to believe that the HD format has been around for 20 years. The first HD televisions went on sale in 1998, and since 2013 the only kinds of TVs available have been HD models.

Unlike the previous standard-definition format, which was analog in nature, HD is a digital format. That means that HD signals are encoded and transmitted digitally, via a series of binary bits. This results in exact fidelity to the original programming source.

More importantly, HD offers much higher resolution than the older standard-definition format. A standard-definition television picture is composed of approximately 300,000 picture elements, called *pixels*. The HD picture is composed of up to 2 million pixels—more than six times the picture information previously. As you can imagine, this results in a much more detailed and lifelike picture.

Pixel Measurements

A pixel (short for "picture element") is a single point onscreen. Video displays are created from thousands (or millions) of pixels, arranged in rows and columns. The pixels are so close together that, from the proper distance, they appear connected—and create a complete picture.

There are actually three HD formats in use today—720p, 1080i, and 1080p.

The 720p HD format (sometimes called *HD ready*) features 1,280 vertical lines of pixels and 720 horizontal ones. When you multiply 1,280 by 720, you get a total resolution of 921,600 pixels. In this format, the horizontal lines (called *scan lines*) that make up the picture are displayed *progressively*, one after the other. (That's the "p" in 720p.) This format is best for programming with lots of motion, such as sports; 720p is used by a handful of broadcasters, primarily ABC and ESPN.

SDTV

The older standard-definition (SD) format employed just 640 vertical and 480 horizontal lines, for a total resolution of 307,200 pixels. Unless, that is, it was a widescreen picture; then it was 720 × 480 lines for a total of 345,600 pixels.

The second HD format is 1080i HD, which features 1,920 vertical lines of pixels and 1,080 horizontal lines. When you multiply 1,920 by 1,080, you get a total resolution of 2,073,600 pixels, or 2 *megapixels*. In this format, half the horizontal scan lines are displayed first, then the other half are *interlaced* between them. (That's the "i" in 1080i.) The 1080i format is sharper than 720p, although, because of the interlaced lines, it's not as responsive to fast movement. This format is used by the majority of broadcast and cable/satellite channels, including CBS and NBC.

The final HD format is dubbed 1080p HD (sometimes called *full HD)*. It has the same 1920 × 1080 resolution as the 1080i format, but the lines are displayed progressively, as in the 720p format. This is the format used by Blu-ray discs and players and most streaming media players—but not by any broadcasters.

Although some budget HD televisions with smaller screens incorporate 1280 × 720 pixel displays, the vast majority of sets (especially those 40" or larger) have

1920 × 1080 pixel displays. These sets can display programming in all three formats—720p, 1080i, and 1080p.

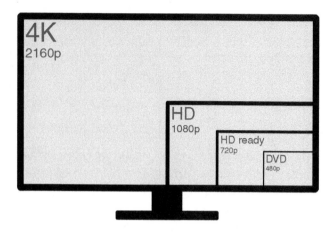

Comparing 480 SD, 720 HD, 1080 full HD, and 4K Ultra HD pictures.

Beyond HD: Ultra HD

As you might expect with any twenty-year-old technology, there have been improvements made in the HD format over the past two decades. These improvements aim to reproduce an even sharper picture than regular HD.

The most noticeable improvement is an increase in resolution. Today's high-end televisions are capable of displaying what is called 4K Ultra High Definition, or Ultra HD. The 4K Ultra HD picture is 3,840 wide by 2,160 pixels tall, for a total of 8 megapixels. That's four times sharper than the normal 2 megapixel HD picture—hence the "4K" moniker. (This format is also called 2160p.)

It doesn't stop there. There's an even newer, higher resolution HD format just now hitting the market, called 8K Ultra HD. This format is 7,680 pixels wide by 4,320 pixels tall, for a total of 33 megapixels. That's a little more than eight times sharper than 4K Ultra HD, and why it's called "8K." (This format is also called 4320p.)

You might think that a TV capable of reproducing 4K or 8K Ultra HD would cost more than a normal HD set—and you'd be at least partially right. That was certainly the case a year or two ago, when 4K sets were very much on the pricey side. Today, however, 4K Ultra HD has kind of hit the mainstream; you can find 55" 4K Ultra HD sets priced just a little higher than comparable HD sets (less than $500 USD), which isn't too pricey at all. The newer 8K Ultra HD sets, however, are considerably more expensive (when you can find them; there aren't a whole lot of models available yet), running well more than $10,000 USD.

Upscaling

All HD televisions will automatically convert lower-resolution programming to the highest resolution available. This is called upscaling, and it involves duplicating scan lines to fill in the space available in the higher-resolution format. For example, normal HD sets upscale standard-definition programming to the 1080p format; 4K Ultra HD sets will upscale not only standard-definition but also regular HD programming to 4K Ultra HD resolution.

But here's the thing—there isn't a lot of 4K or 8K Ultra HD programming available yet. Broadcast and cable networks are committed to the 720p and 1080i formats, so any normal television you watch is limited to those resolutions. DirecTV has a single 4K channel, but that's not much. For a wider variety of 4K programming, you can turn to the various streaming video services; Amazon Prime, Hulu, and Netflix offer some of their original series in 4K Ultra HD. In addition, you can purchase or rent 4K versions of some movies from iTunes, UltraFlix, Vudu, and other online retailers.

Finally, some studios sell 4K Ultra HD versions of their movies on Blu-ray disc. Of course, you need a 4K Ultra HD Blu-ray player (available for $100 to $300 USD) to play them on your 4K Ultra HD television.

Table 1.1 compares the various HD standards you may encounter.

Table 1.1 HD Formats

Format	Resolution (pixels)	Total Pixels (megapixels)	Scanning	Aspect Ratio
SD (standard-definition)	640 × 480	0.3 MP	Interlaced	4:3
720p HD	1280 × 720	0.9 MP	Progressive	16:9
1080i HD	1920 × 1080	2 MP	Interlaced	16:9
1080p HD	1920 × 1080	2 MP	Progressive	16:9
4K Ultra HD (2160p)	3840 × 2160	8 MP	Progressive	16:9
8K Ultra HD (4320p)	7680 × 4320	33 MP	Progressive	16:9

>>>*Go Further*

IS ULTRA HD THAT MUCH BETTER?

Ultra HD technology isn't just for high-end sets anymore; the 4K picture is creeping into lower-priced and smaller-screen models from almost all manufacturers. But is Ultra HD that much better than standard HD?

You'll really notice the difference between HD and Ultra HD if you have a larger screen. If your TV screen is 50 inches or larger, the better picture is noticeable—even more so on super-large screens of 65 inches or more.

On smaller-screen TVs, the difference is hard to spot. If you're watching a TV with a 32-inch or even a 42-inch screen, Ultra HD won't look much, if any, different from regular HD. That's because the pixels are already packed fairly close together; adding more of them just isn't as noticeable as it is on a bigger screen.

So, if you're looking at a smaller-screen set, it might not be worth the extra money for Ultra HD technology. If you're shopping for larger-screen sets, however, paying extra for the sharper picture might make more sense.

Better Contrast with HDR

There's one more feature available on some 4K and 8K Ultra HD TVs today that can improve the picture of high-definition programming. High Dynamic Range, or HDR, is a technology that expands a picture's dynamic range—the contrast between the deepest blacks and the brightest whites. The higher the dynamic range, the more you can see of what was recorded; you'll see more details in both the shadows and the highlights.

There are several different standards for HDR, with names like HDR10, HDR10+, HLG, Dolby Vision, and Advanced HDR by Technicolor. All of these technologies work in a similar fashion and produce similar results.

All 4K Ultra HD TVs sold today are compatible with the original HDR10 standard and will reproduce HDR10 programming available from streaming services or 4K Ultra HD Blu-ray players. That said, some 4K programming uses the Dolby Vision standard, which many experts claim produces a superior picture. In addition, some television manufacturers embrace other standards; Samsung uses its own

HDR+ technology, and LG is supportive of Advanced HDR by Technicolor. For all practical purposes, however, HDR10 is the current standard. You shouldn't worry too much (at least yet) about the other formats.

To watch HDR programming, you'll need the following things:

- A 4K or 8K Ultra HD TV that is HDR-compatible
- A streaming media player (or smart TV with streaming functionality built in) that is HDR-compatible
- Access to HDR-formatted programming on a compatible streaming video service

Note that all manufacturers of streaming devices—including Amazon, Apple, Google, and Roku—offer 4K/HDR-compatible models, which are typically a little higher-priced than their base models.

>>>Go Further

WHERE DO YOU FIND THE BEST VIDEO CONTENT?

Now that you know all about the different HD formats and equipment, where do you find the best sources for HD programming? Broadcast TV, cable, streaming, and Blu-ray sources are all good, but some offer higher-quality video than do others. In order, here's where you can find the best HD programming audio for your viewing pleasure:

- **Blu-ray discs:** The Blu-ray format offers enough storage capacity and bandwidth to carry even the most demanding Ultra HD video content. All Blu-ray discs are in 1080p HD; many newer discs are in 4K Ultra HD with HDR.
- **Streaming video services:** Most streaming services offer 1080p HD video. Some content on some services (on compatible streaming media players) is transmitted in 4K Ultra HD with HDR.
- **Cable television:** Much programming is in 720p or 1080i HD. Some channels still transmit in standard-definition video. Some cable providers offer a few channels of 4K Ultra HD (with HDR) programming.
- **Satellite television:** As with cable television, many satellite channels are in 720p or 1080i HD.

- **Broadcast television:** Broadcast TV is capable of 720p and 1080i HD video. Some digital subchannels may be in standard definition.

- **DVDs:** The original DVD format offers standard-definition video only, although many movies are in widescreen format.

- **VHS tapes:** VHS tapes are in standard definition, but the quality is lower than that available on DVD.

Bottom line, you'll find the most content with the highest-quality video on Blu-ray discs—although streaming video services (along with cable and satellite TV) provide more high-quality content every day.

Different Types of Screens

The days of bulky CRT-type television sets are long gone. In their place are thin, lightweight models with large, widescreen displays. These flat-panel displays are so thin because they contain no picture tubes or projection devices; instead, today's displays employ liquid crystal device (LCD) technology that sandwich tiny liquid crystals between thin layers of lightweight glass.

Understanding LCD and LED Displays

A typical LCD display contains millions of individual picture elements, called *pixels*. Each pixel consists of a liquid crystal suspension sandwiched between two panels of polarized glass and contains three subpixels with red, green, and blue color filters. When electric current is applied to a pixel, it changes the angle of the light passing through the pixel so that the backlight behind it shines through and changes the color. The resulting pattern of bright and dark pixels creates the overall picture shown on the LCD display.

A Sony Bravia Masters series LCD/LED television. (Photo courtesy Sony Corporation, www.sony.com.)

Almost all of today's flat-panel TVs are advertised as having light emitting diode (LED) screens. This is somewhat misleading. These so-called LED screens are simply LCD screens that use small LEDs to illuminate the liquid crystals in the display. All LCD displays need some sort of backlighting to illuminate the screens; in the past, manufacturers used cold cathode fluorescent lamp (CCFL) technology, but that has pretty much been replaced by the more efficient LED technology, at least in higher-end models.

That said, there are two ways to use LEDs to light up LCD displays. *Edge lighting* uses LEDs positioned along the edges of the screen shining in; *full-array back-lighting* uses an array of LEDs behind the entire screen. Not surprisingly, full-array lighting produces a brighter picture with more contrast than does edge lighting, but it comes at a higher cost.

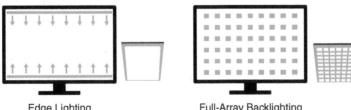

Edge Lighting   Full-Array Backlighting

Edge lighting versus full-array backlighting.

Local Dimming

Some LED LCD screens employ what is called *local dimming* technology, in which the LEDs behind the display are selectively dimmed when that part of the picture is supposed to be dark. This produces deeper blacks than screens without local dimming. (A display with full-array backlighting and local dimming is called an FALD screen—for Full-Array Local Dimming.)

>>>*Go Further*
PLASMA DISPLAYS

Before the proliferation of LCD displays, many flat-panel TVs utilized plasma display technology. Plasma displays sandwiched a layer of ionized gas between two thin layers of glass to produce what some claimed was a higher-contrast picture (with deeper blacks) than LCD displays. On the downside, plasma displays were more expensive, weighed more, used more electricity, and generated more heat than comparable LCD displays.

Today's best LCD displays approach plasma's performance, and newer OLED displays (see the next section) surpass it—making plasma displays old tech. The last plasma displays (for the consumer market) were manufactured in 2015.

Beyond LCD: OLED Displays

Adding LED backlighting makes for a better LCD display, but there's a new technology that's even better than that. Organic light emitting diode (OLED) displays don't use liquid crystals at all; instead, they employ LEDs made from an organic compound that transmits light when an electric current is applied. OLED displays don't need backlighting because they emit their own light. The result is a thinner, lighter panel that displays much deeper blacks and brighter whites than is possible with LCD technology.

Put simply, OLED displays offer the very best picture quality available today. They're also pricier than comparable LCD displays; the lowest-priced 55" OLED models currently start at $2,000 USD or so and go up from there. (Note that prices on OLED TVs are going down each year, as always happens when a new technology becomes more mainstream; by the time you read this book, expect to find even lower priced models.)

LG's ultra-thin 65" ThinQ OLED television. (Photo courtesy LG Electronics, www.lg.com.)

So if you have the money and want the best possible picture, OLED is the way to go. If your budget isn't quite so expansive, instead look for a good LCD display with LED backlighting.

QLED Displays

Just to make things more confusing, Samsung sells televisions that use what the company calls QLED technology. (QLED sounds like OLED, but it's a completely different tech.) A QLED screen is a normal LCD screen with LED backlighting, but it incorporates what Samsung calls "quantum dots," which are tiny filters that produce a purer light than traditional LEDs. Those quantum dots improve the screen's brightness levels and provide deeper blacks and brighter colors. So, QLED is better than normal LCD/LED but not as good as OLED. (Like I said, a little confusing.)

Screens of All Shapes and Sizes

Bigger isn't always better. If your TV screen is too big, the individual pixels in the picture (especially with older or standard-definition sources) will be more noticeable. The optimal screen size depends on how far away from the screen you'll be sitting, as well as the resolution of the TV screen.

Know that screen size is measured diagonally from one corner of the screen to the other. You may be interested in the height or width of a particular set (to see if it fits within a given space), but it's the diagonal measurement that we go by.

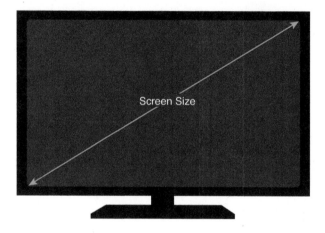

Measuring screen size, diagonally.

Determining the Right Size Display

For today's HD content, the ideal screen size is half the distance between you and the screen. So, for example, if you're watching high-definition programming and sitting 10 feet (120 inches) from the screen, the ideal screen size is half that, approximately 60 inches diagonal.

For higher-resolution 4K Ultra HD screens, however, you can sit closer—or, conversely, use a larger screen. That's because the screen elements are smaller and closer together, and thus can be comfortably viewed from a shorter distance. The rule of thumb here is to take your distance from the screen and divide by 1.5. Taking our previous example of sitting 10 feet (120 inches) from the screen, you could go with an 80" diagonal Ultra HD screen.

Table 1.2 provides a general guide to the best screen size for different viewing distances:

Table 1.2   Viewing Distance Versus Screen Size

Viewing Distance	Ideal HD Screen Size	Ideal 4K Ultra HD Screen Size
6'	36" diagonal	48" diagonal
7'	42" diagonal	56" diagonal
8'	48" diagonal	64" diagonal
9'	54" diagonal	72" diagonal
10'	60" diagonal	80" diagonal
11'	66" diagonal	88" diagonal
12'	72" diagonal	96" diagonal

Viewing Angle

Few living rooms have a single chair positioned exactly in front of the TV screen. If you have seating that is considerably off-axis from the center, consider going with a slightly larger screen.

Dealing with Different Aspect Ratios

Originally, all motion pictures were projected on a squarish screen with an aspect ratio of 4:3—which means that if a screen is four units of measurement wide, it's also three units tall. (Another way to express this aspect ratio is 1.33:1—the width is 1.33 times the height.) When television was first developed, it adopted this same 4:3 aspect ratio.

When the movie industry began to feel threatened by the rise of television in the 1950s, Hollywood responded by producing films in various widescreen formats. These formats—Panavision, Cinemascope, and the rest—provide a much wider picture than that presented by television's "little square box," with aspect ratios ranging from 1.66:1 to 2.76:1. In the widest of these formats, the picture is almost three times as wide as it is tall.

This is why the HDTV format adopted a wider screen ratio than traditional standard-definition displays. Today's HD and Ultra HD TVs have 16:9 ratio screens, so many widescreen movies (and all HD television programming) can be displayed without modification.

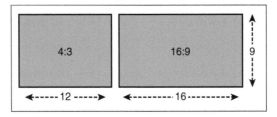

Comparing 4:3 (SD) and 16:9 (HD) aspect ratios.

Pan and Scan

Before widescreen TV displays, many programmers used the "pan and scan" technique to display parts of a film's wider image in the narrower television image area. Essentially they panned across the full image to display only the most important parts (typically the center), cutting off the edges of the widescreen picture. The result was seldom satisfactory, as it often cut off important parts of the picture and interfered with the way the director wanted the movie presented.

There are still many movies, old and new, that are filmed in a wider aspect ratio than 16:9. Some programmers present only the center of these super-wide images, although a better approach is to present the movie at its full width—which leaves some unused areas at the top and bottom of your television screen. This approach, called *letterboxing*, displays the widescreen movie in a strip across the center of your screen, with long black bars above and below the movie image.

A widescreen movie letterboxed on a 16:9 display.

What do you do if you have an older television show with a 4:3 aspect ratio? Displaying a squarish picture on a widescreen display requires some form of compromise. Some channels display older programming with its original 4:3 aspect ratio, leaving dark bars (called *pillarboxing*) on either side of the picture. Other channels zoom into the squarish picture to fill the width of the display, thus cutting off the top and bottom of the picture. Still other channels stretch the picture to fill the width (without cutting off the top and bottom), thus making everyone onscreen appear short and fat.

A 4:3 aspect program pillarboxed on a 16:9 display.

You might not like how a non-16:9 ratio program is displayed on your widescreen TV. This is why television manufacturers let you select different aspect ratios, by using either your remote control or a setup menu. (Look for a button or menu option labeled *aspect, screen, size, format,* or something similar.) You'll typically see options similar to those detailed in Table 1.3, although other options may be available, depending on your manufacturer.

Table 1.3   Typical Aspect Ratio Options

Option	Does This
Normal or Original	Displays the picture at the original aspect ratio. For 16:9 content, the picture fills the entire screen. For 4:3 content, the picture is positioned in the center of the screen with black or gray bars on either side.
Full or Stretch	All content is fit to fill the entire screen. For 16:9 content the picture is displayed at the original aspect ratio. For 4:3 content the picture is stretched to fill the entire width of the screen.
Zoom or Wide Zoom	Zooms into a smaller picture. When you zoom into a 4:3 picture, it fills the width of the screen but crops off the top and bottom.

Getting Smart About Smart TVs

There's one more feature you might want to consider when shopping for a new TV. As you'll discover throughout the balance of this book, there is a ton of great programming available over the Internet, via what we call streaming video services such as Amazon Prime Video, Hulu, and Netflix. Although you can use a separate streaming media device (such as those sold by Amazon, Apple, Google, and Roku) to access these services, many TVs sold today have the capability of receiving these services directly. These TVs are dubbed *Smart TVs*.

Streaming Media Players

Learn more about other freestanding streaming media players from Amazon, Apple, Google, and Roku in Chapter 6, "Getting Streaming Media Devices."

Proprietary Smart TVs

The primary advantage of using a Smart TV instead of a separate streaming media device is one of convenience. With a Smart TV you don't have to connect a separate device and switch to that input to watch streaming video; it's all accessible from your TV's main menu. There are no cables to connect or boxes to plug in. (Naturally, your Smart TV must be connected to the Internet—typically wirelessly, via Wi-Fi—to receive these streaming video services.)

Samsung's Smart TV interface.

Several of today's major television manufacturers—including LG, Samsung, Sony, and Vizio—offer their own proprietary Smart TV interfaces. It's all part of the TV's built-in menu system, typically accessed by a dedicated button on the set's remote control.

Unfortunately, some of these proprietary Smart TVs don't offer as many streaming services as do dedicated streaming media devices, so you might not have access to all the streaming services you want. In addition, many of these Smart TVs don't update their services with new channels as frequently as do Roku and other streaming media devices; if there's a new streaming media service launched, you might have to wait awhile to gain access to it.

Using a Streaming Media Device with a Smart TV

If you're looking at higher-end TVs, you're going to be stuck buying a Smart TV whether you want one or not. Fortunately, you can ignore your TV's built-in streaming options and still connect a separate streaming media device, like an Amazon or Roku box or stick, to your TV and use that, instead.

Fire TVs and Roku TVs

Another class of Smart TVs offers all the channels and options you'll find on a freestanding streaming media device. These are TVs that incorporate the same interfaces and functionality as you get from Amazon's Fire TV or Roku. It's like having a Fire TV or Roku device built into your TV.

A Toshiba-branded 55" 4K Ultra HD Fire TV Edition set. (Photo courtesy Compal Electronics, tvna.compal-toshiba.com.)

These so-called Fire TV Edition and Roku TVs are available from several different manufacturers, including Element, Hisense, Insignia, Sharp, TCL, and Toshiba. These TVs cost a little more than TVs without the smart interface, but are typically a better value than buying a TV and a Fire TV or Roku device separately.

A 43" 4K Ultra HD Roku TV from TCL. (Photo courtesy TCL North America, www.tclusa.com.)

You use the Fire TV or Roku interface to not only access every streaming channel their parent services offer, but also to control all of the TV's inputs and functions, using a modified Fire TV or Roku remote control. Looking at the Roku TV home screen, for example, you see options not only for Netflix, Hulu, and other streaming services, but also for a cable box, external antenna (for over-the-air TV broadcasts), and game console. You select any of these inputs just as you select your favorite streaming service.

These Fire TVs and Roku TVs have become very popular options, and are available even in smaller-screen and lower-priced models. My wife and I have a Roku TV in our bedroom, and I can attest this is both a convenient and functional way to go.

>>>Go Further

HOW TO GET RID OF YOUR OLD TV

After you've purchased a new HD or Ultra HD television, what do you do with your old TV?

Well, one thing you *can't* do is just toss it in the trash. No matter the age, style, or brand, television sets contain a variety of toxic materials—including arsenic, lead, and mercury—that can cause all sorts of harm to people and the environment. We don't want these toxic materials seeping into landfills and creating environmental hazards, so many localities have laws that prohibit the unapproved disposal of these old electronics. (People in the industry call old TVs and other electronic items *electronic waste*, or *e-waste*.)

Bottom line: You cannot put old TVs in your normal trash. You also cannot put them in your normal recycling, where you put bottles and papers and such. Instead, you need to recycle your old TV in a different, responsible manner.

The first thing to do is check with your local government to see if it offers drop-off or pick-up recycling services for old electronics—what some call *e-cycling*. Some municipalities will take your old electronics for a small fee; others offer special days each year where they'll take e-waste for free. Check with the E-Cycling Central website (www.ecyclingcentral.com) to find government-sponsored e-cycling centers and events in your area.

Another option is to check with the dealer where you purchased your new TV. If you're getting a new set delivered, some dealers will take away your old TV, too. For that matter, many retailers, such as Best Buy, offer recycling for old electronics; just drop off your old set and be done with it. (Many retailers charge for this service; for example, Best Buy charges $25 USD to recycle an old TV.)

You may also have dedicated e-cycling firms in your area. Check the Call2Recycle website (www.call2recycle.org) for e-cycling firms near you.

If your TV is still in good working condition, you don't have to throw it away. You could try selling or giving it away, although it's probably too big and heavy to easily ship across the country, which leaves out national sites such as eBay. Craigslist (www.craigslist.org) is a better choice; it's like old school classified ads, except online. If you want to sell it, browse the listings for similar products to gauge an appropriate price, then list your old set and see who's interested!

Shopping for a New TV: A Checklist

If your appetite is now sufficiently whet for a new TV for your living room or bedroom, it's time to consider just which of these many features and options you really need—and what types of sets fit within your budget.

Here are the options you should consider:

- **Price:** First, consider your budget. Prices range from less than $100 USD to more than $15,000 USD, depending on screen size and features. Although that $5,000 USD set might look really nice and have all the bells and whistles you want, it might be out of your price range. Set your top-line budget first, then determine what's the best set for your money.

- **Screen size:** Use the guidance presented earlier in this chapter to determine the right screen size for your room. In general, think of a 32" to 42" screen for most bedrooms, and 55"+ for most living rooms.

- **Screen type:** LCD screens with LED backlighting look better than straight LCD displays. OLED screens look even better than that. (You pay more for a better picture, of course.)

- **Resolution:** Is straight 1080p HD good enough for you, or do you want to pay extra for a 4K Ultra HD display? (Or, if you're looking at a 32" or smaller screen, is 720 HD good enough?)

- **Performance:** This is one you can't judge just by looking at the specs. Go to a store and look at several comparable sets. In particular, look at black levels and white levels, color reproduction, and off-angle viewing (if that matters for your room). Which set looks best to you? That's the one you want.

- **Inputs and outputs:** Almost all external devices today connect via HDMI instead of separate audio and video cables. Make sure the set you're looking at has enough HDMI inputs to handle all the devices you may have (such as cable/satellite box, DVD/Blu-ray player, streaming media device, and game console). In addition, if you're using an external sound bar or audio/video receiver (read more about them in the next chapter), make sure the set has an optical digital audio output to feed the internal sound to the external system.

Digital audio output ⸺

HDMI inputs ⸺

The input/output panel on a typical HDTV—note the HDMI inputs and digital audio output.

HDMI ARC

Some current TVs have an HDMI input labeled "ARC." This stands for Audio Return Channel, and you can use this HDMI connector to feed audio back to an external sound bar or audio/video receiver; think of it as kind of like an HDMI output for digital sound. Just connect an HDMI cable from the ARC connector to your sound bar or receiver, and all the audio from your TV will be heard from there.

- **Smart TV—or not:** Consider whether you want to have your video streaming built into your TV or from a separate media streaming device. See whether you like the streaming channels available from a given Smart TV, and whether you like the built-in interface. If you're a Roku or Amazon Fire TV user, consider a TV with Roku or Fire TV built in.

- **Remote control:** Take a look at the remote that comes with the TV. Make sure it's one you're comfortable with. Some remotes are covered in dozens of buttons for individual functions; others let you navigate with just a few simple buttons. Some remotes can operate other devices in your system; conversely, you might be able to operate your TV from another device's remote, or use a universal remote to operate all your devices.

A typical TV remote control from Sony. (Photo courtesy Sony Corporation, www.sony.com.)

Also consider how you want to mount your new TV. Most sets come with a stand of some sort that works if you want to put it on a table or other piece of furniture. If you'd rather mount your flat-screen TV on a wall, look into the mounting kits that are available. Most TVs have standard-size holes on the back that most any bracket can connect to. (This is called the VESA Interface Mounting Standard, which makes it really easy to choose the right mount.) Many retailers also offer installation services, which is nice if you have to run a few cables inside the wall behind your TV.

Curved Screens and 3D

Every few years TV manufacturers jump on the latest fad, and often those fads don't last. Two cases in point are curved screens and 3D viewing—both of which were widely trumpeted several years back, and both of which are now absent from current models.

>>>Go Further

WHERE TO BUY?

If you're in the market for a new TV, where should you shop? Although I always prefer to shop at local merchants, who typically provide hands-on service before and after the sale, the number of small, locally owned TV retailers has dwindled to almost zero. If you have a local electronics store in your area, that's a great place to shop; if not, there are a number of larger regional and national retailers that offer a good selection of sets at all screen sizes.

When you want someone you can go back to if something goes wrong, it makes sense to buy from a physical retailer in your area. Lots of big-box stores sell TVs these days, including Best Buy (www.bestbuy.com), Costco (www.costco.com), Sam's Club (www.samsclub.com), Target (www.target.com), and Walmart (www.walmart.com). Some even offer delivery and installation.

If you're comfortable unboxing, setting up, and installing your TV yourself, then shopping at an online retailer makes sense. Most traditional retailers (such as those I just mentioned) offer an even larger selection online, and they offer the benefit of returning to a local store if you have issues. There are also many online-only retailers, such as Amazon (www.amazon.com), B&H Photo and Video (www.bhphotovideo.com), and Crutchfield (www.crutchfield.com), that offer a variety of models for sale via their websites. You can even find a variety of new and used TVs for sale from both large and small sellers on eBay (www.ebay.com).

Adjusting Your Set for the Best Picture

Whether you have a brand new TV or a slightly older one, there are several adjustments you can make to get the best picture possible. Here are a few tips to consider:

Choosing a picture mode on a Samsung TV.

- **Use the right preset:** When in doubt, use your set's menu system and switch to Standard or Normal mode; this works best for most content. Avoid Dynamic or Vivid mode (which may be the default); this is a pumped-up picture mode that looks good in the store but is overkill in your living room. Movie or Cinema mode is good for watching movies (as well as most TV programming), Sports mode is good for the rapid motion of sporting events, and Game mode is optimized for playing videogames. Or you can select Custom and adjust all the settings individually for your own personal preferences.

Configuring the expert picture settings on a Samsung TV.

- **Adjust brightness and contrast:** If you select the Custom or Expert mode, your picture will look a little more natural if you back off the brightness control a bit; too bright and everything looks washed out. The contrast control is just the opposite, however—you can turn this one all the way up, in most instances.

- **Tone down the sharpness:** It might sound counterintuitive, but your picture will probably look a little better if you turn down the sharpness control a little. Too sharp and you see all the little flaws in the picture; a little less sharp and things look more pleasant.

- **Adjust the color:** If you're doing custom adjustments, you might want to tweak the color (also called color saturation) control. You probably don't need to touch the tint control (most sets do a good job of this automatically), but you might find that turning down the saturation just a tad makes for a more pleasing picture.

- **Adjust color temperature:** Most sets let you configure the display's color temperature. Neutral isn't a bad choice; going warmer will bring out the oranges and reds in the picture, while choosing a cooler setting will shift the colors toward the blue side of things.

- **Turn off motion smoothing:** Most newer TVs have a feature, typically called Motion or Motion Smoothing, that artificially adjusts the set's frame rate to compensate for the motion blurring that occurs when LCD screens attempt to reproduce rapid motion, like that found in video games and sports programming. (Okay, not golf, but just about every other sport.) Unfortunately, when you turn on motion smoothing, it makes most other programming, including movies, look as if it's a cheap soap opera shot on video tape. (In fact, experts call this the "soap opera effect.") The solution is to turn off or turn down the motion smoothing control when you're not watching sports channels or playing games.

- **Turn on HDR:** If you have a 4K or 8K Ultra HD set that is HDR-compatible, make sure that HDR is turned on. You probably want to select the automatic setting, which chooses the right HDR format for the current programming. (You might also be able to select individual HDR formats, but that's a trickier thing.)

In addition, where you put your set will affect its picture. Avoid placing your screen where it's hit by direct lighting, either from a lamp or open window. A slightly darkened room works best. And the closer you can sit to the center of the screen, the better; many displays look darker or duller when viewed too far off-angle.

>>>Go Further

WHATEVER HAPPENED TO THOSE TV BRANDS FROM THE PAST?

I grew up in a TV family. My father owned a TV and appliance store in Speedway, Indiana, and I spent a good portion of my childhood and young adult years in that store, cleaning and moving and eventually selling all manner of televisions and other electronics. Every few months or so my dad would bring home the latest and greatest set for us to use, which in the 1960s meant a big, heavy piece of furniture known as a console TV, typically with a 23" to 25" diagonal screen. (That was really big at the time, but it pales in comparison to the 55"+ models in most homes today.) Before 1965 or so, the TVs were all black and white; after that, everything changed to living color.

My father was an RCA dealer, and RCA was one of the two big brands throughout the 1960s, '70s, and early '80s. The other big name was Zenith, and the two companies, both U.S.-based, made some very good sets for the time. It was a friendly but intense rivalry.

Of course, there were other, smaller, American TV brands back then, too, including Admiral, Curtis-Mathes, General Electric, Magnavox, Motorola, Philco, and Sylvania. Starting in the late '60s and growing throughout the '70s and '80s, Japanese brands like Hitachi, JVC, Mitsubishi, Panasonic, Sony, and Toshiba came to challenge the American-based manufacturers. Sony especially, with its innovative Trinitron models, became a significant player in the market, as the hardware components inside the sets evolved from vacuum tube-based to solid state (no tubes).

The consumer electronics market became much more competitive (and much less profitable) during the 1980s. In 1985, the struggling RCA Corporation was sold to General Electric, which four years later sold the consumer electronics division to Thomson Consumer Electronics (now known as Technicolor SA), a large French-based electronics manufacturer. The equally struggling Zenith met a similar fate in 1995, when South Korean giant LG Electronics acquired a controlling interest in the company, buying the entire company in 1999.

As to the brands themselves, Thomson/Technicolor really never navigated the move from cathode ray tube (CRT) displays to flat-screen technologies, and the RCA brand faded surprisingly quickly from the scene; today, Technicolor licenses the RCA name to Curtis International, a Canadian company that markets low-end TVs made overseas. Similarly, LG eventually did away with the Zenith brand in favor of its own name, so there haven't been Zenith-branded sets in the market for more than a decade.

The major Japanese manufacturers took advantage of this upheaval in the marketplace and made a big name for themselves in the late 1980s and 1990s. But in the twenty-first century, South Korean and Chinese manufacturers took over the market, producing higher-quality sets at lower prices. Today, the leading global TV manufacturers are LG Electronics (Korean), Samsung (Korean), Sony (Japanese), Hisense (Chinese), and TCL (Chinese). The first three compete at the higher end of the market while the latter two produce some very fine sets at lower price points. There's also Vizio, which is an American-based company that manufacturers all its sets in China and Mexico, and Insignia, which is Best Buy's house brand (also manufactured overseas).

There have been a lot of changes in the electronics industry over the years, and today's TV sets are far better (and bigger!) than anything manufactured in my youth. Still, I miss those days of big, heavy RCA and Zenith television consoles taking a prominent position in living rooms across America. Today's TVs are great, but yesterday's models hold a special place in my memories—and yours too, probably.

Getting Better Sound

Your flat-screen TV includes two or more built-in speakers. They might sound okay to you, especially when you're listening to a news channel or late-night talk show. But those built-in speakers might be inadequate when you're listening to a concert or watching an explosion-filled action movie. You might even have trouble discerning normal dialogue from those tiny built-in speakers.

What can you do if the sound on your new TV isn't as good as its high-definition picture? Fortunately, you have several options—some of which sound really impressive.

Reading What You Hear with Closed Captions

If your room is especially noisy or if you're a little hard of hearing, it may be difficult to make out what people are saying in a television program. Sometimes the only way you can understand what's being said onscreen is to turn on a show's closed captions and read the dialogue. It's a common solution; my wife and I use closed captions all the time, especially for shows where the characters tend to mumble or speak very quickly.

In most instances, you turn on closed captioning from your programming source. This means finding the closed captions setting on your cable or satellite box, streaming media player, or Blu-ray player. Some devices have a "captions" button right on the remote; others force you to hunt through the menu system until you find the right setting.

For example, if you're using a Roku streaming media player, you can activate captions for all installed apps (channels), or within a given app for that particular channel. To turn on universal captions, go to Settings, Accessibility, Captions Mode and select On Always. To turn on or off captions for a specific app/channel, press the Options (*) button on the Roku remote and then select the caption track you want.

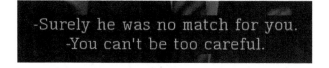

Watching closed captions on a Roku media player.

If you're watching TV from a set-top cable box, press the Menu button on your cable remote control and navigate to settings or setup screen. From there you can find the captions or closed captioning option, and turn it on.

However you do it, closed captioning is a boon for those of us who are a little hard of hearing or have to listen in noisy rooms. Closed captions are also great when you need to mute the sound but still want to watch your favorite program; you can read what's happening without having to hear it!

Getting Better Sound from Headphones

Another low-cost solution when you have trouble hearing what's on your TV is to invest in a set of wired or wireless headphones. A good set of headphones lets you adjust the sound you hear to your taste. You can also use headphones to listen to your favorite programs at night without disturbing others in your home. Just put on your headphones, mute the normal TV sound, and you're watching and listening in your own private world.

Although you can plug any set of earbuds or headphones in the audio jack on the front of most TV sets, a better approach for most living rooms is to invest in a set of wireless headphones. These units let you connect a wireless transmitter to your TV's audio jack so you can listen to your headphones via Bluetooth or RF technology—no wires necessary. Most of these units have their own volume controls; you can control your personal volume level without adjusting the sound on your TV.

A set of wireless headphones (and transmitter) from Sony Corporation.
(Photo courtesy Sony, www.sony.com.)

There are a variety of wireless headphones for TV use available for less than $100 USD, with higher-quality models running up to $400 USD or more. Look for a reputable brand and, if you can, try them out before you buy them. You want headphones that are comfortable when you're wearing them for long periods of time and that deliver the sound you need.

Enhancing TV Audio with a Sound Bar

When you want to improve your TV sound substantially, you can replace your set's internal speakers with a set of external speakers, in the form of a freestanding *sound bar*. A sound bar is simply an array of two or more speakers in a single enclosure. You position the sound bar underneath or in front of your TV screen. The additional speakers replace your TV's built-in speakers, and provide much better sound for music, movies, and dialogue.

How Sound Bars Work

The lowest-priced sound bars include just two speakers—left and right. Higher-priced models include four or more speakers. Almost all sound bars are "active" speakers, meaning they have their own built-in amplifiers, typically more powerful than the amp that drives your TV's built-in speakers.

The sound bar itself is a short and wide enclosure, anywhere from 1' to 5' wide. If your TV is wall-mounted, you can mount the sound bar directly underneath the screen on your wall. If your TV is on a table-top stand, you typically position the sound bar in front of the stand, underneath and in front of the TV screen.

JBL's Bar Studio 2-channel sound bar with four speakers.
(Photo courtesy Harman International Industries, www.harmankardon.com.)

All sound bars reproduce stereo sound, so you'll hear a program's right and left channels more clearly and distinctly than from your TV's speakers. Many sound bars also include a discrete center channel speaker, typically used for dialogue; this will help you hear voices more clearly than you would otherwise.

Some sound bars attempt to simulate surround sound. (I talk more about surround sound later in this chapter.) These sound bars use various audio techniques to trick your ears into thinking you're hearing sound coming from beside and behind you—even though the sound bar itself is very clearly positioned in front of you. Depending on the sound bar, this simulated surround sound might sound a little fake, or it might be surprisingly effective. If you want surround sound from a sound bar, it's worth your time to audition it at a dealer before you buy.

For more authentic surround sound, look for a sound bar with additional surround speakers. These auxiliary speakers are typically wireless, connecting via Bluetooth technology to the main sound bar.

Although most sound bars sound considerably better than your TV's internal speakers, the speakers in a sound bar are still somewhat small and might have trouble reproducing deep bass tones. That is, they might still sound tinny, especially when you listen to music or movies with lots of rumbling and explosions.

For this reason, many sound bars come with a separate speaker, called a *subwoofer*, for those bass notes. The subwoofer is a bigger speaker than those in the sound bar itself, and it does a better job with those low tones. Because the sound of a subwoofer is so low it's nondirectional, which means you can place it anywhere convenient in your room. Just remember that a subwoofer contains its own power amplifier, and you must connect it to a power source to work. Most subwoofers in these systems connect to the sound bar wirelessly, via Bluetooth.

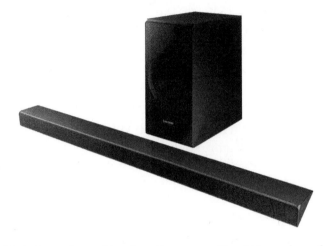

A 3.1-channel sound bar from Samsung with wireless subwoofer.
(Photo courtesy Samsung, www.samsung.com.)

When shopping for a sound bar, you'll find the number of channels it reproduces is indicated by a number, like 2.1, 3.1, or 5.1.2. The first numeral in this designation alignment tells you how many channels of audio the sound bar reproduces. The "2" in 2.1 means two channels, and the "3" in 3.1 means three channels. A two-channel sound bar reproduces two front channels: left and right. A three-channel sound bar reproduces three front channels: left, right, and center. (The center channel is typically for dialogue.) A five-channel sound bar reproduces the front three channels along with left and right surround (side) channels. A seven-channel sound bar adds right and left rear channels to the front and surround channels.

The second numeral in the designation tells you whether the sound bar includes a separate subwoofer for low bass tones. If it does, you'll see the number "1," as in 5.1. If it doesn't, you'll see a "0," as in 2.0.

If a sound bar's numeric designation includes a third number (not all do), such as 5.1.2, the third number indicates the number of Dolby Atmos channels, which add "height" to the bar's sound. I discuss Dolby Atmos in the "Understanding Surround Sound" section, later in this chapter.

There are lots of different sound bar models available from lots of different manu-facturers, including Bose, JBL, LG, Samsung, Sonos, Vizio, and Yamaha. Prices run from less than $100 USD to more than $1,000 USD. The more expensive models typically feature more speakers in the bar (up to a dozen or more!), bigger speak-ers (especially for the subwoofer), and more powerful amplifiers. In general, the more money you spend, the better quality sound you'll hear.

Amplifier Power

Amplifier power is measured in number of watts (W). For example, a 300W amp is more powerful than a 100W amp. Power is sometimes rated on a per-channel basis, as in 40W/channel, or with all channels added together (four channels at 40W/channel equal 160W total system power).

Connect a Sound Bar to Your TV

Connecting a sound bar is as simple as running a cable from the audio output on your TV to the input jack on the back of the sound bar. In most cases you do this with a thin and flexible optical digital audio cable. (Most sound bars include an optical digital audio cable; if not, you can purchase one for less than $10 USD at any store that sells electronics equipment.) It's a quick and simple operation.

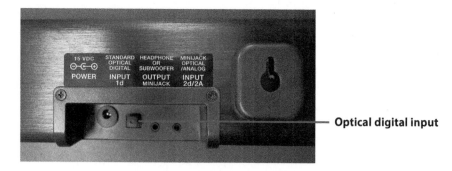

Optical digital input

Connect an optical digital audio cable from your TV to the optical digital input on the sound bar.

Some sound bars let you connect external devices, such as a cable/satellite box or streaming media player, directly to the sound bar itself, instead of to your TV. This lets you use the sound bar's remote to control switching between components. If you want to go this route (and you don't have to, if you're happy switching inputs from your TV), simply connect the HDMI cables from each device to the appropriate HDMI inputs on your sound bar. You then connect an HDMI cable from your sound bar to an HDMI input on your TV.

Turn Off Your TV's Internal Speakers

Because the sound bar has much better-sounding audio than your TV's built-in speakers, you want to turn off those internal speakers when using your sound bar. You do this from your TV's setup menu; it's a little different on each set, but the following general instructions apply.

(1) Open your TV's setup menu and navigate to the Audio or Sound section.

(2) Select the sound output option.

(3) Turn off your TV's internal speaker. Or......

(4) Select the external speaker setting. (On some sets, you can choose which external output you want to use—digital audio or HDMI.)

(1) (2)

Sound		Select your preferred sound output device.
Sound Output		TV Speaker
Sound Mode	·	Standard
Wi-Fi Speaker Surround S...		
Expert Settings		

(3)

Sound Output

Select an audio device from the list to play TV sound.

TV Speaker   ılı

Receiver(HDMI)

Audio Out/Optical   Close

Speaker List

(4)

Understanding Surround Sound

Your TV's internal speakers might be fine if you're listening to simple right/left stereo soundtracks, but most of today's HD programming—both movies and TV shows—uses more audio channels than that. We're living in a world where soundtracks are designed to envelop the viewer from the front, both sides, behind, and even above the TV screen.

Virtually all movies and TV shows made over the past several decades use *surround sound*, which places the soundtrack all around the listener. Dialogue comes from the front of the room, special effects come from behind, and music fills the entire listening space. This is especially noticeable in special effects–laden action/ adventure films; because your television has only front speakers, you need something more to experience these soundtracks as they're meant to be heard.

To experience the full immersive surround sound experience, you need to move beyond your TV's built-in speakers and even beyond sound bars to a full-fledged surround sound system. But before you make that leap, it helps to understand just what surround sound means.

Counting Surround Channels

Surround sound for home video has been around in one form or another for more than 30 years. There are various surround sound formats available today, differing mainly in the number of audio channels available.

The most basic surround format, and the one used in most HDTV broadcasts, is designated as 5.1 surround. The "5" in this format means that it can reproduce up to five main channels of audio—front left, front center (typically located just above or below the television screen), right center, left surround, and right surround. Many listeners mistakenly place their surround speakers at the rear of the room, but these speakers are designed to literally surround the listener by being placed to the sides of the primary listening location, level with or just slightly above your ears.

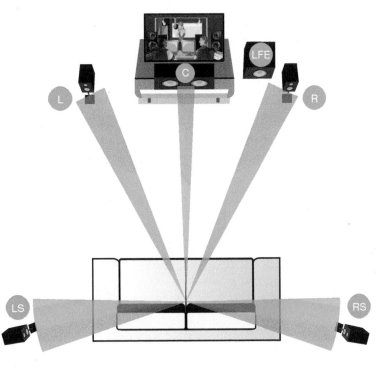

A typical 5.1-channel surround setup.

Different Channels for Different Purposes

In most instances, the center channel in a surround sound system is used primarily for dialogue, where characters are typically speaking from the center of the screen. The front left and right speakers are used for music and off-center dialogue, whereas the surround and rear channels are used for sound effects and reverberation.

The ".1" part of the equation is a separate low-frequency effects (LFE) channel that reproduces the very lowest bass information. This channel is fed to a powered subwoofer, which can be located anywhere within your listening space.

More Subs

Some surround sound systems include more than one subwoofer. This is indicated by a larger number after the "dot;" for example, a 5.2 system would include five primary audio channels and two LFE (subwoofer) channels.

Next up is 7.1 channel surround. In this setup, the sixth and seventh channels are true rear channels; these speakers should be located directly behind the listener. In a 7.1-channel system, you end up with speakers in front of you (left, center, right), speakers beside you (left and right surround), and speakers behind you (left and right rear). With this sort of setup, you're literally surrounded by sound; you're put in the middle of a movie soundtrack, with gunshots, explosions, and other special effects whizzing past your head, all around the room. (The surround and rear channels typically don't carry dialogue—just effects and, in some cases, music.)

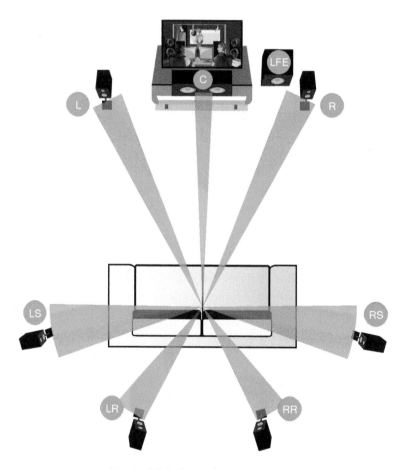

A typical 7.1-channel surround setup.

Choosing the Right Surround Format

The number of channels isn't the only factor that distinguishes one surround format from another.

The most popular format in use today is Dolby Digital. This format delivers 5.1 channels of sound in a discrete fashion, meaning the individual channels are encoded and decoded separately. As the name implies, Dolby Digital sound is all digital, from start to end. Similar to Dolby Digital is the competing DTS format, which also offers 5.1 discrete channels of digital sound. The official HDTV broadcast standard mandates Dolby Digital sound; it's also used in most DVDs and online streaming services.

Older Formats

Before the creation of discrete digital surround sound technology, older surround formats (such as Dolby Pro Logic and DTS Neo:6) didn't keep all the channels separate. Instead, they mixed the surround channels into the front channels during the encoding process; the resulting surround sound (called matrixed sound), when decoded, wasn't as distinct as with the newer discrete technologies. (The newer, discrete, surround formats do a noticeably better job of keeping each channel separate and simply sound clearer.) These older surround formats are used in some older programming available on broadcast/cable TV, DVDs, and streaming video services.

The Dolby Digital Plus and DTS-HD formats add two discrete rear channels to the mix, for 7.1-channel sound. You'll find these surround formats used in the Blu-ray disc format. Also used in Blu-ray discs are the Dolby TrueHD and DTS-HD Master Audio formats. These are also 7.1-channel formats, but with higher-quality lossless audio.

That's a lot of different formats to keep track of; fortunately, today's surround sound receivers automatically recognize and decode whichever format is selected from the source. While you might be able to manually select from different surround formats, your receiver automatically plays either the default format or whichever other format you select, from either Dolby or DTS. Just make sure you have the right number of speakers connected, and you can enjoy all the wonders that surround sound provides.

Dolby and DTS

Two technology companies compete in the home surround sound market. The market leader is Dolby Laboratories (www.dolby.com), with Dolby Digital, Dolby Atmos, and other technologies. Dolby competes with Digital Theater Systems (www.dts.com), with its similar DTS, DTS:X, and other technologies. Although some audiophiles might be able to tell the difference between competing Dolby and DTS formats, for all practical purposes they deliver similar results.

Adding "Height" with Dolby Atmos

The latest improvement in surround sound technology adds height to the normally "flat" audio experience. That added height essentially envelops you in three-dimensional sound, placing individual objects in precise locations within the sound field. For example, with this kind of system you can hear a helicopter flying overhead, instead of just moving from front to back or side to side.

The leading three-dimensional surround technology is Dolby Atmos, from Dolby Laboratories. Dolby Atmos starts with a standard 5.1- or 7.1-channel surround sound setup (that is, five or seven channels plus a subwoofer), but augments the normal front-left and -right speakers with *elevation speakers* that fire upward. These upward-firing speakers bounce sound off your ceiling and into the rest of the room, providing the extra height for the sound. (You can also use dedicated downward-firing speakers, which you position high on your walls or in your ceiling.)

A 7.1.4-channel Dolby Atmos setup, with upward-firing front and rear speakers.

A Dolby Atmos system is designated with a third digit after the second "dot;" the last digit indicates the number of height channels. For example, a 5.1-channel system with two front elevation speakers is designated as 5.1.2; a 7.1-channel system with two front and two rear elevation speakers is designated as 7.1.4.

You can also find sound bars that incorporate Dolby Atmos technology. These sound bars add upward-firing speakers to the normal front-firing array, bouncing the two elevation channels off the ceiling.

A sound bar with upward-firing speakers for Dolby Atmos sound.

Dolby Atmos is the most popular three-dimensional surround technology, but competing company DTS offers a similar system in its DTS:X technology. Like Dolby Atmos, DTS:X works with either upward-firing speakers or separate wall- or ceiling-mounted elevation speakers.

A 7.1.4 DTS:X system with downward-firing ceiling speakers.

As Dolby Atmos and DTS:X are relatively new technologies, there isn't a lot of content yet available that incorporates these extra height channels, although that will change over time. Some Blu-ray discs are available with Dolby Atmos soundtracks, and Netflix and Vudu both offer a limited selection of Dolby Atmos–compatible programming. Don't expect to find Dolby Atmos or DTS:X sound on normal broadcast TV, however.

Assembling a Surround Sound System

When you want to hear surround sound, you have to go beyond the two front speakers built into your flat-screen TV. Some sound bars attempt to simulate surround sound by using audio tricks to bounce sound from their front-mounted speakers off your room's side and rear walls; although the result is sometimes surprisingly effective, it's not true surround sound. For that you need separate speakers for each channel, positioned properly throughout your viewing room.

Choosing the Best Surround Sound Speakers

How many speakers you need depends on the type of surround sound system you want. For a 5.1-channel system (which is the bare minimum for true surround sound), you need the following:

- Two front speakers, positioned to the left and right of your TV screen at the front of the room.

- One center speaker, positioned below your TV screen at the front of the room.

- Two surround speakers, positioned on the left and right walls of your room, beside the main viewing position.

- One subwoofer, positioned anywhere in the room. (For easier installation, most people position their subs near the front of the room, typically in a corner.)

A center channel speaker from Polk Audio. (Photo courtesy Polk Audio, www.polkaudio.com.)

Note that all these speakers except the subwoofer are "passive" speakers, meaning they don't include their own amplification; they get their power through the speaker wire you connect to an audio/video receiver. (The receiver contains the amplifier that powers the speakers.) Subwoofers, however, are powered speakers, meaning they contain their own amplifiers that must be connected to a power source. (For practical purposes, that means you need to plug a subwoofer into a power outlet in addition to connecting it to your A/V receiver.)

A powered subwoofer from Klipsch. (Photo courtesy Klipsch Group, Inc., www.klipsch.com.)

Ideally, the five speakers are similar in their aural characteristics. (That means they sound similar.) However, the surround speakers can be a little smaller than the front speakers because they're carrying less of the "weight" of most soundtracks. (Most programming places the bulk of the sound up front.) The center speaker might also be a little larger than the front left and right speakers because that's where the majority of the dialogue comes from.

If you want a more immersive experience, you can add two more rear speakers, positioned literally behind the primary viewing position. These speakers should be at about the same height as the surround speakers; in most systems, the surround and rear speakers are of the same model for continuity of sound.

If you want to go with a Dolby Atmos or DTS:X system, you'll want your front-left and front-right speakers to include upward-firing speakers in addition to the normal front-firing speakers; you might also want to go with upward-firing speakers in your rear speaker enclosures. In lieu of upward-firing speakers built into the normal speaker enclosures, many manufacturers offer speaker "toppers" that sit on top of your existing speakers and fire upward for the elevation effects. You can also use dedicated elevation speakers mounted or built into your front/rear walls or ceiling.

A pair of dedicated elevation speakers from Klipsch. (Photo courtesy Klipsch Group, Inc., www.klipsch.com.)

Although some speakers can sit on shelves or even on the floor, you might want to mount your speakers, either in stands or on (or in) your walls. (Or, in the case of ceiling-mounted elevation speakers, in your ceiling.) You also need to run speaker wire from each speaker to your audio/video receiver, which will typically be at the front of your room.

What does all this cost? It depends on how much you want to spend.

Many speaker manufacturers—including Bose, Definite Technology, Klipsch, and Polk Audio—offer special surround sound speaker packages with all the speakers you need for 5.1- or 7.1-channel sound included. These packages run from around $400 USD to more than $2,000 USD.

A 5-1 surround speaker package from Definitive Technology.
(Photo courtesy Definitive Technology, www.definitivetechnology.com.)

You also can choose to assemble the speakers you need individually. In this instance, the sky is the limit, depending on whether you want floor standing, bookshelf, or wall-mounted models. Individual front/surround/rear speakers start at less than $100 USD each and go up into the multiple thousands; subwoofers start at less than $150 USD and go up to $500 USD or more.

You can find surround sound speakers at your local electronics or big-box store, or at online retailers such as Amazon or Crutchfield. Make sure you buy enough speaker wire to run around your entire room, too!

Incorporating an Audio/Video Receiver

You can't just connect all these speakers to your TV; it doesn't have a built-in amplifier to drive external speakers. Instead, you need an audio/video receiver, which not only drives your speakers but also functions as the control center of your entire system.

Most A/V receivers let you connect all your audio and video components, and then switch between inputs with a single remote control. Connect your cable or satellite box, streaming media player, Blu-ray player, game console, and more to the inputs of your A/V receiver, then connect the output of the A/V receiver to your TV and external speakers. Whatever you select on the receiver's remote appears on the television screen.

A 5.2-channel audio/video receiver from Denon. (Photo courtesy D&M Holdings, Inc., usa.denon.com.)

The A/V receiver also serves as the main processor/amplifier for your system's audio. Surround sound sources are fed into the receiver, which decodes the surround sound signal using the appropriate technology. Select a source with surround sound content and your A/V receiver creates room-filling sound.

When selecting an A/V receiver, you want to look at the number of inputs and outputs, the types of surround sound technologies supported, how powerful the amplifier is, and how easy it is to use. I discuss each factor separately.

Most video and audio sources today connect via HDMI, and your A/V receiver should offer enough HDMI inputs to handle all the devices you want to connect. The receiver should also have at least one optical digital audio input, so you can run the audio output from your TV into the receiver and hear your TV's sound through your entire system. Look for at least one HDMI output, as well, to send the video signal from all your devices through to your TV.

As to what surround technologies are supported, most A/V receivers today handle all the major Dolby and DTS formats. You might have to pay a little extra to get a receiver that supports the newer Dolby Atmos or DTS:X formats, however.

In terms of amplifier power, the more you have, the better—within limits. A more powerful amplifier not only produces louder sound but also cleaner and clearer sound; that's because it doesn't have to push its limits when you're playing loud content. Don't sweat 10–20 watt per channel differences between models because the difference won't likely be noticeable. Bigger differences, however, matter more.

Finally, consider how you control the receiver because that's likely to be how you control your entire system. Look for a remote control unit that feels comfortable in your hand and is easy for others to figure out and use. Also look for a universal or learning remote that you can program to control all the components in your home theater system.

How much will you pay for a good A/V receiver? As with speakers, there's a wide range of models available at an equally wide range of prices. You can find basic models with 5.2-channel sound, less than 100 watts/channel amplification, and four HDMI inputs for $200 to $300 USD. When you get into the $500 USD range, you'll find models with 7.2-channel sound, more power amplification, and more HDMI inputs and outputs; some models in the higher-end of this range also feature Dolby Atmos and DTS:X processing. Ramp your budget up into the $1,000 USD range (and beyond), and you get top-of-the line performance, compatibility with just about every surround sound format available, enough power to handle the most explosive soundtracks, multiple-room audio and video, a plethora of inputs and outputs of all shapes and sizes, and really fancy universal remotes and onscreen displays. Set your budget and choose the model that best suits your needs.

All the connections available on a high-end 11.2-channel A/V receiver from Onkyo, with 135 watts/channel power, eight HDMI inputs, two HDMI outputs, and Dolby Atmos and DTS:X decoding. (Photo courtesy Onkyo USA, www.onkyousa.com.)

Choosing the Right Options for You

As you can see, there are many different options when it comes to improving your TV sound. Let's look at which options might be best for your individual situation:

- If you're satisfied with the sound from your TV and don't watch a lot of action movies or concerts, don't do anything—just use your set's built-in speakers.

- If you have trouble discerning dialog on certain shows, turn on your source's closed captioning.

- If you want to improve the sound for your listening experience without affecting anyone else watching—or if you want to watch TV while others want silence—invest in a set of wireless headphones.

- If you want to improve the overall sound of your system without investing a lot of time and money, add a soundbar underneath your TV.

- If you want to experience the full effect of surround sound movies and shows—and have the budget to do so—invest in a complete surround sound audio/video system.

As to the last option, consider whether you want a prepackaged system (typically cheaper and easier to assemble) or one that you purchase as separate components (sounds better but costs more, and is more complicated). Finally, if you want the latest and the greatest in fully immersive sound, make sure your system includes Dolby Atmos or DTS:X sound, with additional speakers to add "height" to the sound. (That costs more, too.)

>>>*Go Further*
WHERE DO YOU FIND THE BEST AUDIO CONTENT?

Now that you know all about surround sound formats and equipment, where do you find the best sources for surround sound audio? Broadcast TV, cable, streaming, and Blu-ray sources offer different types and quality of sound. In order, here's where you can find the best audio for your listening pleasure:

- **Blu-ray discs:** The Blu-ray format offers enough storage capacity and bandwidth to carry even the most demanding audio formats. Look for those Blu-ray discs that offer Dolby Digital Plus, Dolby TrueHD, DTS-HD, or DTS-HD: Master Audio formats (along with 4K Ultra HD video!). Some Blu-rays also feature Dolby Atmos and DTS:X soundtracks.

- **Streaming video services:** Most streaming services offer 5.1-channel Dolby Digital surround sound. Some services offer some programming in the higher-quality Dolby Digital Plus format. There is a handful of programming (primarily from Netflix and Vudu) with Dolby Atmos sound. (To hear these higher-quality surround formats, you need a streaming media player that supports those formats.)

- **Cable television:** Most cable programming is in 5.1-channel Dolby Digital. Some cable providers offer selected channels in Dolby Atmos sound.

- **Satellite television:** As with cable television, most satellite programming is in 5.1-channel Dolby Digital. Select programming is offered with Dolby Atmos.

- **Broadcast television:** Broadcast TV offers the capacity for 5.1-channel Dolby Digital surround. Some older programming may be in Dolby Pro Logic surround or plain old stereo or mono sound.

- **DVDs:** The original DVD format specified 5.1-channel Dolby Digital surround; some DVDs may also be encoded in DTS surround. Some older content may be in Dolby Pro Logic surround, stereo, or mono.

- **VHS tapes:** Most VHS tapes are stereo or even mono. Some offer Dolby Pro Logic matrix surround.

Bottom line: If you're looking for the most content with the best sound, Blu-ray is the way to go. Streaming media services are catching up, though, with more and more higher-quality audio available every day.

In this chapter, you learn how to receive local stations and national networks for free, over the air, as well as through other options.

→ Why People Still Watch Broadcast TV
→ Cutting the Cord for Over-the-Air Broadcasts
→ Watching Local Digital Networks
→ Recording Local Channels
→ Other Ways to Watch Local Channels
→ Checklist for Watching Local TV on a Budget

3

Getting Local and Broadcast Television Over the Air

The television we all grew up with, before the advent of cable and satellite, is what is known as *over-the-air* or OTA television. With any television set and the appropriate digital antenna, you can receive digital programming from any local channel within your antenna's reception range—no cable or satellite box or subscription required. These broadcasts are all in glorious high definition, and completely free. It's the first step toward cutting the cable cord!

Why People Still Watch Broadcast TV

If you believe the experts and reviewers, with all the quality programming available on cable channels, pay channels, and streaming channels, nobody is watching broadcast network television anymore. Although it's true that network viewership is down (and binge-watching on cable and streaming services is up), the reality is that most of us still watch our local television stations—a lot.

Why are local stations important? First, there's a lot of great programming on the major broadcast networks that the local stations represent—ABC, CBS, CW, Fox, and NBC. You have popular dramas such as *Chicago PD, Law & Order: SVU*, and *This is Us* (all on NBC); *The Good Doctor* and *Grey's Anatomy* (both ABC); and *Blue Bloods* and the various iterations of *NCIS* (CBS). If you like superhero shows, there's nothing better than *Arrow, Black Lightning, DC's Legends of Tomorrow, The Flash*, and *Supergirl* (all on The CW), as well as *Gotham* (on Fox). Some of the best comedies are on broadcast TV, including *Black-ish* (ABC), *The Good Place* (NBC), *Mom* (CBS), and *The Simpsons* (Fox). There's also tons of reality programming on the major networks, including *Dancing with the Stars* (ABC), *So You Think You Can Dance* (Fox), *Survivor* (CBS), and *The Voice* (NBC).

Let's not forget the major-league sports broadcasts on the major networks, including NFL games, college football, and local football and basketball games. There are also college sports, NASCAR racing, the Indy 500, professional golf, and all the competitive events you can think of during Olympic years. These are all events you watch on the broadcast networks.

In addition to delivering programming from the major broadcast networks, local stations also deliver local news, sports, and weather. You want to know what's going on with your local sports team, or find out whether it's going to rain tomorrow? Tune into your local television station.

Many local stations also produce their own local programming, whether it's documentaries, daytime talk shows, broadcasts of local events and concerts, or children's shows. Your local station serves your local community; streaming video channels on the Internet don't.

So, local channels and the broadcast networks they represent continue to be an important part of our daily television diet. There's a lot you'd miss if you didn't have access to your local stations; you need them every bit as much as you do the latest binge-worthy programming on Netflix or Hulu.

Cutting the Cord for Over-the-Air Broadcasts

Most viewers today receive their local channels as part of their cable or satellite television packages. Local channels are typically part of a service's basic tier of programming but aren't free. In essence, you're paying your cable or satellite provider to receive your local channels and deliver them to you.

Not surprisingly, many viewers are tired of paying hundreds of dollars a month for cable or satellite service, and want to cut the cord to cut their costs. As you'll discover throughout this book, there is a wide variety of programming freely available over the Internet or for a lower cost than you pay for cable or satellite packages. The challenge, however, is how to watch your local channels if you don't have cable or satellite.

Fortunately, you don't have to pay anybody anything to watch your local broadcast stations. That's because all your local stations transmit their signals over the public airwaves, for free. Receiving these over-the-air (OTA) broadcasts is as simple as connecting a receiving antenna to your TV and programming the tuner in your set to find those channels. After that, you get the same programming, in the same high-definition format, without having to pay any monthly charges. What's not to like?

Understanding OTA Reception

To receive the signals transmitted by your local television stations, you must connect your TV to some sort of digital antenna. This is not as simple as it sounds; there are lots of different types of antennas to choose from.

What type of antenna you need depends on where your home is in relation to where a station's broadcasting antenna is. In most instances, stations try to place their antennas on the highest possible ground—in a big city, that might be on top of the tallest nearby skyscraper; in a smaller town, it might be on top of a tall transmitting tower. You'll often see antennas for multiple stations clustered together in a single location, which makes it easier to aim your receiving antenna.

Problems occur if different stations locate their antennas in different locations. In my former hometown of Indianapolis, for example, different stations use one of two transmitting towers located on completely different sides of town; if you aim at one, you completely miss the other. There's no way a single-element antenna can pick up stations from both towers.

It also doesn't help if your home is too far away from a station's antenna. (This is a problem I suffer from; I live in a far southern suburb of Minneapolis, and our main transmitting towers are way north of the city.) If you get too far away from a transmitting antenna, the digital signal simply stops working. It's not like it was back in the old analog VHF/UHF days, where if you got too distant the signal simply got weaker and snowier. With today's digital broadcasting, the signal is either on or it's off; there's no in-between.

Reception can also be made difficult if you're not line-of-sight with any of the stations' antennas. Again, this situation is a problem for me; my house is located in a relatively low valley, surrounded by lots of hills and trees and tall buildings. Consequently, I don't get a clear signal; a simple window-mounted antenna does not do the job for me.

Choose the Right Type of Antenna

Choosing the right antenna, then, requires you to consider where your home is in relation to where your local stations are broadcasting from. The closer you are to a transmitting antenna, and the fewer things between you and the tower, the simpler and lower-priced the antenna you can use. If you're further away or have lots of trees or buildings in the way, then you'll probably have to opt for a more complicated and higher-priced antenna.

Let's start with the best-case scenario. If all your area's broadcasting towers are in roughly the same direction and relatively close, with no major obstacles in the way, you can probably make do with a simple low-cost indoor antenna. This is the kind of antenna you can set on top of or near to your TV; some are flat pieces of plastic that you attach to the closest window. This type of antenna typically costs anywhere from $10 to $50 USD and is easy to connect yourself.

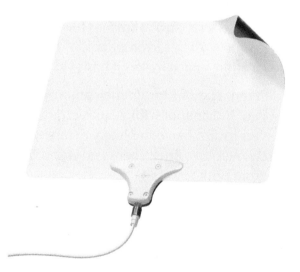

The Mohu Leaf 30 indoor antenna installs on a nearby window pane and is ideal when you're close to the transmitting antenna.
(Photo courtesy Mohu, www.gomohu.com.)

If, on the other hand, different stations in your area use different transmitting towers, you need a different type of antenna. In this instance, you want a medium- or long-range antenna that sits in your attic or installs on your roof and includes two or more different elements—a *multidirectional* antenna. Surprisingly, this type of antenna doesn't cost much more than an indoor antenna, in the $50 to $150 USD range, although you may have to pay for installation.

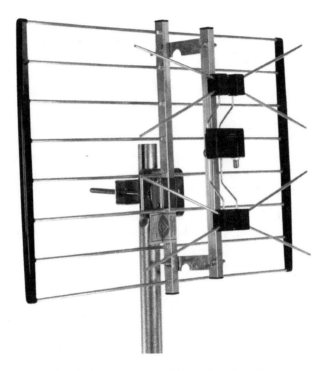

*Channel Master's METROtenna 40 multidirectional outdoor antenna, ideal
if your local stations broadcast from more than one location.
(Photo courtesy Channel Master, www.channelmaster.com.)*

If your local transmitting antennas are too far away, you need an even more powerful antenna mounted on your roof. In this instance, a *directional* antenna with a single element you can aim at the transmitting tower is the way to go. If you have different towers to deal with, add a motor that rotates the antenna from location to location. This type of antenna is priced in the $100 USD range, give or take, plus installation.

The Digital Advantage 60 motorized directional outdoor antenna from Channel Master,
for when you're dealing with distant stations.
(Photo courtesy Channel Master, www.channelmaster.com.)

Amplifiers and Splitters

If the signal you're receiving is too weak, you might need to make it stronger. You do this with a signal amplifier, added in-line between your antenna and your TV. And if you want to connect more than one TV to your antenna, you need to install a signal splitter, which does as its name implies.

To simply things, the Consumer Electronics Association and the National Association of Broadcasters have compiled a list of six different antenna types, identified by color code. These types are detailed in Table 3.1.

Table 3.1 Color-Coded Antenna Types

Color	Antenna Type	Your Distance from Transmitter	Location	Typical Cost
Yellow	Small multidirectional	Up to 10–15 miles	Indoor	$10–$50
Green	Medium multidirectional	Up to 30 miles	Indoor or attic	$50–$100
Light green	Large multidirectional *or* small directional	Up to 30 miles	Attic or roof	$50–$100
Red	Medium directional	30–45 miles	Attic or roof	$75–$125

Color	Antenna Type	Your Distance from Transmitter	Location	Typical Cost
Blue	Medium directional antenna with amplifier *or* large directional antenna	45–60 miles	Roof or tall tower	$75–$150
Violet	Large directional antenna with preamplifier	60+ miles	Roof or tall tower	$75–$150

Use AntennaWeb to Find the Right Antenna

If you're not sure what type of antenna to get, consult the AntennaWeb website (www.antennaweb.org). Just enter your street address and this site will show you what local stations are available, where their transmitting towers are, and what kind of antenna you need for best reception.

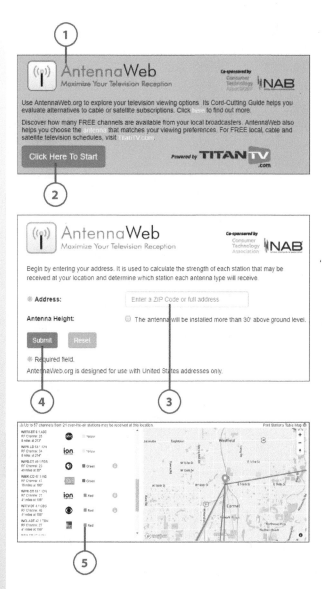

1. From any web browser, go to www.antennaweb.org.

2. Click Here to Start.

3. Enter your street address and ZIP code into the Address box.

4. Click Submit.

5. AntennaWeb displays the appropriate information for your location, as well as a map of transmitting antennas in your area. Scroll down to see recommended antenna types for each station you can receive.

Connect an Antenna to Your TV

Whichever type of antenna you choose, connecting it to your TV is simple. All antennas today use a coaxial cable to connect to the Antenna or Cable input on the back of your TV. All you have to do is connect the coaxial cable from the antenna to the Antenna input (sometimes labeled ANT IN) on the back of your TV. It screws right on.

Program Your TV for Local Stations

The tuner built into your television set automatically recognizes and displays those broadcast channels that your antenna picks up—once you program it for those channels, that is. Programming your TV to scan for local channels is a one-time thing, and it's fairly automatic. (Naturally, this process differs from brand to brand; these general instructions should work on most sets.)

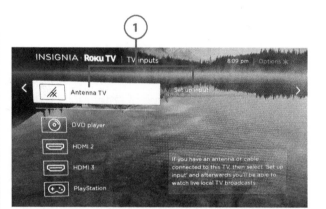

1. On your television set, use your remote control to access your set's setup menu and select the antenna or channel setup option.

2. Select the option to start finding or scanning channels.

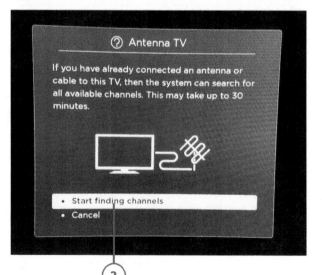

(3) Your set scans for available broadcast channels, including all digital subchannels. (I discuss these in the "Watching Local Diginets" section, later in this chapter.)

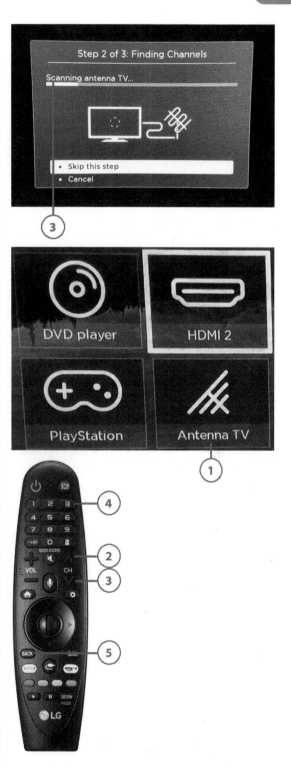

Watch OTA Channels on Your TV

Once your television has been programmed for all available OTA channels, it's easy to watch those local channels on your TV. It's just a matter of selecting the right source and then going to the channel you want.

(1) Use your TV remote to select the antenna or live TV input.

(2) Press Channel Up on the remote to go to the next highest channel.

(3) Press Channel Down on the remote to go to the next lowest channel.

(4) To go directly to a specific channel, enter the three- or four-digit channel number.

(5) Press the Back or Previous button on the remote to return to the previously viewed channel.

(6) Most newer TVs display OTA stations in a channel guide format.
Scroll to the channel you want to
watch, then press Enter or Select
on the remote. Your TV automatically switches to that channel.

Troubleshooting Reception Problems

When you have your antenna installed and your stations programmed, a local
channel on your television set normally is a simple thing. On that rare occasion
where you have trouble finding or viewing a local station, consider the following
options:

- Make sure your TV is switched to the appropriate source or input for antenna
  reception. You can't watch broadcast TV if your set is switched to an HDMI
  input.

- Make sure your antenna is connected to the antenna input on the back
  of your TV. Make sure the coaxial cable is firmly inserted and screwed in.
  Unscrew the coaxial cable and make sure the small copper wire in the center
  is inserted properly; make sure it's not bent and therefore not inserting.

- If you're using an indoor antenna, try moving it to a different position or location. Digital television signals can be tricky; sometimes moving the antenna a
  few inches or rotating it a few degrees will get a finicky signal to come in.

- If you're using an outdoor antenna, make sure that the coaxial cable is firmly
  connected to the antenna itself and there is no break in the cable. Try wiggling
  the cable as it comes into your room; if the signal goes in and out, the cable
  might have a short that requires replacing part of or the entire cable run.

- If you don't see a particular local channel on your TV or its channel guide,
  run the auto setup scan again. If the channel still isn't found, try adding the
  channel manually, if your TV has that option. If your TV still doesn't recognize

that channel, you need to reposition your antenna (or get a different type of antenna) to bring in that station.

- Check to make sure you are using the right type of antenna for the station you're trying to receive. If the transmitting antenna is too far away or if you don't have a clear line-of-sight to the antenna, you might need a different antenna.

- If a signal for a given station goes out during inclement weather, either you have a reception problem or the station has a transmitting issue. Wait for the weather to clear; if the channel comes back in, the problem is probably on the transmitting end. It's also possible that blowing winds could cause tree limbs to interfere with your reception; you might need to cut down the offending tree parts or reposition your antenna so the limbs aren't a problem.

- If you used to receive a specific station and no longer get it, look for any environmental issues that have changed. There might be new electrical interference from a nearby appliance or electronic device. It's possible that a tree limb or another outdoor item has changed position and is now blocking your signal. It's also possible that the television station changed the location of its transmitter, or even changed the frequency on which it transmits; it doesn't hurt to call or email the station to see if anything has changed on their end.

>>>Go Further

DIGITAL TV VERSUS ANALOG TV

On June 13, 2009, all television stations in the United States were required to switch from analog broadcasting to digital broadcasting. Digital television is better than the older analog television in a lot of ways—the picture is sharper, the sound is clearer, and you get more channels of programming.

Analog television transmitted programming in a continuous signal, kind of like the modulations in an old vinyl record. That analog signal was far from perfect; it easily deteriorated over long distances and often suffered interference from other sources, producing ghost images, static, and "snow." Analog picture quality was never as sharp as the original source, the background was sometimes grainy, and the sound suffered from noise and a reduced frequency response.

Digital television is more advanced than that older analog technology. A digital broadcast converts the programming into a stream of binary on/off bits—sequences of 0s and 1s—the same way that computers store information in digital data files. These binary bits recombine to reproduce an exact copy of the original material; the picture and sound received from a digital transmission are always identical to the original source.

Even better, over-the-air digital signals don't weaken over distance as analog signals do. As long as your antenna can receive the signal, the picture is perfect, with no degradation or ghosting.

In addition, digital transmission enables stations to broadcast high-definition programming, which requires a digital signal. Most, if not all, of the programming on your local stations today is broadcast in HD. (Learn more about HD in Chapter 1, "Choosing the Right TV.")

All TVs manufactured in the past decade are built to receive these new digital transmissions. TVs manufactured before 2008 or so do not receive digital broadcasts; thus, they're unusable today (except for watching old VHS tapes). So, if you're watching over-the-air stations on a new flat-screen TV, you're getting all digital, HD broadcasts—much better than the old analog, standard-definition programming of our youth.

Watching Local Digital Networks

Digital television not only brings better sound and HD picture than the old analog service but it's also a more-efficient technology. A digital transmission requires less bandwidth than does a similar analog broadcast; this lets local television stations broadcast two, three, or even four digital channels in the space of a single older analog channel. This "multicasting" technology means you receive more variety in programming from your local stations—all delivered with superior digital quality.

Understanding Digital Subchannels

A local channel starts with a single main channel, but it then can add as many *subchannels* as space (and their budget) allows. Each available subchannel can carry a complete high-definition program, a standard-definition program (in digital format), or specific data streams. Therefore, broadcasters can offer a variety of special data services over their digital channels in addition to offering the normal programming.

For example, a station might start with its main channel, typically offering the feed from its affiliated network, local news, and the like. For example, channel 6 in your town technically would designate its primary channel as 6.1. The station might then offer HDTV programming on one subchannel (designated 6.2), standard-definition programming on a second subchannel (designated 6.3), completely different programming on a third subchannel (designated 6.4), and a local news or weather feed on a fourth subchannel (designated 6.5). That's a lot more programming than the current single channel you're used to!

NOTE

Broadcasters don't have unlimited digital bandwidth, which means they have to choose how many subchannels they offer—and what kinds of programming go on each subchannel. For example, don't expect multiple HDTV subchannels; you'll typically find one subchannel with high-definition programming (typically limited to 720p, which requires less bandwidth), while the other subchannels transmit standard-definition programming.

Enter the Diginet

One result of these new digital subchannels has been the rise of something the industry refers to as *digital networks*, or *diginets*. A diginet is a television network that broadcasts over these digital subchannels. They're typically not major networks; they're offshoots of big media companies, such as those companies that own a chain of television stations across the nation. In many cases, the diginets use programming owned by the network's owner; for example, a CBS-owned diginet might run programming owned by CBS.

What kinds of programming can you find in the world of diginets? Most diginets offer older programming in the form of classic TV shows or older B-movies. It's what we used to call reruns and now refer to as classic television programs and movies, with the occasional lifestyle channel thrown in. You typically won't find newer shows or movies; because the programming is older, it's often presented in standard definition. (Still digital, mind you, just not HD.)

Most diginets target specific genres, eras, or audiences. Grit, for example, offers Westerns and action/adventure programming, targeted at men; Laff is all about comedies; Start TV offers crime procedurals targeted at a female audience. The content of other diginets is similarly targeted.

Table 3.2 details some of the more popular diginets available today. Not all diginets are available in all locations, of course; check your local listings to see what's offered in your market.

Table 3.2   Thirty-One Top Diginets

Diginet	Owned By	Programming
Antenna TV	Tribune Broadcasting	Classic TV comedies, old episodes of *Tonight Show with Johnny Carson*
Bounce TV	Katz Broadcasting	Classic comedies, game shows, and talk shows aimed at the African-American audience
Buzzr	Freemantle North America	Classic TV game shows
Charge!	Sinclair Broadcast Group and MGM Television	Action and adventure movies and TV shows
Comet	Sinclair Broadcast Group and MGM Television	Science fiction, fantasy, and horror movies and TV shows
Cozi TV	NBCUniversal	Classic TV comedies and dramas
The Country Network	TCN Country	Country music videos and other music-based content
Create	Public Broadcasting Service	Cooking, DIY, and how-to programming
Decades	Weigel Broadcasting and CBS	Classic TV comedies and dramas presented in mini-marathon format
Escape	Katz Broadcasting	Crime-focused TV shows and movies

Diginet	Owned By	Programming
getTV	Sony Picture Entertainment	Action and Western TV shows and movies, along with variety shows from the 1960s and 1970s, including *The Smothers Brothers Comedy Hour* and *The Sonny and Cher Comedy Hour*
Grit	Katz Broadcasting	Action and Western TV shows and movies aimed at a male audience
Heroes & Icons	Weigel Broadcasting	Classic TV science fiction, Western, and action/adventure, including *Star Trek*
Ion Television	Ion Media Networks	Recent crime shows and dramas, including *CSI*, *Law and Order*, and *NCIS* franchises
Ion Life	Ion Media Networks	Family-friendly cooking and lifestyle programming
Justice Network	Cooper Media	True crime and investigative documentaries
Laff	Katz Broadcasting	Classic TV comedies
Light TV	MGM Television	Family-friendly and faith-based programming
MeTV	Weigel Broadcasting	Classic TV comedies and dramas
Movies!	Weigel Broadcasting and Fox Television Stations	Feature films
PBS Kids	Public Broadcasting Service	Children's programming
Qubo	Ion Media Networks	Children's programming
Retro TV	Luken Communications	Classic TV comedies and dramas
Rev'n	Luken Communications	Automotive programming
Stadium	Sinclair Broadcast Group	Live sports programming
Start TV	Weigel Broadcasting	Crime procedural TV shows aimed at a female audience

Diginet	Owned By	Programming
TBD	Sinclair Broadcast Group	Original Internet programming
This TV	MGM and Tribune Broadcasting	Feature films and some classic TV shows
WeatherNation TV	WeatherNation	National and regional weather forecasts
World	Public Broadcasting Service	PBS news and documentaries
Youtoo America	ComStar Media Fund	Self-help and reality TV shows

>>>Go Further
DIGINETS: HOME OF CLASSIC TV

Personally, I love diginets. In fact, I find myself watching some of these diginet channels more than I do their host local stations. I'm particularly fond of those channels that offer truly classic television programming, which is most of them.

There's such a wealth of old television programs on these diginets. On any given evening, you might find me watching episodes of *The Saint* on This TV, *The Avengers* or *Danger Man* (aka *Secret Agent*) on Charge!, all versions of *Star Trek* on H&I, *Perry Mason* on MeTV, and old *Tonight Show* episodes on Antenna TV. Antenna TV is also a good place to find reruns of comedies I watched as a kid, including *Bewitched*, *I Dream of Jeannie*, *The Burns and Allen Show*, *The Jack Benny Program*, and more obscure shows like *Good Morning, World* and *The Paul Lynde Show*. MeTV is also good in this regard, with *The Andy Griffith Show*, *The Beverly Hillbillies*, *M*A*S*H*, and *WKRP in Cincinnati*, along with dramas and action programming such as *Mannix*, *Matlock*, *The Twilight Zone*, and *Wonder Woman*. (And cheesy horror movies on Saturday nights with Svengoolie!)

In short, if you like to watch those TV shows you watched when you were younger, you'll likely find them on the subchannels of your local TV stations—which are available free to anyone with a TV set and a good antenna. It's like going home again.

How to Receive Diginets on Your TV

If you're receiving your local television stations on your TV via an OTA antenna, you're all set. All available diginet subchannels should be programmed and displayed automatically. You'll see them listed as .2, .3, .4, and so on after the main channel number (.1). You can enter the channel numbers directly, scroll up and down the channels to them, or select them from your TV's built-in channel guide (if you have one).

Know, however, that most diginets are broadcast in standard definition, not in high definition. There are two reasons for this. First, stations have limited bandwidth available; they want to devote the large chunk of it toward the HD programming on their main channel. Second, most of the old TV shows you find on diginets were produced before the advent of HD; they were made in standard definition so they're broadcast in standard definition.

If you receive your local channels via cable or satellite, however, the situation is not as rosy. Satellite services, by law, cannot carry any diginets. It's better with cable, but not perfect, as most cable providers don't carry all available local subchannels. It's possible that your favorite diginet simply isn't available on your cable service. I've experienced my local cable provider swapping in one subchannel for another without giving a reason save for the cable system only having a limited number of slots available for local subchannels. It's less than ideal.

If you want access to all the subchannels available in your area, you'll probably have to get them over the air rather than via cable or satellite. That's not a bad thing; that's where they're free!

>>>Go Further
WHERE TO WATCH YOUR FAVORITE WESTERNS

I'm a big fan of old Western TV shows and movies. I grew up watching *The Lone Ranger* in syndication, and some of my favorite movies of all time are the James Stewart/Anthony Mann and Randolph Scott/Budd Boetticher Westerns of the 1950s. I even wrote a book about Westerns (*Management Secrets of the Good, the Bad and the Ugly*, available online at www.millerwriter.com/book/management-secrets-of-the-good-the-bad-and-the-ugly-2nd-edition/).

Just about every time I stumble across a decent Western when I'm surfing the channels, I stop and watch it. Really.

So where can find your favorite Westerns on TV? Your local diginets are good places to start.

The Grit network focuses almost exclusively on Westerns, with a large variety of TV Westerns from the 1950s and 1960s, including *Death Valley Days, Laramie,* and *Wagon Master;* it also offers a ton of Western movies, both well-known and more obscure. You also can find a selection of Western movies from the 1940s to 1960s on Charge!, an action-focused network.

MeTV offers a few classic TV Westerns, including *The Big Valley, Gunsmoke* (the black-and-white half-hour episodes), *Have Gun Will Travel, Maverick,* and *The Rifleman.* GetTV schedules some more obscure Western series, including *Guns of Paradise, Hondo, How the West Was Won, Laredo,* and *Shane.* In addition, Retro TV offers *Bonanza* and This TV shows *Bat Masterson, Mackenzie's Raiders,* and the occasional Western movie.

If you're a cable subscriber, you definitely have to check out the Starz Encore Westerns channel, which offers a ton of TV and movie Westerns, 24/7. You can find TV shows such as *Cheyenne, Death Valley Days, Maverick, Wagon Train,* and *Wanted: Dead or Alive,* along with both classic and B-movie Westerns from the 1950s through today. (This is the channel I watch most to get my Westerns fix.)

Also good for Westerns is the INSP network, which runs *The Big Valley, Branded, The Virginian,* and the black-and-white hour-long episodes of *Gunsmoke,* along with a fair number of Western films from the 1950s and 1960s. And if you're looking for the color hour-long episodes of *Gunsmoke,* turn to TV Land. Check 'em out!

Recording Local Channels

Since the days of video cassette recorders are long gone, how can you record programs from your local broadcast stations today? It's possible, but you need to purchase a separate set-top digital video recorder (DVR) designed for OTA recording.

There are several companies that manufacture DVRs for OTA use. These units all work in a similar fashion. The DVR connects between your antenna and your TV and contains its own tuner (or tuners, for recording multiple programs simultaneously). This enables you to record one program while you watch another. The DVR has its own onscreen channel guide; just navigate to the program you want to record and press the Record button. When the program airs, it's recorded to the hard disk drive included in the DVR.

The following sections describe some of the more popular OTA DVRs available.

Subscription Fees

Some OTA DVRs require a monthly subscription to their on-screen channel guides. Others don't. Factor that into your costs.

Amazon Fire TV Recast

Amazon is the newest entrant in the OTA DVR field, with the Fire TV Recast. It works by streaming (or "recasting") what it records to your television set or mobile device.

The Amazon Fire TV Recast OTA DVR. (Photo courtesy Amazon, www.amazon.com.)

There are two models available. A model with a 500 GB hard drive and two tuners ($229.99 USD) can hold up to 75 hours of HD programming. The second model, with a 1TB hard drive and four tuners ($279.99 USD), can hold up to 150 hours of HD programming.

Gigabytes and Terabytes

Hard disk storage is measured in bytes and multiples of bytes. A million bytes is a megabyte, notated as MB. A thousand megabytes (a billion bytes) is a gigabyte, notated as GB. A thousand gigabytes (a trillion bytes) is a terabyte, notated as TB.

To use the Recast, you need to have an Amazon Fire TV streaming media player (sold separately) connected to your TV. (Learn more about Amazon Fire TV in Chapter 4, "Getting Streaming Media Devices.") The Recast connects to your antenna via a coaxial cable, but it streams both live and recorded programming to the Fire TV device (and thus to your TV) via Wi-Fi. You can stream from the Recast to up to two different devices simultaneously.

Unique to the Recast is the ability to use an Amazon Echo smart speaker to control the Recast via voice commands. You also can control the Recast with the Fire TV mobile app on your smartphone or tablet.

The Recast is a good choice if you're tied into Amazon's infrastructure, if you already have a Fire TV streaming media player, or if you have an Alexa device in your living room. Amazon does not offer or require any subscription to use the Recast.

Channel Master Stream+

Channel Master's Stream+ unit is unique in that it is both an OTA DVR and a streaming media player. Connect it to your antenna to record OTA broadcasts, and to the Internet to stream (and record) programming from Hulu, Netflix, and other streaming services.

The Channel Master Stream+ OTA DVR and Streaming Box.
(Photo courtesy Channel Master, www.channelmaster.com.)

That said, the base Stream+ unit alone doesn't offer recording functionality; it only streams video from the Internet. To activate OTA recording, you need to purchase a separate external hard drive. Channel Master offers its own 1TB hard drive for a package price (with the main Stream+ unit) of $178 USD; the unit alone, no hard drive, runs $149 USD.

The Stream+ includes two tuners so you can record two programs at the same time. It connects to your OTA antenna via coaxial cable and to your TV via HDMI. No subscription is required for the unit's onscreen channel guide.

Nuvyyo Tablo

Nuvyyo offers several different versions of its Tablo OTA DVR, differing mainly in recording capacity and how many tuners are included, which determines how many programs you can record at the same time. All Tablo models connect to your antenna via coaxial cable and to your Internet router via Ethernet cable (not Wi-Fi). The Tablo then streams the programs it records through your router to one or more TVs via Wi-Fi or Ethernet. That's right; the Tablo is a network streamer that lets you view your recorded programs from multiple TVs and connected devices.

The Nuvyyo Tablo Dual Lite OTA DVR. (Photo courtesy Nuvyyo, www.tablotv.com.)

Like the Stream+, the base Tablo units don't come with built-in hard drive storage, so you have to add an external hard drive via USB. Tablo doesn't sell hard drives, so you have to buy one separately.

The Tablo Dual Lite unit offers two tuners and sells for $139.99 USD. The Tablo Dual 64GB unit comes with the same two tuners but adds 64GB of built-in storage (which isn't much, for HD programming); it sells for $179.99 USD. The Tablo 4 comes with four tuners (for recording up to four programs at the same time) and sells for $219.99 USD. And remember, you need to supply your own external hard drive for recording, which can run another $100 USD or more.

While you can use any Tablo without a subscription, you get a very, very basic grid guide that shows only 24 hours of upcoming programming. Realistically, you'll want the upgraded TV Guide data service, which runs $4.99 per month or $49.99 per year.

When you add up the cost of the Tablo box itself, an external hard drive, and the TV Guide service, the Tablo is one of the more expensive options available. It's also one of the more complicated to set up and use. If you need the ability to stream recordings to multiple devices, however, it might be worth the cost and trouble.

TiVo Bolt OTA

When most people think of freestanding DVRs, they think of TiVo, the company that pretty much invented the category (long before cable companies put DVRs in their set-top boxes). Over the years, TiVo has offered various DVRs for OTA recording; the current model is the TiVo Bolt OTA, which comes with four built-in tuners, for recording up to four programs at the same time.

The TiVo Bolt OTA DVR. (Photo courtesy TiVo, www.tivo.com.)

The Bolt connects to your antenna via coaxial cable, and to your TV via HDMI. You select the programs you want to record from TiVo's industry-leading onscreen channel guide. It comes with four tuners so you can record up to four programs simultaneously.

Like the Channel Master Stream+, the Bolt also functions as a streaming media player for Internet-based content. It comes with more than 20 apps for streaming video services, including Amazon Prime Video, Hulu, Netflix, and YouTube. Just connect it to the Internet and you'll see your favorite streaming programs alongside your local channels.

TiVo ships the Bolt with 1TB of storage; the company claims this will hold up to 150 hours of HD programming. It costs $249.99 USD. You also need to subscribe the TiVo service to get the online channel guide; that runs $6.99 per month or $69.99 per year.

Bottom line, the TiVo Bolt is not the lowest-cost option out there, but it's one that is easy to set up and easy to use. It's also a tried-and-true solution, with the most number of users over time. If you want simplicity and everything all in one set-top box and don't mind the higher price tag, the Bolt is the way to go.

Comparing OTA DVRs

Now that you know all about the various OTA DVRs currently available, how do you choose the one that's right for you? Perhaps Table 3.3 can help; it compares the features and pricing for all available DVRs.

Table 3.3   Features of OTA DVRs

Device	Built-in Storage	Tuners	Internet Streaming Video	Wireless Streaming to Other Devices	Subscription	Price (USD)
Amazon Fire TV Recast 500GB	500GB	2	No	Yes	No	$229.99
Amazon Fire Recast 1TB	1TB	4	No	Yes	No	$279.99
Channel Master Stream+	None	2	Yes	No	No	$149.00
Nuvyyo Tablo Dual Lite	None	2	No	Yes	$4.99/month	$139.99
Nuvyyo Tablo Dual 64GB	64GB	2	No	Yes	$4.99/month	$179.99
Nuvyyo Tablo 4	None	4	No	Yes	$4.99/month	$219.99
TiVo Bolt OTA	1TB	4	Yes	No	$6.99/month	$249.99

>>>*Go Further*

FOUR STATIONS ON THE VHF DIAL

When I was a kid, we didn't have cable or satellite or movies on DVDs. (Or even VHS tapes!) We had broadcast television only, and not a lot of that. Where I grew up, in Indianapolis, Indiana, we had just four local stations—the affiliates for ABC, CBS, and NBC, plus one independent station. We watched shows when they aired, and if we weren't home, we missed it; there was no time-shifting or streaming yet.

Back then, local stations transmitted in analog format on either the Very High Frequency (VHF) or Ultra High Frequency (UHF) bands, in glorious black and white (until 1965 or so, when everything started to switch to color). VHF stations were numbered 2 through 13 (there was no channel 1), and UHF stations went up from there.

In Indianapolis, the ABC station was channel 13, WLWI; it was part of the WLW Television Network out of Cincinnati, and during the daytime it broadcast regional shows such as *The Ruth Lyons 50-50 Club* and *The Paul Dixon Show*. The CBS station was channel 8, WISH. The NBC station was channel 6, WFBM. And our final station was the independent channel 4, WTTV, which showed lots of cartoons and syndicated programming, including my favorite show, *The Adventures of Superman*. (WTTV was technically based about 100 miles south of Indianapolis in Bloomington, Indiana, and because of that distance offered the worst reception.)

Receiving these stations meant connecting some sort of antenna to your TV set. Portable TVs had built-in "rabbit ear" antennas in those days; a console TV had to be connected to either a set-top antenna or a rooftop one. My father's television store installed a lot of outdoor antennas on local rooftops and in people's attics.

In the 1970s, we started seeing more local stations. The Public Broadcasting Service (PBS) entered the scene in 1970 (in Indianapolis, on channel 20, WFYI). Many cities saw an influx of independent stations, often broadcasting on the UHF band; our city had a couple of religious broadcasters up in the high numbers on the television dial.

The later '70s also saw the introduction of cable television, which had dozens of channels, including all the local channels plus some. Cable let us see all the channels as clear as a bell, no snow or ghosts. It also brought us more national channels, including the first cable news channel, CNN. Cable changed the nature of broadcasting forever, adding more and more channels every year and making the local channels less and less important. Still, those days as a kid growing up with just four channels on the VHF dial remain something special in my memories. Even with that limited choice, there always seemed to be something good on.

Other Ways to Watch Local Channels

As you've learned, watching local channels (and national broadcast networks) over the air, via antenna, is free and relatively easy to do. It might not be the best solution for all, however—which is why you also can view your local channels via cable, satellite, or the Internet.

Watch via Cable

Cable TV started out as a way for viewers to get crystal clear reception on local channels that they otherwise have trouble receiving via antenna. It makes sense that most viewers today still receive their local channels via their cable TV providers.

All cable providers in the United States provide at least the major stations in any given area over their cable systems, in widescreen HD. Some providers also offer channels from nearby cities. Check with your cable system to see what local channels are available, and for how much. (Local channels are typically part of a provider's basic tier of channels; sometimes you can subscribe to just the local channels for a relatively low price.)

Some cable providers also offer at least some local subchannels, although not all subchannels are always available. So, if you're a fan of MeTV, AntennaTV, or any other particular diginet, make sure that subchannel is offered by your cable provider.

The advantage of getting your local channels over cable is one of reliability. If you have trouble receiving a given channel via antenna, getting it via cable will solve your problems. You also don't have to worry about bad weather knocking out your locals; they're always there on cable. (Unless the cable system has a reception or delivery problem, that is.)

The primary disadvantage of receiving local channels via cable is the cost. With local-over-cable, you're paying for something you'd otherwise receive for free. If you're okay with that, fine, but cutting the cable cord completely (and watching your local channels via antenna) can put money in your pocket.

More About Cable

Learn more about cable television in Chapter 4, "Getting Cable TV."

Watch via Satellite

Similarly, both major U.S. satellite television services include local channels as part of their programming packages. In these cases, the providers receive the local channels via antenna, beam those signals up to their satellites, and then beam them back down to your receiving dish. It's kind of a long way to go for a signal that's pulsing through the air outside your home, but that's the way satellite works.

As with cable services, the satellite services don't always offer all local channels (especially some of the low-power ones) or all local subchannels. This last issue is a deal-breaker for many; if your favorite diginet isn't available over satellite, you might not want to go this route.

In addition, weather plays a big role in satellite reception, so getting your local channels (especially your local weather) could be an issue during heavy rains or snows. I found it intolerable to have the satellite reception of my local weathercasters go blank just when I needed them to tell me what was happening during inclement weather. I personally prefer the more reliable reception of local stations I get via cable or antenna.

The major upside of receiving your locals via satellite, then, is convenience. If you use a satellite provider to receive all your other programming, it's just easier to receive your local channels that way, too. The downsides are cost (paying for what you could otherwise get for free) and reliability during inclement weather.

More About Satellite

Learn more about satellite television in Chapter 5, "Getting Satellite TV."

Watch on Hulu

If all you care about is network programming, not local programming (such as news and sports), and you don't mind watching shows a day or two after they air, then check out the offerings on the Hulu streaming service. Hulu offers recent programming from most of the major broadcast networks, but the shows aren't streamed in real time as they air on the networks. You browse or search for the show you want, then choose from a selection of recent episodes. New episodes typically go online within a day or so of their broadcast airing.

To watch Hulu you need an Internet connection and some sort of streaming media device, such an Amazon Fire TV or Roku device. (Most smart TVs also have the Hulu app built in.) There's also a fee; a basic Hulu subscription costs $5.99 per month. (If you'd prefer to minimize—but not eliminate—commercial interruptions, you can do so for an additional $6 per month.)

I recommend Hulu if you don't care about local news, weather, or sports, and if you can wait a day or two before viewing your favorite network shows. Obviously, if local programming is important to you, or if you need to watch your shows when they air, then this is not the best option.

More About Hulu

Learn more about Hulu in Chapter 7, "Watching the Big Three Streaming Services: Amazon Prime Video, Hulu, and Netflix." (And don't confuse basic Hulu with the similar-sounding Hulu with Live TV service; that one does offer programming from local channels, but it costs $49.99 per month.)

Watch via Live Streaming Video Services

If you're going full-bore with the cord-cutting thing, you don't want to pay for your local stations via cable or satellite. If you also have trouble receiving your locals via antenna, there's another option for you: getting local stations over the Internet as part of a streaming video service.

A growing number of these streaming video services let you watch live video over the Internet on your TV, computer, phone, or other device. These live streaming video services essentially work like a cable service for your TV, but without a cable box (or cable subscription). You get access to dozens if not hundreds of live cable channels, as well as the local affiliates of the major broadcast networks.

The most popular of these services include AT&T's Watch TV, DirecTV Now, Fubo TV, Hulu with Live TV, Philo, PlayStation Vue, Sling TV, and YouTube Live, and they all work in a similar fashion. You need an Internet connection, of course, and the faster the better. You also need a streaming media player, such as Amazon Fire TV, Apple TV, Google Chromecast, or Roku. You connect the media player to your Internet and to your TV (typically via HDMI), and then you're ready to go. Launch the app for the live streaming service and you see a grid of available channels, like the cable channel guide you're probably used to. Check out what's currently showing and then click to watch a given channel.

Not all local channels are available on all live streaming services in all areas. You're more likely to find your local stations offered if you live in a major metropolitan area; these services often haven't negotiated transmission rights with smaller stations out in the hinterlands.

In addition, you're likely to find only the affiliates of the major broadcast networks on these services. You probably won't find a lot of smaller and independent stations, nor any digital subchannels. (If you're a fan of the classic TV reruns you find in the diginet universe, you're likely out of luck.)

Receiving your local channels over the Internet in this fashion isn't cheap. These live streaming services offer different tiers of service at different pricing levels, just like cable or satellite. Expect to pay anywhere from $20 to $50 USD to receive your locals online, depending on the service and where you live.

The upside of viewing your locals via a live streaming service is that you get service, especially in those areas where antenna reception is variable or nonexistent. Also, if you play your cards right, the cost of one of these services could turn out to be a little less than what you're currently paying for cable or satellite service.

The downside of these live streaming services is cost; as with any other subscription service, you're paying for local stations you could otherwise receive for free. In addition, you probably won't be able to receive all your local stations and diginets. And if your Internet connection is slow… well, get used to freezes and stutters while you watch.

I recommend using live streaming services if you want to cut the cable/satellite cord but don't get good over-the-air reception. They're actually very easy to set up and use, and put all your local, cable, and streaming favorites in one place.

More About Live Streaming Services

Learn more about watching local TV live over the Internet in Chapter 10, "Watching Live Broadcast and Cable TV with Live Streaming Services."

Checklist for Watching Local TV on a Budget

Given all the various ways you access local and national programming these days, which way will save you the most money? Here are some tips and advice for watching local TV when you're on a budget:

- If you get good reception, the lowest-cost approach in the long run is watching your local channels on your TV via antenna. You have a minimal outlay upfront for that antenna, but after that you have zero monthly costs.

- If you don't get good reception, consider subscribing to one of the many live streaming video services. It costs you a little less than cable or satellite, plus you need to pay for a monthly Internet subscription, but it could save you money every month.

- If you want or need to keep your cable or satellite subscription, ask about so-called "skinny" bundles that offer fewer channels for a lower price. You might even be able to find a plan that offers only your local channels; then you can watch all those other cable channels for free (or lower cost) over streaming services online.

Bottom line, there are ways to save money when it comes to watching your local television channels. It might require a little effort on your part to get everything changed over and set up, but it could be worth it in the long run.

>>>*Go Further*

BROADCAST TELEVISION IN CANADA AND THE UK

Broadcast television outside the United States is a little different than what American viewers might be used to.

In Canada, for example, there are fewer national broadcast networks. The government-run Canadian Broadcasting Corporation runs two of them, CBC (English-language) and Ici Radio-Canada Télé (French-language). The major privately run networks include Citytv, CTV, CTV2, Global, TVA, and V. Most local stations are owned by one of the national networks; the networks are available over the air, of course, and also via local cable systems and satellites from Bell TV and Shaw Direct. As in the United States, all Canadian OTA broadcasts are in 720p and 1080i HD.

These networks run a mix of Canadian and international programming, including many programs from the United States. To avoid over-reliance on U.S.-produced programming, however, Canadian regulations dictate that 60 percent of the broadcast content be produced in Canada. Of course, those Canadians near the U.S. border also can pick up local stations—including affiliates of the major U.S. networks—from nearby American cities and towns, if they have a good enough antenna.

Over-the-air broadcasts in the United Kingdom are delivered via the Freeview HD service. Freeview HD tuners are built into all newer TV sets sold in the UK and need to be connected to either an indoor or outdoor aerial (what the British call an antenna). The Freeview service broadcasts digitally in 1080i and 1080p HD, depending on the programming. And, as the name implies, it's free—no subscription necessary.

Networks available via Freeview include the BBC, Channel 4, Channel 5, and ITV. Freeview also delivers a variety of commercial channels, such as those from Sky and UKTV, as well as some pay TV services.

In this chapter, you learn how to watch your favorite shows on cable—and save money doing so.

→ Watching Basic Cable
→ Watching Premium Cable
→ Watching On-Demand Programming
→ Recording Cable Programming
→ Reducing Your Cable Bill

Getting Cable TV

Many people get their TV service from cable companies, such as Charter Spectrum, Comcast XFINITY, and Verizon. You pay your cable company a monthly fee and they run a physical cable to each TV in your house, through which you receive access to hundreds of national networks and local stations, as well as on-demand entertainment.

These monthly fees, however, can get expensive, and many users are looking to reduce or eliminate what they pay for cable. Some customers are cutting the cable cord completely, replacing cable service with Internet streaming services. Others find cable to be the easiest and most reliable way to watch their favorite shows, but are looking for ways to save money on their cable bills. Fortunately, there are many ways to save money on your monthly cable bill and still watch the programs you want.

Watching Basic Cable

Most cable providers offer several different tiers of service you choose from when you sign up. At the lowest level, you get so-called "basic" cable channels, as well as your local channels (and some—but probably not all—digital subchannels). Higher-priced tiers offer additional channels, often around some sort of theme—children's programming, sports, movies, that sort of thing.

Examining Different Plans

If you find all your favorite channels at the basic tier, that's great. More likely, you'll have to upgrade to a different tier to get all the channels you like to watch. That's when the costs start creeping up.

For example, XFINITY, the provider in my area (the southern suburbs of the Twin Cities, Minnesota), offers a half-dozen plans. Their Limited Basic plan offers 10 or so local and government channels, the Economy plan offers 100 channels, the Starter plan offers 140 channels, the Preferred plan offers 220 channels, the Preferred Plus plan has 230 channels, and the Premier plan gives you 260+ channels. Prices range from $35 USD per month to more than $100 USD per month.

It's Not All Good

Where's the Most Basic Plan?

Most cable companies are required by law to provide a low-cost basic plan with just local and public access channels. That doesn't mean they have to advertise it. If you don't see the most basic plan on your provider's website, call and ask about it.

You can save money with the Economy plan, if it includes all the channels you want to watch. Chances are, however, that you'll want at least one of the channels in the more expensive tiers, so you'll pay an extra $10 or $20 USD a month.

By the way, the plans offered in your area might be different from those offered elsewhere in the country—even from the same cable provider. And, of course, different providers offer different tiers of pricing and combinations of channels. You can find out what's available in your area by calling your cable provider or going to the company's website and entering your street address. (Because, yes, even the same local provider will offer different channels and tiers and pricings from one neighborhood or municipality to another.)

It's Not All Good

The Charges Add Up

You'll pay more than the stated subscription fee each month. If you use the cable company's set-top box, for example, you'll pay a rental fee for that. (And you'll pay extra fees for multiple boxes.) You'll also probably pay extra for additional lines in your house for additional TV sets. And there are various fees and taxes. If you have cable in your living room and a couple of bedrooms, you'll end up paying well over $100 USD per month.

Take, for example, my cable bill. My cable provider is XFINITY (also known as Comcast), and I have cable in four different rooms—living room, basement, and two bedrooms—which isn't unusual. That's four lines of cable and four cable boxes—two of which are DVRs. My latest bill included the following charges:

- XFINITY Preferred Triple Play Package (which includes Internet and voice service, along with XFINITY's Digital Preferred TV plan, Starz add-on, and HD Technology Fee): $160.00

- Equipment and services ($9.95 times two for extra non-DVR lines, $19.90 for extra DVR line, $9.95 for primary DVR service, and $11.00 for Internet/voice equipment rental): $60.75

- Other charges (various broadcast, sports, and regulatory fees): $16.01

- Service fees (franchise fee, PEG fee): $9.39

- Taxes and surcharges (state and local taxes, 911 fee): $13.69

That adds up to a whopping $259.84 every single month. To be fair, the package includes my Internet service, as well as telephone (voice) service (that I do not use) to supposedly save me a few bucks on the bundle. But the $60.75 for "equipment and services" and $16.01 for "fees" are nothing more than hidden charges for normal usage—what some would consider outrageous overcharging. This, folks, is why more and more people are cutting the cable cord. The monthly fees are completely out of hand!

Local Channels

The first tier of service on almost all cable plans includes the major local channels in your area. These are normal over-the-air (OTA) channels, typically in HD, delivered via cable. Learn more about OTA local channels in Chapter 3.

It's likely that your cable provider will also include some of the digital subchannels offered in your area—but probably not all of them. For example, my local cable provider used to deliver the WeatherNation TV diginet, which I found tremendously useful. But they kicked WeatherNation off the channel list in favor of another rerun diginet. Bandwidth, even on digital cable, is limited, and they have to make choices.

Most cable providers, as part of their contract with the local government, offer one or more public access channels. You might get local government, local education, and other informative but definitely amateur channels—along with C-SPAN (and maybe C-SPAN2 and C-SPAN3).

Major Cable Providers

Back in the early days of cable, a lot of local cable companies offered service across the nation. Today, however, the industry has consolidated so that you have only a handful of national companies offering service. The largest include Altice, AT&T, Charter Spectrum, Cox Communications, Frontier Communications, Mediacom, Verizon, WOW!, and XFINITY (Comcast). You'll typically have services from just one of these companies where you live.

News and Weather

Most cable providers offer a variety of national news, sports, and weather channels as part of their basic tiers—although some cable news channels might be slotted into a higher-priced tier, for no good reason.

The Weather Channel is a staple here, providing national forecasts and other weather-related programming. Most cable providers insert local weather conditions and forecasts into the national Weather Channel feed every few minutes, so that's good.

In terms of news, expect to find the big three—CNN, Fox News, and MSNBC. Some cable providers also offer Al Jazeera, BBC World News, CNN International, HLN, Newsmax TV, Newsy, and RT America, each of which offers its own slant on current news stories.

In addition, most providers include a few business news channels as part of their basic tiers, such as Bloomberg Television, Cheddar, CNBC, and Fox Business.

Pay Cable Channels

Once you get past the local and news channels available as part of the basic tier, cable offerings begin to fragment—and cost more. For a few dollars more each month, you get access to what the industry refers to as *pay cable*—more than 100 different channels of programming, each in its own niche.

Some of these pay channels, such as TBS and the USA Network, are more general in their offerings. Some specialize in movies, such as AMC and TCM. Some are more into specific do-it-yourself or reality niches, such as the Cooking Channel, DIY Network, the Food Network, and the Travel Channel. Other are somewhat educational in nature, such as Animal Planet, the History Channel, and the National Geographic channel. And there's always a lot of children's oriented channels, such as the Cartoon Network, Disney Channel, and Nickelodeon.

Most cable companies sort these pay channels into several different pricing tiers. Some might be available as part of the provider's basic plans; most are offered as part of their "preferred" or deluxe plans. Some of these channels might not be available at all from your cable provider; not everything is universal. See Table 4.1 for a listing of the most popular of these pay cable channels.

Table 4.1   Popular Pay Cable Channels

Channel	Programming
A&E	Non-fiction and reality programming
AMC	Movies and original programs
American Heroes Channel (AHC)	Formerly Military Channel and Discovery Wings Channel; military history, science, and warfare-related programs
Animal Planet	Nature and animal programs
Aspire	Programming for African-American audiences
BabyFirst	Programming for babies and toddlers
BBC America	Primarily British television programming (including *Doctor Who*), with some American science fiction (*Star Trek* and *The X-Files*)
BET (Black Entertainment Television)	Programming for African-American audiences

Channel	Programming
BET Her	Programming for African-American women
BET Jams	Hip-hop and urban contemporary music videos
Black Music America (BMA)	Music programming from and about black artists
Boomerang	Classic cartoons
Bravo	Reality programming, including *Top Chef* and *The Real Housewives* franchises
Cartoon Network	Animation
CMT	Formerly Country Music Television, now offers general entertainment programming
Comedy Central	Comedy and humorous programming, including *The Daily Show*
Cooking Channel	Cooking how-to programming
Destination America	Lifestyle and reality programming
Discovery Channel	Non-fiction and reality programming
Discovery Family	Children's and family programming
Discovery Life	Non-fiction and reality programming
Disney Channel	Animated and live-action Disney programming for the entire family
Disney Junior	Animated Disney programming for kids aged 2-7
Disney XD	Animated and live-action Disney and other programming for kids aged 6 to 11
DIY Network	Do-it-yourself programming
E!	Entertainment news and original series
El Rey	Grindhouse-style content, targeted at Latino audience
ePix	Older and recent movies, original programming, boxing
EWTN (Eternal World Television Network)	Catholic-themed programming
Flix	Movies from the 1970s to current day

Channel	Programming
Food Network	Cooking and competition shows
Freeform	Formerly ABC Family and The Family Channel, now airs family-friendly reruns and movies
Fuse	Music videos and lifestyle and reality programming
FX	Original programming and movies
FXM	Movies from 20th Century Fox
FXX	Comedies and other general entertainment programs targeted at young men aged 18 to 34
FYI	Lifestyle and reality programming
Game Show Network (GSN)	New and classic game shows
Golf Channel	Golf tournaments and instructional programming
Great American Country (GAC)	Country music programming
Hallmark Channel	Family-friendly series and original movies
Hallmark Drama	Family-friendly series and movies
Hallmark Movies & Mysteries	Family-friendly mystery movies
HGTV (Home and Garden Television)	Home improvement and real estate programming
History Channel	History-related non-fiction programming
HSN (Home Shopping Network)	Home shopping
HSN 2	More home shopping
IFC	Formerly known as the Independent Film Channel, now offers original series and independent films
Impact Network	Uplifting programming for black viewers
IndiePlex	Domestic and foreign independent films
INSP	Family-friendly programming, including classic Westerns

Channel	Programming
Investigation Discovery (ID)	True-crime documentaries
JTV (Jewelry Television)	Home shopping
Lifetime	Movies and television series for women
Lifetime Movies (LMN)	Original movies for women
Logo	Classic TV shows and movies, many targeted at LGBTQ audience
MGM HD	Legendary MGM studio films
MoviePlex	Older and more recent films
MTV	Reality and music-related programming
MTV 2	Reality and music-related programming
MTV Classic	Classic music videos from the 1980s to the 2000s
MTV Live	Music videos, concerts, and music-related programming
Nat Geo People	From National Geographic, outdoor adventure and travel programming
Nat Geo Wild	From National Geographic, animal-related programming
National Geographic	Non-fiction nature and science programming
National Geographic Music	International music videos
Nick Jr.	Programming for kids ages 2 to 7
Nickelodeon (NICK)	Children's programming; Nick at Nite evening block runs classic TV programs
NickMusic	Current music videos
Nicktoons	Live action and animated programming for kids
OWN (Oprah Winfrey Network)	Talk shows, documentaries, and reality programing
Oxygen	True crime programming for women
Paramount Network	Formerly Spike TV, original series, Paramount films, and reruns

Channel	Programming
Pop TV	General entertainment and reality programming
QVC	Home shopping
Reelz	General entertainment programming
RetroPlex	Classic movies from the 1910s to 1980s
Revolt	Hip-hop music-related programming
SBN (SonLife Broadcasting Network)	Religious programming
Science Channel	Science-related non-fiction programming
Smithsonian Channel	History, science, and cultural non-fiction programming
Sportsman Channel	Outdoor sports
Starz Encore	Movies from 1970s to today
Starz Encore Action	Action, horror, and martial arts movies
Starz Encore Black	Movies and television series targeted at African-American audience
Starz Encore Classic	Classic movies and television series
Starz Encore Family	Live action and animated films for a family audience
Starz Encore Suspense	Mystery and suspense films and television series
Starz Encore Westerns	Classic and contemporary Western movies and television series
Sundance TV	Independent films and reality programming
Syfy	Formerly the Sci-Fi Channel, science fiction movies and series
TBS	Atlanta-based superstation offering general entertainment programming and some sports
TeenNick	Live-action and animated programming for teenagers and young adults
TLC	Formerly The Learning Channel, reality and lifestyle programming
TNT	General entertainment programming and some sports

Channel	Programming
Travel Channel	Travel and lifestyle programming
Tres (Tr3s)	Lifestyle and music-related programming targeted at Latino audiences
Trinity Broadcasting Network (TBN)	Religious programming
Tru TV	Comedy- and reality-based programming
Turner Classic Movies (TCM)	Classic movies
TV Land	Classic TV programs from the 1950s to the 2000s
TV One	Newer and classic programming targeted at an African-American audience
Universal Kids	Formerly PBS Kids Sprout, offering programming for kids aged 2 to 12
UP TV (Uplifting Entertainment)	Family-friendly movies and TV shows
USA	General entertainment programming and some sports
Velocity	Automotive-themed programming and racing events
VH1	Reality programming and some music videos
Viceland	Lifestyle and reality programming targeted at millennials
WE TV	Lifestyle and entertainment programming for women
WGN	Chicago-based superstation offering general entertainment programming

Browse the Channel Guide

You find all these channels via your cable provider's onscreen channel guide. This is typically a grid-like guide that lets you scroll up and down through all the available channels.

Different cable companies use different cable boxes with different interfaces, and some onscreen guides are fancier than others, but they all work pretty much the same way. You use the up and down arrow button on your remote to scroll sequentially through the available channels. And you use the left and right arrow buttons to scroll through the guide in half-hour increments. When you find a program you want to watch, just press the Enter or Select button on your remote, and you go directly to that channel.

The channel guide for XFINITY's X1 service—most guides are similar to this one.

You can also go directly to a channel by entering the channel number on your remote (if you know the channel, that is). Many cable providers also let you set up lists of favorite channels, so you don't have to scroll through a hundred channels to find the ones you like best.

>>>Go Further
SPANISH-LANGUAGE CHANNELS

Many cable providers offer a variety of channels targeted at a Spanish-speaking audience. These channels typically include the three major Latino networks—Galavision, Telemundo, and Univision—along with several more niche channels, including Canal Once and Cine Latino. You'll also find Spanish-language versions of traditional cable channels, such as CNN, ESPN, and HSN.

Some cable services offer these Latino channels as part of their normal plans. Others offer separate plans with these Latino channels only. Ask your cable provider what Spanish-language channels and plans it offers.

Sports Channels

One thing that cable excels at is offering a variety of sports-oriented channels. This goes well beyond ESPN (and ESPN2, ESPN3, ESPN Classic, ESPNews, and ESPNU). Most cable providers offer packages of local, regional, and (sometimes) national pro sports games, for Major League Baseball, Major League Soccer, the National Basketball Association, the National Football League, the National Hockey League, NASCAR racing, and NCAA college sports.

Some of these channels (typically one or more of the ESPN family, as well as Fox Sports and the NBC Sports Network) are offered as part of one of the basic tiers. Other channels might be included with more expensive plans or as part of separate sports packages. There might also be access to one-time-only sporting events (such as boxing and wrestling matches) on a pay-per-view basis.

Cable sports packages can get pricey, depending on which sports you follow. For example, XFINITY's NBA League Pass, which offers access for up to 40 out-of-market games each week, runs almost $200. The service's NHL Center Ice package is a little less expensive, at just $140 USD.

These packages significantly expand (but also include) the sports programming available on your local broadcast channels. Yes, you'll get your local teams' games, but also a ton of out-of-market games. This is one instance where cable offers much more variety than what you can get from your local channels—or even online streaming services.

>>>Go Further
CHOOSING A CABLE PROVIDER

When it comes to choosing a cable service, people in most locations have a single choice. That's because cable licenses are granted by city or county governments, and they typically only grant one. If you're like most of us, you have the grand number of one cable provider to choose from.

Other locales, however, have more competition. Some local governments are now granting multiple licenses for cable service, so you might have more than one provider to choose from. If that's the case for you, that's good. It's also beneficial to have competition; compare services and prices and choose the service that works best for you.

Watching Premium Cable

As you've seen, there's basic cable (your local channels, news and weather channels, and a few other essentials) and there's pay cable (most of the topic-specific cable channels). Then there's *premium cable*—those individual cable channels that you typically pay extra for.

Understanding Premium Channels

Premium cable channels are able to charge a premium because they offer programming you can't get elsewhere. These channels began by offering first-run movies, but over the past several years have added a variety of original movies and series programming. Premium cable is where you find such modern classics as *Game of Thrones* and *Westworld* (HBO), *Homeland* and *Ray Donovan* (Showtime), and *Outlander* and *Power* (Starz).

Premium channels are not typically offered as part of a cable service's normal plans. Instead, you pay extra to add individual premium channels to an existing plan. Some premium channels are groups of channels; for example, an HBO subscription gets you access to the HBO, HBO 2, HBO Comedy, HBO Family, HBO Latino, HBO Signature, and HBO Zone channels, each with its own focus and programming. You might pay from $6 to $15 USD per month or more for each premium channel; some cable companies offer bundles of two or more premium channels at a reduced rate.

Discovering Premium Channels

What premium channels/packages are available? Table 4.2 details those channels that are typically offered on a premium basis. (Your cable provider might not offer these channels.)

Table 4.2   Popular Premium Channel Packages

Main channel	Included channels	
Cinemax	5StarMax	MoreMax
	ActionMax	MovieMax
	Cinemax	OuterMax
	Cinemax Spanish	ThrillerMax
ePix	ePix	ePix Drive-In
	ePix2	ePix Hits
HBO	HBO	HBO Latino
	HBO 2	HBO Signature
	HBO Comedy	HBO Zone
	HBO Family	
The Movie Channel	The Movie Channel	The Movie Channel Xtra
Showtime	Showcase	Showtime Extreme
	Showtime	Showtime Family Zone
	Showtime 2	Showtime Next
	Showtime Beyond	Showtime Women
Starz	Starz	Starz Edge
	Starz Cinema	Starz in Black
	Starz Comedy	Starz Kids & Family

Saving Money on Premium Channels

The easiest way to save money on premium channels is not to subscribe to them. If your viewing needs are perfectly satiated with the hundreds of basic and pay channels available, you don't have to spend the extra money for premium channels.

If there's a program on a premium channel on your must-view list, then by all means subscribe to that channel—but to that channel only. If you subscribe to every pay channel available, you'll add $60 or more to your monthly bill. Instead, subscribe to a single channel and add $12 per month or so to your bill.

If you've subscribed to one or more premium channels, observe your viewing habits over time. If you, like I did, find that you seldom if ever watch a given premium channel, cancel your subscription. You shouldn't pay for anything you don't watch.

Finally, if you do watch programs on a variety of premium channels, ask your cable company if it has some sort of premium bundle that might lower your price. Companies like to bundle channels together in a single package for a single price; take advantage of any savings that are available.

>>>*Go Further*

COMPETING TECHNOLOGIES: CABLE VERSUS FIBER

What we call cable TV might actually be delivered by one of two competing and very different technologies.

The older and most popular technology is literally delivered via a cable—a coaxial cable, to be precise. The cable company sends the signals of hundreds of different stations from its distribution branch to your local neighborhood via fiber optic cable. A tap is then made into the main line, and a coaxial cable is run from that tap into the cable box on top of the TV in your home. This system uses a radio frequency (RF) signal with 550MHz of digital bandwidth, enough to handle hundreds of individual stations, most in HD.

The newer "cable" technology doesn't use traditional cable at all. Instead, it uses fiber optic technology from beginning to end, with signals transmitted via optical digital signal. This system (dubbed *fiber optic service*, or *FIOS*) offers more bandwidth than the older radio frequency technology, which means space for more HD stations. The FIOS technology has enough bandwidth for high-speed Internet and phone service to piggyback on the same cable.

FIOS is theoretically a faster technology with greater bandwidth than traditional cable, but recent advancements have increased both the speed and bandwidth available via copper coaxial cable. In reality, both technologies deliver an HD picture with hundreds of channels, with both Internet and phone service piggybacking on the same cable into your home. There is no practical advantage of one over the other.

Watching On-Demand Programming

The advent of digital cable in the late 1990s (before that, cable signals were analog) enabled the option of on-demand programming. This lets you order individual movies and TV shows and view them immediately after your request. You're no longer limited to watching shows when they're broadcast; on-demand functionality lets you watch a wide variety of cable programming and first-run movies on your own schedule.

How On-Demand Technology Works

On-demand technology starts with a large bank of servers at the cable company—or more precisely, somewhere in the Internet "cloud." On these servers are stored copies of the on-demand programming offered by the cable company—movies, TV shows, you name it.

When you order an on-demand program, your request is sent upstream to the cable company's control center. This triggers the playback of the program from the cable company's servers. (It also triggers the billing of that program to your account, if it's a program with a fee attached; some on-demand programming is free.)

The requested program is transmitted via cable to your set-top cable box, and playback begins. You have full interactive control over the on-demand program; when you pause, fast forward, or rewind the program, those requests are sent upstream to the network server, which affects playback of the programming you're viewing.

What's on On-Demand

What types of programs can you watch on-demand from your cable provider? Most cable companies offer hundreds of different programs, including

- **Movies:** After a movie is done playing in theaters, it's typically available next on-demand. These are the most recent films—blockbusters and not—available for a fee.

- **Recent TV and cable shows:** You'll find the most recent episodes of your favorite shows, typically for free, so you can catch up on your viewing.

- **Older TV and cable shows:** You might also find previous season's' episodes of your favorite shows. These often are available for a fee.

- **Children's programming:** Want to occupy the small fry in your house? Check out the (mostly free) on-demand programming from Disney, Nickelodeon, and other kids' channels.

- **Adult programming:** Yes, you can rent your favorite "adult programs" on-demand, too. (These are never free.)

Ordering an on-demand program is relatively simple. Most cable providers let you select an on-screen menu item to browse through or search available on-demand programs. These programs are typically organized by category—movies, TV shows, children's programming, and so forth. Click to view details about a program (including the cost to view, if it's a pay-per-view item), then click again to begin playback.

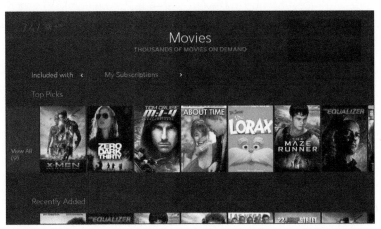

Browsing through the on-demand offerings from Charter Spectrum.

Much on-demand programming is free. Free programming typically includes recent TV programs, so you can catch up if you've missed anything. Prior-season shows and most current movies, however, cost money to watch—anywhere from a buck or two for an individual TV show to $15 USD or more for a first-run movie. When you click the buy or rent button, the appropriate charge will be added to your current cable bill.

>>>Go Further

WHERE TO WATCH SCIENCE FICTION

If you're a science fiction buff, cable is the place for you. Tons of sci-fi shows and movies play every day on a variety of cable channels.

The first channel to check out is the venerable Syfy. (It used to be called the Sci-Fi Channel, but I guess "Syfy" sounds more hip.) Syfy offers a variety of original and made-for-cable series, miniseries, and movies. It's not classic sci-fi (at least not anymore), but it is where you'll find all those cheesy *Sharknado* movies.

If you like *Doctor Who*, the new Who in particular, then BBC America is the channel for you; it's where you'll find the latest shows starring the current Doctor. This channel airs a lot of American *Star Trek*, as well.

For classic *Doctor Who*, subscribe to the BBC's BritBox streaming video service. It has all the pre-relaunch episodes, including everything from my favorite Doctor, Tom Baker.

Another must-see streaming media service for sci-fi buffs is CBS All Access. This where you'll find the new *Star Trek: Discovery* series. (And more new *Trek* series are in development for viewing here!)

The subchannels of your local TV stations are also good places to watch classic sci-fi shows and movies. The Comet diginet is all sci-fi all the time, with a ton of 1950s sci-fi flicks as well as sci-fi TV shows such as *Andromeda, Babylon 5, Space: 1999, Stargate SG-1*. The Heroes & Icons channel is your place for everything *Star Trek,* from the original series up to *Star Trek Enterprise*, including *Star Trek: The Next Generation*. And MeTV runs the original *Battlestar Galactica, Buck Rogers in the 25th Century, Lost in Space,* and *Voyage to the Bottom of the Sea,* as well as the occasional 1950s sci-fi film on *Svengoolie*.

Finally, Amazon Prime Video, Hulu, and Netflix all have a good variety of science fiction programming, old and new. Their offerings change monthly, so check the listings to see what's currently available.

Recording Cable Programming

With over a hundred channels available on cable, chances are you won't be able to watch everything you want the moment it airs live. Fortunately, your cable provider offers a cable box with a built in digital video recorder (DVR). This box lets you record the programs you want, and store them for viewing at a future time and date.

Types of Cable DVRs

Know that your cable company's DVR box is going to cost you more than a standard cable box without recording capabilities. You're renting the box, of course, but you might pay $10 USD or so a month extra for the recording capability. (And that's just for the box; some cable companies charge another $10 USD for the line going into the DVR.)

Traditional cable DVRs use hard disk technology, the same as you have in your notebook or desktop computer. The bigger the built-in hard drive, the more programs you can store. Although most cable companies don't give out detailed specifications, most DVR boxes come with hard drives in the 200GB to 1TB range. That'll let you record anywhere from 20 to 180 hours of HD programming, depending on the model.

The ARRIS DCX3510 cable DVR box with 500GB storage, used by many cable companies.
(Photo courtesy ARRIS, www.arris.com.)

Some cable companies offer cloud-based DVRs. In this system, the recording is not stored on your local cable box. Instead, whatever you set to record is actually recorded on the cable company's "cloud" servers. This theoretically provides more storage capacity, although most providers limit the amount of cloud storage you get. And they'll typically only store your cloud-based recordings for a limited length of time; with a hard disk DVR, you can store your programs as long as you want.

All DVRs include at least one cable tuner. Some include two or four or even six built-in tuners, which let you record (and view) multiple programs at once. For example, a box with two tuners lets you record two shows at once, or view one show while you're recording another. The more tuners the better.

Schedule a Recording

If you're watching a program and decide you want to record it (if you must leave in the middle of a program, for example), all you have to do is press the red Record button on your remote. Your cable DVR will record from that point to the end of the program—and, with some systems, back to the beginning of the program, as well.

Most people, however, set their cable DVRs to record programs in advance. Maybe there's a movie or sporting event coming up that you want to record. Or maybe you have a favorite TV series that you want to record all new upcoming episodes. Whatever the case, setting your cable box to record a future program is relatively easy.

1 From your onscreen program guide, navigate to and select the program you want to record.

2 From the available options, select the option to set a recording.

3 If you're recording a single program, select the option to record this program.

4 If you want to record an entire series, select the option to set up a series recording.

5 Select the appropriate options. In most cases, this means recording only new episodes, and saving them until space is needed.

6 Select to record the program or series with these settings. Your DVR is set record those programs you selected.

View a Recorded Program

Viewing a program you recorded is as simple as selecting it from your list of saved programs.

1 From your cable's onscreen menu, navigate to where your recorded programs are stored.

2 Your recordings are listed by program. Select a program to view all recorded episodes.

3 Select the episode you want to watch.

>>>Go Further

A SHORT HISTORY OF CABLE TELEVISION IN THE UNITED STATES

Cable television was first developed for entirely practical reasons. Many rural American viewers were located too far away from big-city transmitting antennas and couldn't receive the signals of many (if any) major television stations. Cable was used to transmit these far-away broadcast television stations to rural customers.

The first cable network in the United States was established in 1948, when remote Pennsylvanians solved their reception problems by putting antennas on the nearest hills and running cables to their houses in the valleys. In the 1950s, rural cable systems began using microwave transmitting and receiving towers to capture even more-distant signals. This made television available to people who lived outside the range of standard broadcasts—and, in some instances, gave cable customers access to several broadcast stations of the same national network.

By the early 1970s, many cable operators began offering additional channels, obtained from satellite broadcasters. Some of these channels, such as Atlanta's WTBS and Chicago's WGN, were simply local channels from elsewhere in the country. Other, more targeted channels were developed specifically for the cable market. These new cable channels included the Cable News Network (CNN) and Home Box Office (HBO), the latter of which was the first "pay" channel.

Today, cable systems deliver hundreds of channels to more than 30 million American homes. That's down from a peak of 68 million subscribers in the year 2000 (lots of cord-cutters have defected to Internet streaming video services in recent years), but it's still a lot of people who are connected to that ubiquitous cable box.

Reducing Your Cable Bill

As you've learned, cable TV can get very expensive very fast. When you add all the different packages and channels and options, as well as all the different lines and boxes you need, your bill can very quickly become three figures.

Fortunately, there are some things you can do to reduce your monthly cable bill. Let's examine a few.

Choose a Skinnier Package

Your cable company offers several different monthly plans, each with its own selection of channels. Examine the channels you actually watch and see if you really need that higher-end, higher-cost plan you're probably on. If you watch only a handful of channels on a regular basis, you might be able to go with a less-expensive plan. Even better, consider using Hulu to watch your favorite shows a day or two after they air, and go with a very skinny cable plan. And remember, you might have to ask for a lower-priced plan; the skinniest packages might not be offered on your cable company's website.

Choose a Bigger Bundle—If You Need It

Cable companies like you to spend as much money with them as you can. To that end, they often offer additional services beyond just cable television—your cable company may offer Internet, telephone, and even home security services.

If you need some or these services, you might be able to save money by getting them all from your cable provider. Most cable companies offer "double play" or "triple play" or even "quadruple play" bundles that include TV, Internet, phone, and home security services. You shouldn't go with a bundle unless you really need these services, but the bundled savings are often substantial.

Negotiate a Better Price

Here's one you might not know. You might be able to negotiate a lower price for your service. I've been able to negotiate a lower price by calling up my cable company and threatening to disconnect my service. "My cable bill is just too expensive," I say, and then I mention that I'm considering disconnecting everything and going with Internet streaming only. More often than not, the cable company responds with some sort of deal.

This offer will probably be presented as a one-time thing and require a one- (or more-) year commitment. You might also have to subscribe to a higher-end plan or multi-services bundle—but at a lower price. Evaluate what the company is offering and make your decision.

Of course, the cable company might also say that you're already getting a good price and it can't go any lower. It never hurts to ask, in any case.

Supply Your Own Equipment

If you get both TV and Internet service from your cable provider, chances are it gives you (or, more accurately, rent you) what it calls an Internet gateway. This little box combines a cable modem to receive Internet service and a wireless router to broadcast your Internet signal via Wi-Fi. You pay the cable company a monthly fee to rent this device.

You can save money by buying your own cable modem and wireless router. Yes, you pay a few hundred bucks up front for the equipment (which you can get from Best Buy or any similar store), but you save the monthly rental fees you pay to the cable company. You'll probably have to call the cable company's tech support to switch over to your boxes, and then you return the cable company's gateway. You'll save at least $10 a month, which should pay for your new hardware within a year or so. After that, you pocket the savings.

Cut the Cable Cord Completely

Many viewers are tiring of their increasingly high cable television bills; they deal with it by unsubscribing from cable entirely. This is referred to as *cord-cutting*, and involves replacing traditional cable delivery with a combination of over-the-air broadcasts and Internet streaming services.

Much cable programming is available for free or relatively low cost over the Internet. Many cable companies offer their own streaming apps that you can view via a Roku or similar streaming media player. Other cable programming is available for a slight monthly fee via Hulu and Netflix; some cable channels offer their own subscription streaming services, as well.

Internet Streaming Services

Learn more about streaming video services in Chapter 7, "Watching the Big Three Streaming Services: Amazon Prime Video, Hulu, and Netflix" and Chapter 8, "Watching Premium Network Streaming Services."

Local channels (and their corresponding broadcast networks) are available over the public airwaves for free, of course. All you have to do is connect the appropriate antenna to your TV and you're ready to go.

Getting Local and Broadcast TV for Free

Learn more about receiving local and broadcast TV in Chapter 3, "Getting Local and Broadcast Television over the Air."

If you want live broadcast and cable TV over the Internet, you need to subscribe to a live streaming service, such as PlayStation Vue, Sling TV, or YouTube TV. These services offer a variety of plans, much like cable providers do, but at a somewhat lower monthly cost.

Live Streaming Services

Learn more about these cable replacement services in Chapter 10, "Watching Live Broadcast and Cable TV with Live Streaming Services."

Of course, cutting the cable cord requires you to continue to keep Internet service, typically from your cable company. But all cable companies offer Internet-only service, for as little as $30 USD or so per month. You'll pay more for higher-speed service as well as if you need to rent a cable modem or router (or combination gateway) from the cable company. Still, that's a lot less than you're probably spending today on a full-blown cable plus Internet package, and that's your savings.

>>>Go Further

CABLE TELEVISION IN CANADA AND THE UK

A number of local and regional cable providers operate in Canada, such as Bell Canada, Rogers, Shaw, and Vidéotron. As in most of the United States, these companies do not really compete with one another; most cities and territories license a single company to provide cable service to customers in that area.

Canadian cable companies offer a variety of Canadian and U.S. channels, as long as those U.S. channels do not compete directly with available Canadian channels. For this reason, U.S. channels such as Comedy Central, ESPN, HBO, and Nickelodeon are not available on Canadian cable systems; instead, similar Canadian channels (or Canada-specific versions of those channels) are offered. For example, Canadian cable systems offer NickCanada instead of the U.S. Nickelodeon channel, and the Canadian Sportsnet and TSN sports channels instead of ESPN.

By law, all Canadian cable providers must offer a basic package that includes all Canadian broadcast networks, all local and regional broadcasters, and various public service channels. This package must cost no more than $25 CAD per month, and typically includes the major U.S. broadcast networks, too. Higher-priced plans are also available that include hundreds more specialty channels, most in HD.

In the United Kingdom, Virgin Media is the single dominant cable operator, covering 95% of the market. Virgin Media offers more than 200 digital channels, many in HD, along with Internet and telephone services. Prices start at £26 per month and go up from there.

Getting Satellite TV

Aside from over-the-air (OTA) broadcasts and cable transmission, there is another way to receive your favorite programming. Satellite television delivers similar programming as cable but without any cables necessary. All you need is a smallish satellite dish—and a clear view of the southern sky.

Beaming TV from Space!

To those of us who grew up with three or four local channels and a set of rabbit ears on a black and white TV, satellite television sounds a little like science fiction. After all, it involves beaming signals from a satellite orbiting in outer space.

How Satellite Television Works

Consumer satellite television initially was an option that only viewers in remote areas chose because they had no access to traditional broadcast or cable signals. The only way these remote viewers could receive television programming was to pick it off from the existing networks' private satellites—the same satellites that transferred programming from network head-quarters to local affiliates.

The dishes used to receive this early satellite programming were huge things—six or eight feet in diameter. You found these dishes at homes in the country; they were too big for the typical suburban back yard.

The next stage in satellite television came about in the mid-1990s with the advent of smaller direct broadcast satellite (DBS) systems. These systems use powerful satellites that orbit in a stationary spot over the earth; this enables the use of smaller satellite dishes on the ground. Today, DBS satellite systems are offered in the United States by only two providers: DirecTV (owned by AT&T) and the DISH Network.

DBS signals are capable of transmitting high-definition programming. They travel from the satellite provider's transmitting dish on Earth approximately 22,300 miles through space to one of the provider's satellites, which are positioned in orbit over the equator. For this reason, satellite dishes should be pointed toward the southwest with an unobstructed view of the southwest sky.

Satellite signals travel from the provider's Earth-based transmitting dish to an orbiting satellite back down to a small dish on the subscriber's home.

The DBS signals bounce off the satellite back to Earth (another 22,300-mile trip), and are received by a small (20"-24") round or oval satellite dish mounted to the subscriber's house. The signals are then sent from the satellite dish to one or more set-top receiver boxes that are connected to the subscriber's television sets, typically via HDMI cable.

Like cable subscribers, satellite TV subscribers pay for various tiers of programming. Subscribers also have to pay for the satellite dish and to have it installed. This initial investment is typically subsidized by the satellite providers, who offer free installation as part of an initial subscription package.

Watch Satellite Programming

Watching satellite TV is much like watching cable. You operate the satellite box, like a cable box, with the included remote control. The box displays an on-screen channel guide, similar to the kind used by cable companies.

You can go directly to a channel by entering its channel number, or you can browse through available channels in the guide. Use the up and down arrow buttons on the remote to scroll up and down the channel numbers; use the right and left arrow buttons to scroll forward and backward in time. Press the Enter or Select button on the remote to tune into the selected channel.

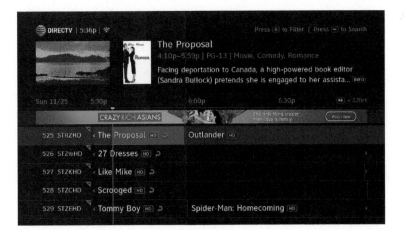

Browsing through the channels with DirecTV's program guide.

Record Satellite Programming

Both DirecTV and DISH Network offer set-top boxes with DVR capability, making it possible for you to record programs on the DVR's hard drive. You can then watch your recordings at a convenient time in the future.

If you want to record a program you're currently watching, all you have to do is press the red Record button on your remote. Your DVR records from that point to the end of the program—and, with some systems, it even records from the beginning of the program.

Recording a program in advance is equally easy, using the program guide.

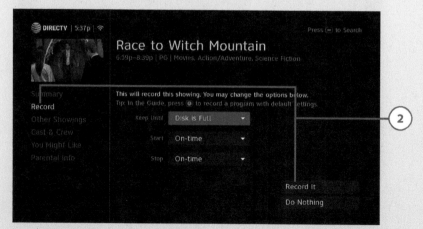

(1) From your onscreen program guide, navigate to and select the program you want to record by pressing the Enter or Select button.

(2) If you're recording a single program, select the option to record this program.

(**3**) If you want to record an entire series, select the option to record a series.

(**4**) Select the appropriate options. In most cases, this means recording only first-run epi-sodes, and saving them until space is needed.

(**5**) Select to record the program or series with these settings. Your DVR will record those programs you selected when they air.

View a Recorded Program

Viewing a program you recorded is as simple as selecting it from your list of saved programs.

(**1**) From your cable's onscreen menu, navigate to where your recorded programs are stored.

(**2**) Your recordings are displayed. Select the program you want to watch.

Watch On-Demand Programming

DirecTV and DISH Network also offer on-demand programming, including both TV shows and recent movies. Some of this programming (TV shows, primarily) is free; some of it costs money.

To order a program, just navigate to the on-demand section of your provider's program guide. On-demand programs are typically organized by channel, genre, or type; you also can choose to search for a particular program. Click to view details about a program (including the cost to view, if it's a pay-per-view item), then click again to begin playback.

Browsing through DirecTV's on-demand offerings.

DirecTV Versus DISH: Comparing Satellite Providers

In the United States, we have two competing satellite TV services: DirecTV and DISH Network. Both work in similar fashion with similar (but not identical) equipment. Both offer similar programming at similar prices, although the pricing and content of individual package plans vary somewhat. How do you choose which provider is best for you? It's all in the details.

Comparing Equipment

The two satellite providers use different equipment; you can't use a DirecTV dish to pick up signals from a DISH satellite. Each company fields its own contingent of geosynchronous satellites, each in their own unique positions in orbit above the Earth. Not only do you have to use a company's satellite dish but you have to position that dish appropriately for that company's satellite.

When it comes to dishes, they're similar but not identical. DirecTV uses an elliptical dish, and the size varies according to your location; the typical dish is 22.5 inches by 32.5 inches. DISH, on the other hand, uses an oval dish, 23 inches in diameter. The dishes differ slightly as dictated by the companies' individual technologies; the differences don't affect performance. (Locations on the fringe of the satellite's range, such as in Alaska or Hawaii, might require a slightly larger dish.)

A typical DirecTV home satellite dish.

The bigger differences come in the companies' set-top boxes. Interestingly, the set-top technology used by DirecTV and DISH Network is somewhat more advanced than what you find in the typical cable box.

DirecTV calls its set-top box the Genie. A single Genie box transmits programming to up to 8 secondary Genie Mini boxes connected in other rooms of your home. Genie lets you record up to five shows simultaneously and store up to 200 hours of HD programming on its 1TB hard drive.

DirecTV's Genie DVR. (Photo courtesy DirecTV, www.directv.com.)

DISH's set-top box is called the Hopper; you install a single Hopper DVR and then beam live and recorded programming to other rooms with secondary boxes, called Joeys. The latest version, the Hopper 3, lets you record up to 16 shows at the same time. It also offers a 2TB hard drive that can store up to 500 hours of HD content.

DISH's Hopper 3 DVR. (Photo courtesy DISH Network, www.dish.com.)

Table 5.1 compares the basics of the two systems.

Table 5.1　Comparing DirecTV and DISH Network Systems

	DirecTV	**DISH Network**
Dish size	Elliptical, 22.5 × 32.5 inch	Round, 23-inch diameter
Main set-top box	Genie	Hopper 3
Secondary boxes	Genie Mini (up to 8)	Joey (up to 6)
DVR tuners	5	16
DVR capacity	1TB (200 hours)	2TB (500 hours)

Comparing Programming

Both DirecTV and DISH Network offer more than 300 channels of programming, much of it in HD. The channels offered are similar (if not identical) to those provided by the major cable TV services.

Cable and Satellite Channels

For a more complete discussion of the channels offered by cable and satellite providers, see Chapter 4, "Getting Cable TV," in particular Table 4.1.

Both satellite providers offer basic, pay, and premium channels. Programming is similar between DirecTV and DISH; they all have all the major networks, although there are some minor or niche channels that you might find only on one system. If there's a channel you absolutely must have, check the DirecTV or DISH channel guides (available on their websites) to see who carries that channel.

DirecTV and DISH both rebroadcast the major local stations in your area (in HD), although not those stations' digital subchannels. That means no Antenna TV or Heroes & Icons. For that, your best option is to connect an antenna to your TV and watch over-the-air.

The big difference between the two providers comes in the form of sports programming; DirecTV carries more and more diverse sports channels than does DISH. Of particular importance is the fact that DirecTV offers the NFL Sunday Ticket package, and DISH does not. So, if you want to watch all your favorite NFL games, it's an easy choice—DirecTV has them, but DISH doesn't.

In addition, both satellite providers offer a variety of music-only channels for your listening pleasure. DISH has a slight advantage here in that it offers 60 channels of music and talk programming from Sirius XM Satellite Radio. If you like listening to Sirius XM in your car, DISH enables you to continue listening at home, too.

Comparing Pricing

To get all the channels you want, you'll end up spending $100 USD or more per month with either DirecTV or DISH. Of course, both companies package their channels in different tiers and plans, so you might have to pay a little more to get the channel you want from one provider or another.

DirecTV's basic package starts at $35 USD per month with 155 or so channels. Plans top out at $110 USD per month with 330+ channels available. Some premium and sports channels are optional and extra above that. (These prices are for the first 12 months of a new contract and go up after that.)

DISH's basic package starts at $59.99 USD per month with 120 channels. Plan pricing goes up to $89.99 USD per month with a slightly lower 290+ total channels available. Again, some premium channels and sports packages are extra beyond that. (These prices are for the first 24 months of a new contract and go up after that.)

Both DirecTV and DISH Network offer free installation. Most plans require a one-year (or more) commitment.

Making a Choice

Given the similarities and differences between the two satellite services, which is best for you? As always, it comes down to what you want to watch, and how you want to watch it.

If you're a sports fan, DirecTV is the better choice; you simply have more channels available. This is especially true if you're into football, due to DirecTV's exclusive NFL Sunday Ticket package.

On the other hand, if you want the most advanced technology, DISH might be your choice. The Hopper 3 DVR has both more tuners (16 versus 5 with DirecTV's Genie) and more storage space (2TB versus 1TB). So if you do a lot of recording of a lot of different programs, DISH is the way to go.

Aside from these differences, it all comes down to what channels you want, what packages they're in, and how much you'll have to pay for those packages. For many customers, it's a coin flip.

>>>Go Further

WHERE TO WATCH CLASSIC MOVIES

When it comes to watching classic films—true classics, not just old B-movies—there's one channel to turn to: Turner Classic Movies, also known as TCM. TCM is a cable and satellite channel that specializes in feature films from the silent era through the mid-1980s, with a sweet spot in the 1940s and 1950s. It's *the* place to get your fix of film noirs and serials, dramas and comedies, foreign films and musicals. It's where you'll find *Citizen Kane, Casablanca, Singin' in the Rain*, and other true classics, as well as a fair number of more obscure movies. If you're a real movie buff you *must* have TCM on your cable or satellite plan.

Also good is the Retroplex channel, owned by Starz, which offers an eclectic mix of films from the 1920s through the 1980s; it's not as purely classic as TCM, but it does have a lot of old movies on tap. Retroplex is available on DISH Network and many cable systems, but it's not currently on DirecTV.

Beyond these two channels, the pickings for classic films on cable and satellite get a little slim. There are a few cable/satellite channels that run some classic films as part of their genre-specific programming (such as the Starz Encore channels) but none that specialize in the classics.

You can find more channels offering older films (not all of them true classics) on the diginets carried on the subchannels of your local TV stations. Of particular interest are the Charge!, Comet, Grit, Movies!, and This TV. All of these channels schedule some older movies as part of their daily programming.

If you have an Amazon Fire TV, Apple TV, or Roku streaming media player, check out the Film Detective streaming app. This app offers dozens of mostly pre-1950 classic movies, all digitally remastered. You'll pay $3.99 USD per month for a subscription. Other good streaming services for classic (and other) films are Fandor, Popcornflix, and Shout Factory TV.

Perhaps surprisingly, Hulu and Netflix, two of the big Internet streaming services, don't offer a lot of classic movies. You'll find a few older films there, but mainly they focus on newer movies, TV shows, and original programming. It's worth looking there, but you won't find much.

Outside of these streaming apps, the best online source for classic films is Amazon Prime Video. The main service doesn't offer a lot of classic films as part of its subscription, but Amazon does offer a huge variety of classic and foreign films for rental or purchase. Just access the Amazon Prime Video app via your Roku or other streaming player, pay for your selection, and stream the films you love. (And if you have an Apple TV box, the iTunes Store offers a similar selection for purchase or rental.)

By the way, there *used* to be a really great streaming service for classic and foreign films that is unfortunately no more. FilmStruck was owned by the Warner Bros., the parent company of TCM, and carried a lot of TCM-like programming, along with Criterion releases and other classic movies. Unfortunately, Warner decided that FilmStruck, even though it was a subscription service, wasn't making enough money, and pulled its plug at the end of 2018. That's a shame, and it leaves true movie lovers with no good streaming source for classic movies. (Know, however, that Criterion intends to launch its own streaming service for classic and foreign films in 2019; that will fill some of the space left by FilmStruck's exit.)

Cable Versus Satellite: What's Best for You

If you live way out in the country, you don't have much of an option; if cable doesn't reach you, you have to get your programming via satellite. If you live in the city or suburbs, however, you probably have a choice. If you have both cable and satellite TV available, which should you choose?

Comparing Programming

All cable and satellite providers offer similar content from basic, pay, and premium channels, as well as local broadcast stations, with a few major exceptions:

- **Local channels:** While DirecTV and DISH offer the major local channels in most major metropolitan areas, they might not rebroadcast smaller independent stations, or any stations in rural locations. Cable is going to cover all your local stations all the time, as required by their licensing from local authorities. You'll also find local educational and public access stations on cable that no satellite provider carries.

- **Diginets:** Most cable providers offer at least some of the diginets broadcast on the local stations' subchannels. Satellite providers do not (actually, cannot) offer these diginets. So if you like the vintage TV and movies you find on your local diginets, cable is your only choice.

- **Sports:** If you're looking for the most sports channels and packages, DirecTV has everybody beat. Cable comes next, with most providers offering decent sports packages, and DISH Network brings up the rear.

It's Not All Good

No Diginets on Satellite

The reason you won't find diginets on satellite services is that the diginets themselves only have digital subchannel broadcast rights to the programming they offer. With a few exceptions (Ion Television on DirecTV and MeTV on DISH in some locations) the satellite providers cannot legally rebroadcast these diginet channels.

Comparing Installation

In terms of installation, cable has satellite beat, hands down. The cable company runs a simple coaxial cable into your home, then runs off that cable into set-top boxes in different rooms. Satellite TV requires installation of what some might call an ugly satellite dish somewhere on the outside of your house or apartment. That makes for a somewhat more complicated installation with more equipment.

That said, the ability of today's satellite companies to beam programming from a single box to secondary boxes in other rooms negates the need to run cable throughout your house. So advantage satellite for that.

In addition, some locations do not lend themselves to one or the other type of providers. If you live out in the country, you might not have cable available, making satellite your only choice. Conversely, if you live in the city surrounded by tall buildings, or in the burbs with lots of tall trees around, those elements might block your view of the southern sky, which you need to pick up satellite signals. In either instance, your choice might be made for you.

Comparing Technology

Speaking of those beaming boxes, the equipment you get with satellite TV is more technologically advanced than what you typically get from your cable company. The DVRs available from DirecTV and (especially) DISH offer more built-in tuners and hard drive storage than you get with the average cable box. The satellite companies have always been on the cutting edge of interface design, as well, which makes for a cleaner, easier-to-use program guide. And the ability to beam programming from a single main box to secondary boxes in other rooms sure beats having to rent individual cable boxes for every room in your house.

In addition, many cable companies don't do a great job of upgrading their equipment. If you've had cable for a half-dozen years, you probably still have that original set-top box, which isn't near as advanced as the newer boxes available today. If you want more built-in tuners and storage, you'll have to turn in your old cable box for a new one—which can be a time-consuming and often frustrating experience. In my experience, both DirecTV and DISH Network are much better about upgrading their equipment so that you have the latest and greatest available.

Comparing Reliability

In general, cable is typically more reliable than satellite. That's because satellite reception is dependent to some degree on the elements. You need a clear line of sight between your dish and the orbiting satellite, and anything that gets in the way of that can cause your signal to deteriorate or go out completely. Heavy rain, snow, and even fog can cause reception problems, as can errant branches and leaves. (When this happens during a rainstorm, it's called "rain fade.") The last thing you want is not being able to access your local weather coverage because your satellite went out during a storm.

Cable, on the other hand, has fewer variables to deal with and ends up being more reliable. Although the cable company can always have issues that interrupt your service for periods of time, you're not dependent on the weather. You're more likely to have uninterrupted service during extreme weather with cable than with satellite.

Comparing Costs

Prices on the surface might seem to be comparable, but cable ends up costing a little more than satellite for most people. Cable companies have an annoying habit of charging extra fees for every little thing—extra rooms, extra boxes, DVRs, HD service, you name it. Satellite companies are a tad more transparent in their pricing, and they throw in more extras for free.

That said, if you just want the bare minimum of what's available, in terms of both channels and boxes, cable might have lower pricing. Most cable companies offer basic plans with local and public access channels for less than you'd pay for the lowest-tier satellite plan—which typically includes a lot more channels than you might want. So, for bare-bones customers, cable has the advantage.

As you can see, when it comes to cost, your mileage may vary. The best thing to do is to compare the same situations (number of rooms, DVRs, channels you want, and such) with both cable and satellite providers to see which is the lowest-priced for you.

Making a Choice

Should you go with satellite or cable? Assuming that the programming you want is available on both (it isn't always, especially with diginets, sports, and local public access programming), look at the difficulty of installation, the look and feel of the program guide, the DVR features and capacity you need, and the total monthly cost involved. Also consider whether you have a clear view of the southern sky; too many trees or tall buildings might make the choice (against satellite) for you.

Reducing Your Satellite Bill

As you've no doubt realized, satellite TV can be just as costly as cable. When your satellite bill gets too high, what can you do to bring it down? Here are some tips.

Switch to a Lower-Cost Plan

You might not need the most expensive satellite package. Evaluate the channels you really watch and see if you can switch to a plan that costs a little less each month. Saving $10 USD per month on the next-lower plan amounts to $120 USD per year, which is real money.

Downgrade Your Equipment

Yes, DirecTV and DISH offer some truly state-of-the-art set-top boxes. But you might not need the latest and greatest. If you don't need as much hard-disk storage or don't intend to record 16 channels at once (who even does that?), then you might be able to save a few bucks a month by going with older or second-tier satellite boxes.

Negotiate a Lower Rate

Just as with cable providers, your satellite TV company might be able to offer you a lower monthly rate if you do a little negotiation. Threatening to disconnect sometimes encourages the satellite company to offer you discounts you wouldn't receive otherwise. When your bill's getting too high, call up DirecTV or DISH and tell them that, and see what they offer. You might be pleasantly surprised!

Bundle Other Services

DirecTV is owned by AT&T, which means they also offer (not via satellite, of course) telephone and broadband Internet services. If you need these (and you probably do), you might be able to save a little by getting them all from one provider.

It's the same with DISH, which partners with local Internet service providers (ISPs) to offer TV/Internet bundles. If bundling services makes sense for you, it's something to look into.

Disconnect the Dish

Just as many viewers are cutting the cable cord to go full-in with streaming Internet video, many satellite users are taking down the dishes to do the Internet streaming thing, too.

Most of the programming you get via satellite is available at relatively low cost over the Internet. Hulu is a good way to catch up on recent programming from most of the major networks, for a small monthly fee. Some networks offer their own subscription streaming services, as well.

Internet Streaming Services

Learn more about streaming video services in Chapter 7, "Watching the Big Three Streaming Services: Amazon Prime Video, Hulu, and Netflix" and Chapter 8, "Watching Premium Network Streaming Services."

As for your local channels (and their digital subchannels), more of them are available over the public airwaves at no charge than what's available via satellite. All you have to do is connect the appropriate antenna to your TV and you're ready to go.

OTA TV

Learn more about receiving local and broadcast TV in Chapter 3, "Getting Local and Broadcast Television Over the Air."

If you want live broadcast and cable TV over the Internet, you need to subscribe to a live streaming service, such as PlayStation Vue, Sling TV, or YouTube TV. These services offer a variety of plans, much like your satellite provider does, but at a somewhat lower monthly cost.

Live Streaming Services

Learn more about these cable replacement services in Chapter 10, "Watching Live Broadcast and Cable TV with Live Streaming Services."

To go this route you need a fast broadband Internet connection, but you're going to have that anyway. So keep your Internet connection, disconnect the satellite service, and get just about everything you need over the air and over the Internet. You'll spend a lot less than you're currently spending on satellite-only service.

>>>*Go Further*

SATELLITE TV IN CANADA AND THE UK

There are two primary satellite TV providers in Canada: Bell Satellite TV and Shaw Direct. Bell uses a 50 cm (20") circular dish, whereas Shaw uses a 45 cm × 60 cm elliptical dish. Both offer a similar number of Canadian and U.S. channels, many in HD, along with on-demand programming. Both also offer similar sports packages, including NHL Centre Ice and NFL Sunday Ticket. Pricing is similar between the two providers, with basic plans starting at around $45 CAN per month.

In the UK, viewers have the choice of two free and one subscription satellite services. (You have to pay for your own equipment with the free services, of course.) The free services are Freesat (owned by the BBC and ITV) and Freesat from Sky (owned by Comcast); Freesat offers around 200 channels, and Freesat from Sky has around 250. The Sky TV subscription service (also owned by Comcast) offers more channels (300+) and DVR capability; pricing starts at £20/mo.

In this chapter, you learn how to cut the cable and satellite cord and view your favorite programs with a streaming media player.

→ Understanding Internet Streaming Video

→ Watching Amazon Fire TV

→ Watching Apple TV

→ Watching Google Chromecast

→ Watching Roku

→ Comparing Streaming Media Players

→ Optimizing Streaming Media Playback

Getting Streaming Media Devices

Cable and satellite TV are so *yesterday*. Today there's a new way to watch your favorite programming, called *streaming video*, and you get it over the Internet—via a small stick or set-top box called a *streaming media player*.

With a streaming media player and an Internet connection, you have access to practically any channel, network, or program available on cable, satellite, or antenna TV. It's the perfect way to "cut the cord" and reduce or eliminate your monthly cable or satellite bill!

Understanding Internet Streaming Video

As you've learned, local television stations broadcast their programming via radio waves over the air. Cable systems transmit their hundreds of stations over a coaxial or fiber optic cable to your home. And satellite systems transmit their programming by bouncing it off a satellite orbiting tens of thousands of miles in space.

Streaming video services, however, use the Internet to deliver their programming. By connecting a streaming media player to the Internet and your TV, you gain access to hundreds of streaming services—in full HD. Many of these streaming services are free; others require a monthly subscription.

Welcome to the World of Streaming Video

Streaming video, sometimes called IPTV (that's short for *Internet Protocol television*), sends video programming over the Internet as a stream of digital data. When you choose to watch a streaming program, playback starts almost immediately and continues until the program is done; there are no files to download or store on a computer or hard drive. The streaming playback can be paused, stopped, fast forwarded, and rewound, same as you would do with a program on a DVD or Blu-ray disc. You control what you watch; it just happens to come to you via the same connection that brings your other Internet content.

The technical wizardry behind all this is similar to that behind your cable or satellite company's on-demand video. All the programming offered by a given streaming video service is stored in digital data files somewhere in the great big Internet cloud. When you select to watch a given program, it is streamed from the video service's servers across the Internet to the Internet modem in your home. From there the signal goes to your Wi-Fi router and is transmitted wirelessly to your Smart TV or the streaming media player connected to your TV. The media player plays the selected program and you view it on your TV, controlling playback with your media player's remote control. It's that sophisticated and that simple.

Discovering Streaming Media Players

A streaming media player is a standalone device that connects to your TV, typically via HDMI. Some media players are small set-top boxes; these connect to your TV's HDMI input via an HDMI cable. Others are in so-called "stick" format; they look like USB memory sticks and connect directly to your TV's HDMI input.

HDMI

HDMI stands for *high-definition media interface*, and it enables the transmittal of uncompressed audio and video data between devices. HDMI is the standard used to connect most consumer electronics devices today.

A typical set-top streaming media player, the Roku Express+. (Photo courtesy Roku, www.roku.com.)

A typical stick-type streaming media player, the Amazon Fire TV Stick.

Either type of streaming media player—set-up box or stick—needs to connect to a power source and to the Internet. For power, just plug the unit's power cable into a wall socket. For the internet, all have built-in Wi-Fi capability so they can connect via your home wireless network; a select few also have Ethernet ports so they can connect via a wired connection, too.

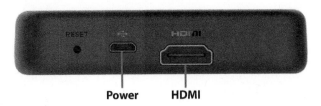

The connections on the rear of a typical streaming media player, the Roku Express.
(Photo courtesy Roku, www.roku.com.)

Streaming media players are available from four major suppliers: Amazon, Apple, Google, and Roku. These companies offer a variety of models in different form factors, with different capabilities, at various price points. The lowest-priced streaming media players today sell for under $30 USD; the highest-priced ones get closer to $200 USD. I'll go into the pros and cons and pricing later.

In addition to these freestanding streaming media players, streaming media playback is built into many of today's so-called "Smart" TVs. Some of these Smart TVs have their own proprietary menus and operation; others offer the same look and feel as the freestanding players—in particular, the Amazon and Roku systems.

Streaming on the Go

You can also view streaming video from smartphones, tablets, and computers. Learn more in Chapter 12, "Watching Streaming TV on Your Phone, Tablet, or Computer."

How Streaming Media Players Work

All streaming media players and smart TVs offering streaming content work in pretty much the same fashion. You start by connecting the player to your TV, typically via HDMI. Then you connect the player to a power source and to your wireless home network. This is typically made easy by a step-by-step setup routine; just follow the onscreen instructions and you'll be done in a few minutes.

You then have to select which streaming services you want to view on the streaming media player. Individual streaming services are available as "apps" in that device's app store. (Roku calls these services "channels," and its app store a Channel Store.) Select which apps/services you want to access, and tiles for those apps appear on the device's home screen.

Browsing for new apps in Roku's Channel Store.

To watch a specific streaming service, select that service's tile on your player's home screen. The app for that service launches, and you can browse or search for something to watch on that service. Click to select a specific episode or movie, and playback starts on your TV screen.

You can use your player's remote control (or, in some cases, the player's smartphone app) to control playback. Press the Pause button to pause playback; press Play to resume playback. Press the Fast Forward (or right arrow) button to skip forward through a program; press the Rewind (or left arrow) button to skip backward to rewatch a program. Viewing progress is typically noted via an on-screen "scrubber" or slider control. In many cases, you can press the Enter or Info button to view more information about the current program.

The remote control unit for Amazon's Fire TV players.

What's Available on Streaming Video

Just about every channel available on cable or satellite is available on streaming video. There are even streaming services that offer access to your local over-the-air (OTA) broadcast channels!

Most cable networks offer streaming apps that play on most streaming media devices. Many networks are available as part of streaming services that offer multiple channels in a single interface. And many network shows, old and new, are available as individual programs on one or more streaming services, such as Hulu and Netflix.

Many streaming services also offer first-run and older movies. Newer movies might cost money to view; older movies might be offered for free or included as part of a general subscription price.

Streaming video services also offer a significant amount of original programming. Netflix, for example, offers both original series, such as *Fuller House, House of Cards, Stranger Things*, and *Unbreakable Kimmy Schmidt*, and original movies, including the Coen Brothers' *The Ballad of Buster Scruggs, The Little Prince*, and *To All the Boys I've Loved Before*. Amazon Prime Video, Hulu, and other streaming services are equally invested in original programming of all types.

How much does all this cost? Many streaming video services are free of charge, supported by their advertisers. Other services have a low monthly subscription fee, anywhere from a few dollars per month to $15 USD or so. More inclusive services that stream multiple channels of live TV and cable programming can cost up to $80 USD or so a month. So the amount you spend depends on which streaming services you watch and subscribe to. (That's in addition to the purchase price of the streaming media player and your monthly Internet service, or course.)

>>>*Go Further*
WHAT'S PLAYING AND WHERE

When you want to find a particular program on streaming video, you can search through dozens of individual services. Or you can take advantage of the universal search available with some streaming media players. For example, Roku offers a search function that searches across all the streaming apps you have installed to discover which apps are playing the program you want.

There are also several websites that serve as universal program guides for a variety of popular streaming services. The most popular of these include

- Can I Stream It? (www.canistream.it)
- GoWatchIt (www.gowatchit.com)
- JustWatch (www.justwatch.com)
- Reelgood (www.reelgood.com)

All these sites work in pretty much the same fashion. Enter the name of the program you're searching for, and these sites tell you on what services you can find what you're looking for. (If the program is available, that is; not every TV show or movie is currently playing on streaming video.)

Watching Amazon Fire TV

You might know Amazon as a giant online retailer, but it's also a manufacturer of many different high-tech devices. Among the company's most popular tech products are its line of Fire TV streaming media players.

Amazon's Fire TV players are available in both stick and set-top boxes. All players come with voice-activated remotes that let you operate the players and select programming with simple voice commands. These Fire TV devices also are compatible with Amazon's Alexa voice assistant, so if you have an Amazon Echo smart speaker you can instruct it to control your Fire TV device, too.

Another unique feature to Fire TV is that your Fire TV device is automatically connected to your Amazon account. This makes it easy to order paid streaming programming from Amazon; Amazon's programming, not surprisingly, is prominently featured on screens throughout the Fire TV service.

Comparing Models

As of early 2019, Amazon offers three Fire TV models—two sticks and a cube-like set-top box. The basic Fire TV Stick is 1080p HD only and sells for $39.99 USD. A step up, the Fire TV Stick 4K adds 4K Ultra HD resolution, HDR, and Dolby Atmos sound for ten dollars more ($49.99 USD). The Fire TV Cube has the same specs as the Fire TV Stick 4K but also includes an Ethernet port for wired Internet connections; it sells for $119.99 USD.

The Amazon Fire TV Stick 4K and remote control. (Photo courtesy Amazon, www.amazon.com.)

The Amazon Fire TV Cube. (Photo courtesy Amazon, www.amazon.com.)

Table 6.1 compares the Fire TV models; learn more at www.amazon.com/FireTV.

Table 6.1.   Comparing Amazon Fire TV Models

	Fire TV Stick	Fire TV Stick 4K	Fire TV Cube
Format	Stick	Stick	Set-top box
Voice-controlled remote with Alexa	Yes	Yes	Yes
1080p HD	Yes	Yes	Yes
4K Ultra HD with HDR	No	Yes	Yes
Dolby Atmos sound	No	Yes	Yes
Wi-Fi	Yes	Yes	Yes
Ethernet connection built in	No	No	Yes
Price (USD)	$39.99	$49.99	$119.99

Amazon Fire TV Edition TVs

Several television manufacturers offer Smart TVs with the Fire TV interface and service built-in. These so-called Fire TV Edition sets come in a variety of sizes and functionality, and they work just like freestanding Fire TV devices.

Using Fire TV

You can operate Fire TV from its supplied remote or via voice commands (from the remote control or a connected Amazon Echo device) .

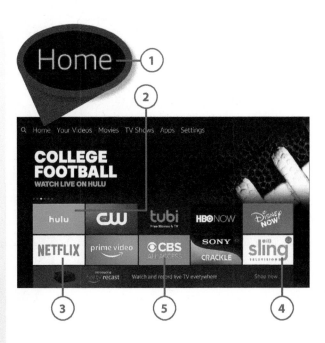

(1) Select a tab at the top of the screen to go to that content. Select Home to view the Home screen.

(2) Press the down arrow button on the remote to go to the first row of app tiles. This row displays your most recently viewed apps.

(3) Press the down arrow button again to go to the bottom row of app tiles. This row displays all the apps you've added to your Fire TV.

(4) Press the right and left arrow buttons to scroll right and left through all the installed apps.

(5) Press the Enter button on the remote to open a selected app.

(6) With the row of tabs selected, press the right and left arrow buttons on your remote to select other tabs.

(7) Select the Search icon to search for shows and movies across all your installed apps.

(8) Select Your Videos to display content you've watched on Amazon Prime and other services, as well as recommended TV shows and movies from Amazon Prime Video.

(9) Select Movies to view movies available on Amazon Prime Video.

(10) Select TV Shows to view television series (including original series) available on Amazon Prime Video.

(11) Select Apps to select new apps/streaming services to install on your Fire TV device and to manage those apps you've previously installed.

(12) Select Settings to configure your device's settings.

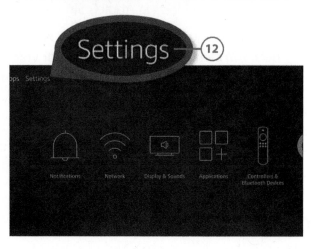

>>>Go Further
HOW TO WATCH YOUTUBE ON FIRE TV

Because Amazon and Google (which owns YouTube) are competitors, no Google content is available in Amazon's app store. This means there's no YouTube app for Fire TV. However, you can still watch YouTube on a Fire TV device, via Fire TV's web browser, called Silk.

You first need to download the Silk app for Fire TV (it's on the Apps tab, or just search for it). Then launch Silk, navigate to the YouTube site (www.youtube.com), and create a bookmark for it. If you search for YouTube on Fire TV, you'll find some apps that are pre-made bookmarks that do this for you.

The YouTube bookmark looks like any other app tile on Fire TV. To watch YouTube, just navigate to and select that tile. YouTube is automatically launched within the Silk browser and looks and works like any other streaming service on your device.

Watching Apple TV

Apple was one of the first companies to offer a streaming media player, in the form of its Apple TV device. Apple TV is a smallish set-top box that connects to your TV via HDMI. It works pretty much like competing streaming media players, but it has a definite Apple feel to it.

Some of this Apple feel is seen in the unit's remote control, which lets you operate the unit by pressing physical buttons or issuing voice commands. The voice control is provided via Apple's Siri intelligent assistant.

Another unique feature of Apple TV is the way it interfaces with other Apple products. You can stream photos, music, or videos you've stored on your Apple iPhone, iPad, or Mac computer to your Apple TV using Apple's Airplay functionality. It's easy.

Using AirPlay
Learn more about using AirPlay to stream content to an Apple TV in Chapter 12.

Apple TV is also unique in offering access to the iTunes Store. This makes it easy to rent or purchase movies for streaming that aren't available from other streaming services.

iTunes Store

Learn more about streaming video from the iTunes Store in Chapter 9, "Watching Paid and Rented Programs."

Comparing Apple TV Models

As of early 2019, Apple offers two Apple TV models, both set-top boxes. The basic Apple TV box is 1080p HD and offers both Wi-Fi and Ethernet connectivity; it sells for $149 USD. The higher-priced Apple TV 4K unit adds 4K Ultra HD, HDR, and Dolby Atmos sound for $179 USD. There's also a version of the 4K unit with additional built-in storage; this sells for $199 USD.

The Apple TV set-top box.

These prices make Apple TV the most expensive streaming media players out there. But if you have other Apple devices and want to share content among them all, the higher price might be worth it.

Table 6.2 details the differences between the two Apple TV units. Learn more at www.apple.com/tv/.

Table 6.2   Comparing Apple TV Models

	Apple TV	Apple TV 4K
Voice-controlled remote with Siri	Yes	Yes
1080p HD	Yes	Yes
4K Ultra HD with HDR	No	Yes
Dolby Atmos sound	No	Yes
Built-in storage	32GB	32GB, 64GB
Wi-Fi	Yes	Yes
Ethernet connection	Yes	Yes
Price (USD)	$149	$179 (32GB), $199 (64GB)

Using Apple TV

When you first connect and turn on your Apple TV box, it leads you through an on-screen setup process. This includes connecting the device to your existing Apple account, so it can share content with your other connected Apple devices.

The Apple TV remote differs a bit from the remotes from the other streaming players. Instead of physical buttons, the top part of the remote has a kind of touch pad. Swipe your finger up or down to scroll or move the onscreen focus up or down; swipe left or right to scroll or move the onscreen focus left or right. You also can press on the top, bottom, left, or right edge to move the focus in that direction. Press in the middle of the touch pad to make a selection; this is essentially the "enter" key.

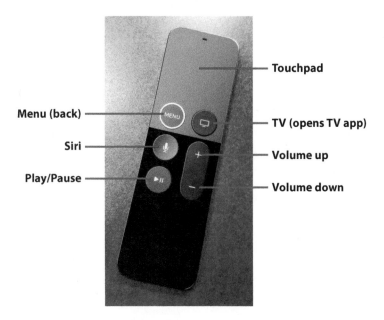

Touchpad

Menu (back)

TV (opens TV app)

Siri

Volume up

Play/Pause

Volume down

The Apple TV remote.

The bottom part of the remote has physical buttons. The Menu button essentially functions as a "back" button to move to the previous screen. The TV button opens the TV app. (More on that later.) The Microphone button opens Siri for voice commands. The Play/Pause button does what you would expect; the + (up) and – (down) buttons raise and lower the volume.

It's Not All Good

Apple TV Remote

The Apple TV remote definitely looks, feels, and works differently than standard remote controls. The touch pad takes a bit of getting used to, and it might be especially difficult to operate if you have any physical challenges. Personally, I found it not entirely intuitive and somewhat challenging to use. The remote alone might make Apple TV a poor choice for some users; it's awkward enough to be a deal breaker for me.

(1) Featured programming appears at the top of the home screen. The first row of tiles beneath that is called your Top Shelf, five tiles for Apple TV's most-used features. From left to right you find tiles for TV, the App Store (to install new apps for additional services), Movies for purchase in the iTunes Store, TV Shows for purchase in the iTunes Store, and Music from iTunes. Swipe the touchpad left or right to select a tile.

(2) Scroll down to view your installed apps for streaming services. Select a tile to open that app/service.

(3) Select the Settings tile to configure Apple TV settings.

(4) Select the Search tile to search for content across your apps and in the App Store.

(5) Select the App Store tile to search for and install apps for additional streaming services.

(6) Select the TV tile to open the TV app.

(7) The TV app consolidates content from across all the streaming apps you've installed. Select the Watch Now tab to view selected content by genre—Sports, News, TV Shows, Movies, and the like.

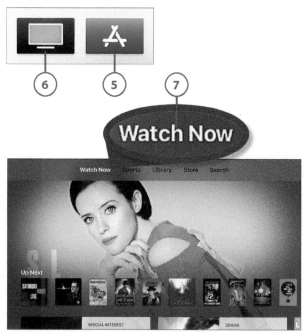

8 Scroll down to the Browse by Category section to view programming in selected categories—TV Shows, Movies, Kids, and Collections.

9 Within a category, scroll down to browse by genre. Select a genre to view related content.

10 You see all TV shows or movies within that genre. Select a tile to view that particular program or movie.

11 Apple TV shows what streaming services offer this particular movie or TV show. Select Open In to select your desired streaming service and begin playback.

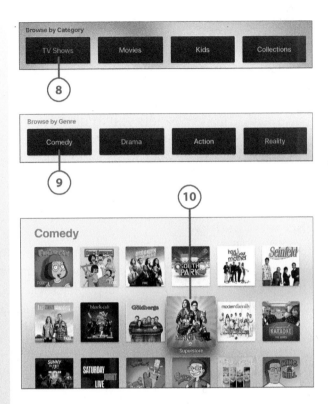

Voice Commands

You also can use the Apple TV voice remote to launch apps. Press the Microphone button on the remote and tell Siri to "open *appname*," where *appname* is the name of the specific app you want to use." For example, to launch Netflix, say "Open Netflix."

Watching Google Chromecast

Google Chromecast is unlike the other streaming media players discussed here. What makes Chromecast different is that it doesn't have its own native interface or home screen or anything like that. It doesn't even come with a remote control.

Instead, Chromecast lets you to broadcast ("cast") content from your phone to your TV. You open the streaming service or app on your phone that you want to watch, select the Chromecast icon in that app, and then what's on your phone is cast to your TV, via the Chromecast device.

Screen Casting

Saying that Chromecast "casts" content from your phone to your TV is a little misleading in this instance. After you select a program on your phone, it streams directly over the Internet to the Chromecast device. You control playback with your phone, but the actual streaming goes direct to the Chromecast, not through your phone. (Learn more about casting in Chapter 12.)

Chromecast works with Android and Apple smartphones and tablets. You also can cast content from any computer running the Google Chrome web browser.

Comparing Chromecast Models

As of early 2019, Google offered two Chromecast models. The basic Chromecast offers 1080p HD resolution and sells for $35 USD. The Chromecast Ultra adds 4K Ultra HD with HDR, as well as an Ethernet connector, for $69 USD.

Google Chromecast. (Photo courtesy Google, www.google.com.)

Both Chromecast models are technically *dongles*; they're not sticks per se, but disc-shaped devices that connect directly to (and hang off of) your TV's HDMI input. They are *not* set-top devices.

Table 6.3 compares the two Chromecast models. Learn more at store.google. com/category/connected_home.

Table 6.3   Comparing Google Chromecast Models

	Chromecast	Chromecast Ultra
Voice-controlled remote	No	No
1080p HD	Yes	Yes
4K Ultra HD with HDR	No	Yes
Dolby Atmos sound	No	No
Wi-Fi	Yes	Yes
Ethernet connection	No	Yes
Price (USD)	$35	$69

Using Google Chromecast

You set up and configure your Chromecast device (and connect it to your home Wi-Fi network) from the Google Home app on your mobile device. You control any given streaming service from within that service's app on your phone or tablet, or with voice commands via any Google Home smart speaker or connected device.

Most streaming mobile apps are compatible with Chromecast. The big exception is Amazon Prime Video, which is excluded due to the ongoing Amazon/Google feud. All the other major streaming services, including Hulu, Netflix, and YouTube, cast just fine to any Chromecast device.

>>>*Go Further*

CASTING AMAZON PRIME VIDEO

Although the Amazon Prime Video app is not compatible with Chromecast, you can cast Amazon Prime Video content from within the Google Chrome browser on any computer. (But not on a phone or other mobile device, unfortunately.) Chrome is obviously compatible with Chromecast, so anything you do from within Chrome can be cast to your TV.

Just make sure the Chrome browser is installed on your computer, then open Amazon's site in the browser. Click the Customize and Control (three dot) menu in the top right, select Cast, and then select your Chromecast device. Anything currently playing in your computer's browser—such as Amazon Prime Video—is now cast to your Chromecast device and your TV.

(1) On your mobile phone or other device, open the app for the streaming service you want to watch. For example, to watch Netflix, open your phone's Netflix app.

(2) Navigate to the TV program or movie you want to watch and tap the Cast button. (In some apps, you might need to select and start watching a video for the Cast button to appear.)

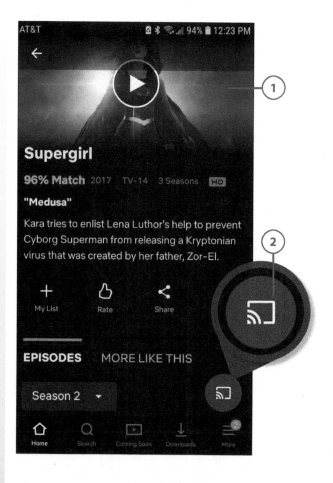

3) Select which device you want to cast to.

4) The streaming content displays on your TV screen. Use the streaming app on your phone to stop, start, pause, resume, fast forward, and rewind what you're watching.

5) Tap the Cast button again in your phone app to stop casting.

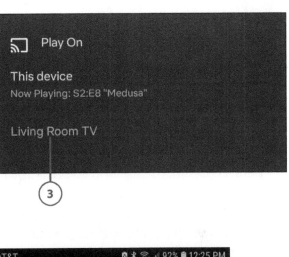

Watching Roku

The most popular streaming media players today are those from Roku. Roku offers a variety of models in both stick and set-top form factors, at a variety of price points.

What makes Roku so popular? First, Roku players have been around for more than a decade, so there are many apps and services available. Second, Roku is agnostic in terms of streaming services; unlike Amazon and Google, which compete in both hardware and streaming services (and block each other's services on their own devices), Roku plays nice with everybody and offers just about every streaming service available. Third, Roku devices just work; plug 'em in and start watching, few hassles involved. Finally, Roku offers a nice variety of models at affordable price points, so you can easily find the right unit to fit your needs.

Comparing Roku Models

As of early 2019, Roku offers seven different models in the U.S. market—two sticks and five set-top boxes, ranging in price from $29.99 to $99.99 USD. Here's how they break down:

- **Streaming Stick:** This is Roku's lowest-priced stick model, with 1080p HD resolution and a voice-controlled remote. It sells for $49.99 USD.

Roku Streaming Stick.

- **Streaming Stick+:** Priced at $10 more than the basic Streaming Stick, the "plus" model adds 4K Ultra HD playback, HDR, and Dolby Atmos sound. It sells for $59.99 USD.

- **Express:** This is Roku's lowest-priced set-top box. It offers 1080p HD resolution and sells for $29.99 USD. (If you don't need 4K UHD, this is the model to buy.)

- **Express+:** This is the same as the Express, but it has a composite audio/video cable output in addition to HDMI, in case you need to send audio to a separate receiver. It sells for $35 USD.

- **Premiere:** This set-top box is Roku's lowest-priced model with 4K Ultra HD, HDR, and Dolby Atmos support. It sells for $39.99 USD—just $10 more than the non-4K Roku Express.

Roku Premiere streaming media box and remote. (Photo courtesy Roku, www.roku.com.)

- **Premiere+:** This unit, sold only at Walmart, adds a voice-controlled remote to the basic Premiere unit. It sells for $49.99 USD.

- **Ultra:** This is Roku's top-of-the-line unit, adding a headphone output to its voice-controlled remote, as well as an Ethernet connection. It sells for $99.99 USD.

Table 6.4 compares all of these Roku models. Learn more at www.roku.com.

Table 6.4   Comparing Roku Models

	Streaming Stick	Streaming Stick+	Express	Express+	Premiere	Premiere+ (Walmart only)	Ultra
Format	Stick	Stick	Set-top box	Set-top box	Set-top box	Set-top box	Set-top box
Voice-controlled remote	Yes	Yes	No	No	No	Yes	Yes

	Streaming Stick	Streaming Stick+	Express	Express+	Premiere	Premiere+ (Walmart only)	Ultra
Remote with headphone output	No	No	No	No	No	No	Yes
1080p HD	Yes	Yes	Yes	Yes	Yes	Yes	Yes
4K Ultra HD with HDR	No	Yes	No	No	Yes	Yes	Yes
Dolby Atmos sound	No	Yes	No	No	Yes	Yes	Yes
Wi-Fi	Yes	Yes	Yes	Yes	Yes	Yes	Yes
Ethernet connection	No	No	No	No	No	No	Yes
Price (USD)	$49.99	$59.99	$29.99	$35.00	$39.99	$49.99	$99.99

Roku TVs

Several television manufacturers offer smart TVs with the Roku interface and service built-in. These so-called Roku TVs come in a variety of sizes and functionality, and work just like freestanding Roku devices.

Using Roku

All Roku devices—including Roku TVs—have the same interface. You find apps for your favorite streaming services on an easy-to-navigate Home screen.

(1) Select the Home tab or press the Home button on the Roku remote to display the Home screen. Use the up and down arrow buttons on the remote to scroll through the available tabs.

2 Press the right or left arrow buttons to scroll left and right through the tiles, or press the up or down arrows to scroll up or down through the tiles.

3 To launch an app, select the tile and press the OK button on the remote.

4 Select the Featured Free tab to view selected programming available for free.

5 Select the Search tab to search for programs across all the services available on Roku.

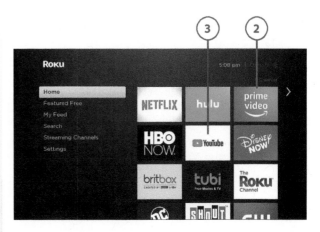

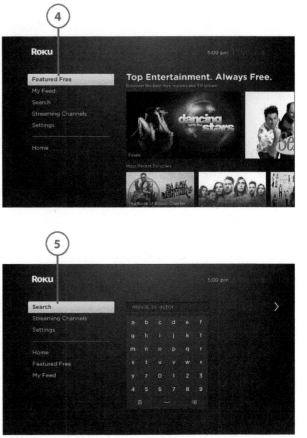

6. Select the Streaming Channels tab to add new apps/services to your Roku device.

7. Select the Settings tab to configure various settings for your Roku device.

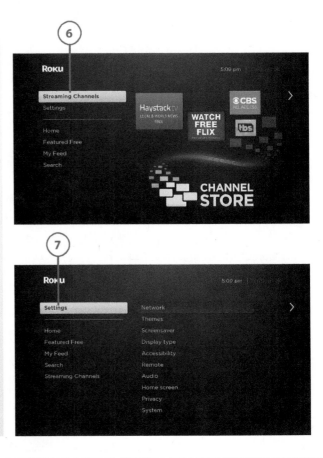

>>>Go Further
NVIDIA SHIELD

There's one more streaming media player worth noting. The Nvidia Shield ($179-$299 USD) is a combination streaming media player and game console. It offers access to hundreds of streaming media apps and even more online games.

The Nvidia Shield is probably more optimized for gaming than media streaming (it comes with a game controller as well as a standard remote control), but it's good at that, too—even though it's the priciest streaming player out there. It offers 4K Ultra HD with HDR, Dolby Atmos surround, and voice control with Google Assistant. It's also a lot faster than competing streaming players because of its gaming roots. Content offerings are similar to Roku, meaning just about every streaming service is available.

As noted, however, the Shield's gaming functionality is probably unnecessary for those of us who just want to watch streaming videos. Still, it's a high-end streaming player that might be worth your consideration if you want the latest and the greatest—and do a lot of gaming. Learn more at www.nividia.com/shield/.

Comparing Streaming Media Players

So, which of the four major streaming media players is right for you: Amazon Fire TV, Apple TV, Google Chromecast, or Roku? They all work in a similar fashion but have their own unique pros and cons. It's likely that any one of these four devices will do the job for you, but there are things that might sway you toward one or the other.

Comparing Features

Table 6.5 compares the important features for the major streaming media players.

Table 6.5   Comparing Streaming Media Players

	Amazon Fire TV	Apple TV	Google Chromecast	Roku
Stick format	Yes	No	Yes	Yes
Set-top box	Yes	Yes	No	Yes
Voice-activated remote	Yes	Yes	No	Yes (some models)
Amazon Alexa voice control	Yes	No	No	No
Google Assistant voice control	No	No	Yes	Yes
1080p HD	Yes	Yes	Yes	Yes

	Amazon Fire TV	Apple TV	Google Chromecast	Roku
4K Ultra HD and HDR	Yes (Fire TV Stick 4K, Fire TV Cube only)	Yes (4K model only)	Yes (Chromecast Ultra only)	Yes (Premiere, Premiere+, Streaming Stick+, Ultra only)
Dolby Atmos sound	Yes (Fire TV Stick 4K, Fire TV Cube only)	Yes	No	Yes (Streaming Stick+, Premiere, Premiere+, and Ultra only)
Wi-Fi connection	Yes	Yes	Yes	Yes
Ethernet connection	Fire TV Cube only	Yes	Chromecast Ultra only	Roku Ultra only
Smartphone app	Yes	Yes	Yes	Yes
App store for new apps	Yes	Yes	Yes	Yes
Amazon Prime Video and store	Yes	Yes	No*	Yes
Hulu	Yes	Yes	Yes	Yes
iTunes Store	No	Yes	No	No
Netflix	Yes	Yes	Yes	Yes
YouTube	No*	Yes	Yes	Yes
Website	www.amazon.com/firetv	www.apple.com/tv/	store.google.com/category/connected_home	www.roku.com
Price (USD)	$39.99–$119.99	$149–$199	$35-$69	$29.99-$99.99

* = No dedicated app available, but can play in the device's web browser.

Making a Choice

In many ways choosing a streaming media player comes down to what services/apps are available on each—which is where we get down to the peculiarities of each streaming system. Yes, Hulu and Netflix are available on all four devices, but they're not the only streaming services you might want to watch.

Knowing that Amazon and Google are bitter competitors, for example, you quickly realize that you won't find apps for Google services, such as YouTube, on Amazon Fire TV devices. Nor, for that matter, will you find Amazon services, such as Amazon Prime Video, on Google Chromecast devices. It's just not gonna happen.

This is why many users choose Roku devices. Roku doesn't have a horse in the content race, and thus makes both Amazon and Google (YouTube) services available on all of its devices. Roku players provide access to just about everything; Amazon and Google devices, not quite so much.

Then there's Apple. The Apple TV player is a fine device, and it provides access to content from both Amazon and Google. However, it's much higher priced than competing devices; you can buy three or four Fire TV or Roku players for the price of one Apple TV box. If you're heavily invested in the Apple infrastructure (that is, you have an iPhone and an iPad and maybe even a Mac computer), then Apple TV fits right in without a lot of manual configuration necessary, and you can share media among all of those devices. But if you're not a heavy Apple user, you get similar functionality from a Fire TV or Roku player at a considerably lower cost.

Finally, consider the quality of the content you want to stream. If you have a brand-spanking-new 4K Ultra HD TV with HDR, you want a player that can stream 4K Ultra HD HDR content. That automatically shifts you into higher-end models from Amazon, Apple, and Roku; lower-cost models are regular old HD only. (The situation is similar if you want Dolby Atmos sound, which is supported only by higher-end Amazon, Apple, and Roku devices.)

>>>*Go Further*

WHERE TO WATCH CLASSIC TV COMEDIES

Between Internet streaming services, cable and satellite channels, and your local OTA diginets, there are lots of places you can find those classic TV comedies you watched when you were younger. Of course, what you deem as classic might differ from what others in your family view as such. If you're of a certain age, you're looking for those 1950s vintage shows, such as *The Honeymooners* and *I Love Lucy*. If you're a little younger you're looking for 1960s comedies, such as *The Beverly Hillbillies* and *Gilligan's Island*. If you were a child of the 1970s, then it's shows like *The Bob Newhart Show* and *M*A*S*H*. Move into the 1980s (not that long ago, I know), and you're talking classics like *Cheers* and *Taxi*.

Whatever your personal vintage, there are lots of places to find the funniest shows from your youth. Starting in the streaming world, Crackle, Hulu, Netflix, and Shout Factory TV offer a variety of older TV comedies, although you might have to hunt for them. Hulu is probably your best bet here, with shows such as *The Addams Family, I Love Lucy* and *The Lucy Show, The Bob Newhart Show, The Brady Bunch, The Dick Van Dyke Show, The Mary Tyler Moore Show, Mister Ed,* and *The Odd Couple*. You can also pay to stream many classic TV series from Amazon or Google Play (or the iTunes Store, if you have an Apple TV box).

Surprisingly, cable and satellite aren't that great a place for truly classic sitcoms. You'll find a lot of 1990s and more recent comedies, but not much from before then.

There's a much better selection of classic TV comedies on the subchannels of your local broadcast stations. Several diginets, including Antenna TV, Bounce TV, Cozi TV, Decades, Laff, MeTV, and Retro TV, specialize in classic TV programming, with a big emphasis on classic comedies. Antenna TV is a particular favorite, with *Barney Miller, Bewitched, The Burns and Allen Show, Coach, Dennis the Menace, Family Ties, Hazel, I Dream of Jeannie, The Jack Benny Program, McHale's Navy, The Partridge Family, Three's Company,* and many more. You'll probably need an OTA antenna to receive these channels, unless they're carried as part of your cable package. (They're not to be found via Internet streaming, unfortunately.)

Optimizing Streaming Media Playback

Some people find that streaming video looks every bit as good as—and maybe even better than—what you get from cable or satellite. Other viewers are plagued by fuzzy or pixelated pictures, stuttering playback, or even problems loading individual channels or programs. What can you do to make sure you get the best possible playback from your streaming video services? Here are some tips.

Get a Fast (and Reliable) Internet Connection

Because streaming video streams over the Internet, you want as fast and reliable an Internet connection as possible. An inferior Internet connection results in all sorts of streaming playback problems—and might not even work at all.

Let's look at the worst-case scenario. If, heaven forbid, you have a dial-up Internet connection (some people still do), you might as well not even try to do the streaming thing. A dial-up connection isn't fast enough for the demands of video streaming. It just won't work.

What you want is as fast a broadband connection as you can get and afford. Streaming video is very demanding and takes up a lot of bandwidth; the faster the connection, the more videos you can stream, more reliably.

A fast Internet connection is even more important if you have multiple people watching multiple streaming programs at the same time. Let's say you're watching a streaming show on your living room TV, your spouse is watching a different streaming program in the bedroom, and your kids or grandkids are watching streaming YouTube videos on their phones or tablets. All that data coming down your Internet connection at the same time can slow everything down unless you have a really fast (high-bandwidth) connection.

That means looking at the Internet packages offered by your Internet service provider (ISP) and choosing the one that best fits your viewing habits. You want to look at download (not necessarily upload) speeds, and the faster the better. A package that promises 200 megabytes per second (Mbps) is going to be considerably faster and more reliable than a 50 Mbps plan.

How fast do you need? To watch a single stream in standard definition, you need a 3 Mbps connection. To watch a single stream in HD, you need a 5 Mbps connection. And to watch a single stream in 4K Ultra HD, you need a 25 Mbps connection.

Multiply these numbers if you want to stream multiple programs simultaneously to multiple devices. For example, to watch two HD streams on two devices, you need a 10 Mbps connection (two times 5 Mbps). If you have three people in your house, all watching HD, then you need 15 Mbps. And so forth.

Most ISPs offer a variety of plans at different speed levels. For example, XFINITY in my area offers a Starter plan with 15 Mbps speed for $29.99 USD per month, a Plus plan at 60 Mbps for $39.99 USD per month, a Pro plan at 150 Mbps for $54.99 USD per month, and a Blast! Pro plan with 250 Mbps for $69.99 USD per month. Other ISPs offer speeds up to 1 gigabyte per second (Gbps)—that's 1,000 Mbps!

It's Not All Good

Your Speeds Might Be Lower

Just because your ISP promises speeds of up to a given number doesn't mean that your actual connection speed will be that fast, at least all the time. Lots of factors, including inefficient equipment and other users on the line in your neighborhood, can negatively affect Internet connection speed. The speed listed by your ISP, then, is a theoretical maximum; your actual speed will probably be lower.

Although the top plans may be overkill for casual viewing, you'll probably find that the most basic plans aren't fast enough. If you experience freezes and long load times and pixelated pictures, it might be time to upgrade your Internet plan. If you're watching mostly HD programming and have two or three people in your home watching simultaneously, I recommend at least a 50 Mbps plan (especially given that you won't always get 50 Mbps speeds).

By the way, while you're figuring out what Internet package is best for your viewing habits, don't forget to include the cost of that Internet service in your entertainment budget. You might save $100 or more by disconnecting your cable or satellite service, but remember you're adding at least some of that back as part of a speedy Internet plan.

Get a Fast (and Powerful) Wi-Fi Router

Most people connect their streaming media players to the Internet wirelessly, via Wi-Fi. That means you need a decent Wi-Fi router in your home—one that can deliver blazing speed over the longest distance in your home.

Without getting too technical, you want a router that uses the latest Wi-Fi technology and a streaming player that matches. Many lower-priced routers and players use the standard labeled 802.11n, although the newer 802.11ac standard is faster and has a greater range, which you need if you have a large house. You should also look for routers and players that use multiple antennae and a technology called MIMO (stands for multiple input, multiple output); these enable more efficient transmitting of multiple streams. Routers that transmit in both the 2.4 GHz and 5 GHz bands (and streaming players that receive both bands) are also good; you can dedicate the faster 5 GHz band for video streaming and leave the lower 2.4 GHz band for regular household Internet.

Netgear's Nighthawk R7000 router—dual-band, MIMO, 802.11a/b/g/n/dc Wi-Fi for superior video streaming. (Photo courtesy Netgear, www.netgear.com.)

A newer, faster, more expensive router not only has more bandwidth for your streaming video but it also should have a longer range. This is important if you have several streaming devices to feed and if some of them are quite distant from the router.

Supply Your Own Equipment

Most ISPs provide their own Internet modem and Wi-Fi router, often in the form of a combination modem/router called an Internet gateway. You typically pay a monthly rental fee for this equipment, and it's seldom state-of-the-art. You often can get better performance—and lower your monthly bills—by returning the ISP's equipment and buying your own.

Move Your Router—or Your Streaming Player

For the best streaming performance, you need the strongest possible Wi-Fi signal. If your streaming player is on the opposite side of a large house from the Wi-Fi router, chances are the signal you receive might be too weak for reliable playback.

You can improve the strength of the wireless signal that your streaming player receives by moving either your streaming player or the wireless router.

If the signal you receive is very weak (check the network settings on your streaming player), try moving the player and the router closer together. That might mean moving the player (and the TV to which it's connected) or moving the router. Sometimes a few feet closer makes all the difference in the world.

The solution might be for you to move the streaming player a little bit. Different objects—walls, doors, other electronic devices—can interfere with the Wi-Fi signal. Moving the streaming player (or the router) one direction or another, or even higher, may give you a clearer path for the signal.

For that matter, you might need to move anything else that's in between the player and the router that could be interfering with the signal. If the router is in a closed office, open the door—or open the door to any bedroom where the streaming player is located. Move other electronics or wireless devices that are near the router—things like computer monitors, cordless phones, microwave ovens, and the like. You also might want to move your streaming player a little further from your TV—and if you're using a streaming stick, connect an HDMI extender cable so that it doesn't have to connect directly to the back of your television.

Connect via Ethernet for Best Playback

Wireless connections are convenient, but they're not as fast or as reliable as a direct wired connection. If you want the best, most reliable picture from your streaming media player, connect to your router via Ethernet cable, not Wi-Fi, if that's an option with your device. A wired Ethernet connection is rock solid, not prone to the connectivity issues you sometimes get with Wi-Fi.

The problem is that not every streaming media player has an Ethernet connection. Of the current generation of players, only the Amazon Fire TV Cube, Apple TV and Apple TV 4K, Google Chromecast Ultra, and Roku Ultra devices have Ethernet connections. Those are also the most expensive streaming media players, but if you want to connect via Ethernet, they're the ones to look at.

Ethernet

The Ethernet connection on the back of the Roku Ultra player. (Photo courtesy Roku, www.roku.com.)

Choose the Right Streaming Player for Each TV

If you want to stream content from different TVs in your home, you need some sort of streaming player connected to each set. You don't have to use the same model or even brand of player on each TV, however; feel free to mix sticks and boxes as necessary.

In fact, it's probably a good idea to choose different streaming players for different TVs and rooms. Although you might want to decide on a single infrastructure (Amazon or Apple or Google or Roku), just because you get used to using the same menus and options, you can choose appropriate devices from that manufacturer for each room's specific needs. For example, you might want a Roku Ultra box in your living room so that you can connect via Ethernet, play back in 4K Ultra HD, and listen in Dolby Atmos. But a simple Roku Stick might be all your need on a smaller bedroom TV that has only HD resolution. You don't have to buy the most expensive model for every TV you have.

Buy a TV with Fire TV or Roku Built In

For that matter, if you like Amazon Fire TV or Roku and also need a new TV, consider buying a smart TV that has Fire TV or Roku built-in. These so-called Fire TV Edition televisions and Roku TVs offer the exact same interface and functionality of the separate Fire TV and Roku devices, no separate player necessary. In many cases, a Fire TV Edition set or Roku TV ends up being a considerably lower price than a similar non-smart TV and separate Fire TV or Roku player. (And most Fire TV Edition sets and Roku TVs have Ethernet connectors on the back, so you can connect via faster wired connection if you want.)

Pick the Right Streaming Services for You

One mistake a lot of first-time streamers make is to spring for too many subscription-based streaming services. Yes, most everybody wants Netflix. You also might want standard Hulu, for watching recent TV shows. But do you really need Amazon Prime Video and CBS All Access and DC Universe and HBO Now? They each have their own monthly subscription fees, and those fees start to add up when you subscribe to multiple services. Yes, it's tempting to subscribe to *everything*, but it's unlikely there will be more than one or two shows on any given service to justify the monthly subscription cost. Check your viewing habits and subscribe only to those services you really watch—a lot.

>>>Go Further

STREAMING VIDEO PLAYERS IN CANADA AND THE UK

If you're in Canada, you have the same choice in streaming media players as do those of us in the lower 48. Prices are comparable to those in the United States.

There is a slightly different mix of players available in the United Kingdom. In addition to the standard streaming players from Amazon, Apple, Google, and Roku, there also are streaming sticks and boxes from NOW TV, which are unique to the UK market.

NOW TV manufactures its Smart Stick and Smart Box in conjunction with Roku; in fact, their products greatly resemble similar Roku products. The NOW TV players are unique in that they're closely tied to content from Freeview and Sky, and not much else. There are several different Sky passes available, for example, but no Amazon Prime Video. (Netflix is recently available, however.) NOW TV Smart Sticks start at £14.99; the NOW TV Smart Box starts at £45.99.

What sorts of streaming services are available outside the United States? I discuss this topic in more depth in the following chapters, but suffice to say that due to country-specific licensing restrictions and channels and networks unique to each area, the offerings are both familiar and wildly different. For example, in the UK a Roku streaming player provides access to UK versions of Amazon Prime Video and Netflix (but not Hulu), but also All 4, BBC iPlayer, ITV, STV, and more channels familiar to Brits but foreign to Americans. Wherever you live, make sure you check out your device's app store to see which streaming channels and services are available.

In this chapter, you learn what's showing on the big three streaming video services—Amazon Prime Video, Hulu, and Netflix—and how to watch them.

→ Watching Amazon Prime Video
→ Watching Hulu
→ Watching Netflix
→ Comparing the Big Three

Watching the Big Three Streaming Services: Amazon Prime Video, Hulu, and Netflix

Streaming Internet video is the way to cut the cable/satellite cord and reduce your monthly entertainment expenditures. With an Internet connection and a streaming media player or smart TV, you're ready to stream all sorts of television programs and movies over the Internet.

The question is, what's the best streaming media service to use? There are lots of them out there, and they all charge some sort of subscription fee each month. With all the choices available, however, three services come to the forefront; Amazon Prime Video, Hulu, and Netflix are far and away the most popular streaming video services today, and the ones you should consider first.

Watching Amazon Prime Video

Amazon offers a streaming video service called Amazon Prime Video. You can watch it on just about any streaming media player, as well as your computer, phone, or tablet. Not surprisingly, it plays very well on Amazon Fire TV devices.

Amazon Prime Video Basics

Amazon Prime Video is an extension of Amazon's Prime service, which gives you free two-day shipping on selected Amazon purchases. If you're a Prime member, your subscription to Amazon Prime Video is free. (Prime membership costs $119 USD per year.) If you're not a Prime member, you can subscribe to Prime Video only for $8.99 USD per month (which comes to $107.88 USD a year). Given the minimal difference in price, most people are better off getting the whole Prime membership (with Prime Video thrown in free) than paying for Prime Video separately.

Like Hulu and Netflix, Amazon Prime Video offers free streaming of thousands of movies, TV series, and original programming. Unlike competing services, Amazon, an online retailer, also sells or rents streaming versions of tens of thousands more titles. When you browse Prime Video, look for those titles or categories labeled "Included with Prime" or that have a "Prime" banner on the thumbnail—that's the free content included with your Prime Video subscription. You have to pay separately for anything not labeled as Prime content. Still, the combination of free subscription streaming and paid/rental titles gives Amazon the most content of any online service.

Some Prime Video content is in 4K Ultra HD with HDR and Dolby Atmos sound. (Unlike other streaming services, Amazon does not charge extra for you to view its 4K content.) The majority of Amazon content, however, is in 1080p HD and Dolby Digital 5.1-channel surround sound.

Learn more at www.amazon.com/av/.

What's Playing?

What kind of content can you find on Amazon Prime Video? Amazon offers a selection of new and older movies and TV series as part of its Prime Video subscription. This selection is weighted toward newer movies and shows (as is the case with most streaming video services), although many older movies and TV series are available for rental or purchase through the Amazon online store. You can browse the for-purchase content from within the Amazon Prime Video app, which is convenient.

Amazon also offers a variety of original programming, which it calls Prime Originals. Prime Original series include *Bosch, Forever, Homecoming, The Man in the High Castle, The Marvelous Mrs. Maisel, Tom Clancy's Jack Ryan,* and *Transparent.* Prime Original movies include *The Big Sick, Manchester by the Sea, The Lost City of Z,* and *Zoe.*

In addition, Amazon offers content from other providers as part of (or in addition to) its Prime Video subscription. This additional content is offered as Prime Video Channels, and includes BritBox, HBO, Showtime, Starz, and similar streaming services. Some Channels are included free with your Prime Video subscription; others (typically premium cable channels) incur an additional fee of anywhere from $4.99 to $14.99 USD per month.

Ever-Changing Content

The content available on all streaming media services is constantly changing. New titles are added to the Amazon, Hulu, and Netflix catalogs on a monthly basis, and older titles are periodically retired.

>>>Go Further

BUYING AND RENTING MOVIES AND SHOWS FROM AMAZON

When you can't find a given movie or TV series on any of the major streaming services, it's time to turn to Amazon. Not Amazon Prime Video, mind you, but Amazon proper. The same online retailer that sells you books and clothing and electronics also sells (and rents) tens of thousands of videos that aren't available anyplace else.

Amazon offers all manner of movies and TV series—pretty much anything also available on DVD or Blu-ray—for online sale or rental. When you rent a title, you have 30 days to start watching and 3 days after that to finish. When you purchase a title, you have endless access to that title. Rental typically runs less than $5 USD or so per movie or episode; purchase price is in the $20 USD range.

With the demise of the FilmStruck streaming service, which specialized in classic and foreign films, purchasing or renting from Amazon (or its Apple competitor, the iTunes Store) is now the primary option for fans of classic cinema, foreign films, and independent movies. If you're looking for fare from Ozu or Tati (and if you know who they are!), you can always purchase or rent *Tokyo Story* or *Monsieur Hulot's Holiday* for streaming from Amazon, via the Prime Video app.

Learn more about buying streaming video from Amazon and other online retailers in Chapter 9, "Watching Paid and Rented Programs."

Where You Can Find Amazon Prime Video

You can watch Amazon Prime Video on most streaming media players, Smart TVs, smartphones, tablets, and computers (via your web browser). When I say "most" I mean every streaming player *except* Google Chromecast. Because of the ongoing Amazon/Google competition, Amazon Prime Video is not available on any Google product, nor are Google services available on Amazon products. (Don't you just love technology feuds?)

That said, if you have an Amazon Fire TV, Apple TV, or Roku device, there's an Amazon Prime Video app in your device's app store. Download the Prime Video app and you can watch all Prime Video content on your device and connected TV.

Table 7.1 details the availability of Amazon Prime Video across all four major streaming media player platforms.

Table 7.1   Amazon Prime Video on Streaming Media Player Platforms

Platform	Amazon Prime Video app
Amazon Fire TV	Yes
Apple TV	Yes
Google Chromecast	No
Roku	Yes

Using Amazon Prime Video

Amazon Prime Video looks and works like most online streaming services. Use the right and left arrow buttons on your device's remote to scroll left and right, and the up and down arrow buttons to scroll up and down the page.

1. Select the Home tab to view featured programming in a variety of categories. There's also a row of tiles titled Watch Next; these are programs you've watched previously and you can easily resume watching.

2. Select a tile to view that item.

3. If you select a series, select the season and episode you want to watch, then press Enter or Play on your remote.

4. Select the Originals tab to view Amazon original series and movies.

5. Select the Movies tab to display featured movies.

6. Select the TV tab to display featured TV series.

7. Select the Kids tab to display featured children's programming.

8. Select Video Library to display movies and TV episodes that you've previously purchased from Amazon.

9. Select Watchlist to display items you've added to your watchlist to view in the future.

(10) Select Settings to configure various Prime Video settings.

(11) Select Search to search for programs on Amazon.

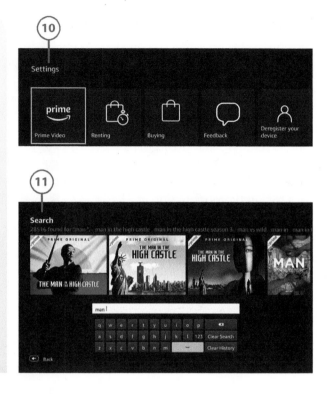

X-Ray

Amazon is unique in that it offers additional information about much of its programming. Amazon's X-Ray feature offers cast and character information, behind-the-scenes photos and stories, bonus video content, and more while you're watching a program. To access X-Ray, press the up button on your device's remote control while the video is playing.

Watching Hulu

Like Amazon Prime Video, Hulu is a subscription service that offers free streaming of movies, TV series, and original programming. Hulu is a joint venture between AT&T, Comcast, and The Walt Disney Company, and it offers content from all the other companies these big guys own.

Unlike Prime Video and Netflix, Hulu is available in the United States only. Outside of the United States, much content from Hulu's owners is available on other streaming services.

Hulu Basics

At its inception, Hulu was conceived as a place to watch recent episodes of current TV series—kind of a "catch-up" service. It still offers access to recent TV shows but has added all manner of other content, including older TV series, movies, and original programming.

If you're watching on a Smart TV or streaming media player, Hulu offers two plans, with and (sort of) without commercials. The basic Hulu plan runs $5.99 USD per month and inserts commercials into the programs you watch. If you want to minimize the number of commercials you see, sign up for the $11.99 USD No Ads plan—but know that you'll still see commercials on some programs, but fewer of them.

Hulu with Live TV

Hulu also offers a live streaming service for broadcast and cable/satellite channels, for an additional monthly cost. Learn more about this service in Chapter 10, "Watching Live Broadcast and Cable TV with Live Streaming Services."

As of early 2019, Hulu programming is broadcast in 1080p HD with stereo sound on most devices. Although Hulu does not yet offer 4K Ultra HD video, it does offer 5.1-channel surround sound for some programs on some devices—specifically, Amazon Fire TV and Google Chromecast players, as well as most current-generation video game consoles.

What's Playing?

Like its competitors, Hulu offers free viewing of thousands of television series, movies, and original programs. Although it's branched out from its original mission, Hulu still offers a significant number of current broadcast and cable/satellite series, with a focus on each show's most recent episodes. This makes Hulu a great place to catch up on your recent television viewing, and for some people Hulu could replace cable or satellite as a source for live viewing. (You typically don't have live access to these shows, but can watch the latest episodes a day or so after their initial airing.)

Hulu also offers a decent selection of vintage television series, which makes it a good choice for fans of classic TV. The service also offers a number of current and older movies, but not near as many as you find on Amazon or Netflix.

In terms of original programming, Hulu is starting to make a name for itself. You'll find a number of well-regarded original series, including *Castle Rock, The First, Future Man, The Handmaid's Tale,* and *The Looming Tower.* Hulu has not yet delved into original movies, instead focusing its efforts on these and other series.

Where You Can Find Hulu

Hulu is pretty much ubiquitous across all streaming players in the United States. You'll typically find it as part of the default home screen on Amazon, Apple, Google, and Roku devices, as well as most Smart TVs and video game systems. You can also access Hulu from your personal computer, smartphone, or tablet.

Table 7.2 details the availability of Hulu across all four major streaming media player platforms; it's available for all of them.

Table 7.2   Hulu on Streaming Media Player Platforms

Platform	Hulu app
Amazon Fire TV	Yes
Apple TV	Yes
Google Chromecast	Yes
Roku	Yes

Using Hulu

Hulu offers the same type of home screen and menu interface as you find with Amazon Prime Video and Netflix. It's easy to browse or search for the programming you want.

1. Select the Home tab to view everything that's on Hulu.

2. Select a sub tab to view specific content. Lineup displays content selected for you. Keep Watching displays programs you've previously watched. Other sub tabs display TV shows, Movies, Kids programming, Hulu originals, and so on.

3. Select My Stuff to view movies and TV shows you've previously looked at or watched.

4. Select a tile to view that show or movie.

5. If you selected a TV show, select the season and episode to watch, then press the Enter or Play button on your device's remote.

(6) Select the Browse tab to view programming by category—Networks, TV Shows, Movies, and so forth.

(7) Select the Search tab to search for a specific program.

(8) Select the tab with your name on it to configure various Hulu settings.

>>>*Go Further*

WHERE TO WATCH CURRENT TV SHOWS

Whether you like the current broadcast network fare or follow your favorite shows on basic or pay cable/satellite, you have more options than you might think in terms of where to watch them.

First, of course, is at the source—live from the broadcast or cable/satellite network. For major network fare (shows from ABC, CBS, CW, Fox, and NBC), this could be watching your local channel on your cable or satellite feed or getting the programming over-the-air (OTA) via antenna.

Next, you can capture the OTA or cable/satellite feed and record the program when it airs for viewing at a later time. Time-shifting, this is called, and you do it with a digital video recorder (DVR) built into your cable/satellite set-top box or a separate DVR box for OTA recording.

There also are Internet streaming services that serve up live broadcasts from your local and cable/satellite services. These services, such as fuboTV, PlayStation Vue, and Sling TV, come with a (sometimes hefty) monthly subscription fee, but let you receive (and often record) live channels over the Internet, no cable or satellite subscription (or OTA antenna) required.

Finally, there's Hulu. Basic Hulu (that is, *not* the Hulu with Live TV option, which is covered in Chapter 10) offers recent episodes of just about every broadcast and cable/satellite show in the United States. Most episodes are posted within a few days after initial airing and stay available for several weeks or months. If you don't really need to watch your favorite shows when they air, or you just prefer to view them at your convenience, then Hulu is a viable option.

Watching Netflix

Netflix is the most popular streaming service today, with more than 137 million subscribers worldwide. It's the granddaddy of streaming video services, and the default (sometimes the only) service offered across a variety of devices.

Netflix DVD Service

Netflix started out as a delivery service for DVD rentals. It still offers this service, although online streaming has become the dominant part of the company's business. If you still watch DVDs and Blu-rays, Netflix's DVD Plan may be of interest; prices run from $7.99 to $13.99 USD per month. Learn more at dvd.netflix.com.

Netflix Basics

Like Amazon Prime Video and Hulu, Netflix offers unlimited video streaming for a monthly subscription price. It started out offering mainly movies but shifted over the years to add a variety of newer and classic TV shows, plus a plethora of original programming.

Netflix lets you include multiple users on your account; it's not uncommon for children (even grown-up children!) to share their parents' or grandparents' account. You can also stream Netflix to more than one device simultaneously—depending on the plan you sign up for.

Which plan you sign up for also determines whether you can receive 4K Ultra HD content. Netflix's Basic plan is in standard definition, but the Standard plan delivers 1080p HD with Dolby Digital surround sound. The highest-priced Premium plan gives you 4K UHD video with HDR, along with Dolby Atmos sound.

Table 7.3 details what you get with each of Netflix's U.S. plans.

Table 7.3 Comparing Netflix's Subscription Plans

	Basic	Standard	Premium
Monthly price (USD)	$8.99	$12.99	$15.99
Number of screens you can watch at the same time	1	2	4
Maximum resolution	Standard definition	1080p HD	4K Ultra HD
HDR	No	No	Yes
Dolby Digital surround sound	No	Yes	Yes
Dolby Atmos	No	No	Yes

What's Playing?

Whereas Hulu leans a little toward recent TV shows, Netflix has become a fairly well-rounded service. It still offers a good selection of movies (but not nearly as many as it used to) and also provides a good number of recent and (some) older TV series.

Unfortunately, Netflix's selection of classic and foreign films has diminished over the years, but it's still a good source for popular movies from the past couple of decades. That said, it's not the first service to turn to for classic TV shows from the 1950s, 1960s, and 1970s.

Netflix is the leader, however, in original programming, both series and movies. Its original series are well known and well respected, and include *Black Mirror*, *Chilling Adventures of Sabrina*, *The Crown*, *Daredevil*, *Fuller House*, *Grace and Frankie*, *House of Cards*, *Lost in Space*, *Orange is the New Black*, and *Stranger Things*. Netflix's original movies are fewer in quantity (and perhaps in quality); recent examples include *The Ballad of Buster Scruggs*, *Father of the Year*, *The Kissing Booth*, and *The Princess Switch*.

Where You Can Find Netflix

Table 7.4 details the availability of Netflix across all four major streaming media player platforms. As you can see, Netflix is available on every player platform. It's also available on most, if not all, Smart TVs, smart Blu-ray players, and videogame consoles; it's also included with a handful of high-end cable services.

Table 7.4 Netflix on Streaming Media Player Platforms

Platform	Netflix app
Amazon Fire TV	Yes
Apple TV	Yes
Google Chromecast	Yes
Roku	Yes

Using Netflix

As noted, Netflix is available for just about every streaming media device out there. The Netflix app is easy to use, and there's lots of content to discover. Just select a tab or section on the left side of the screen and go from there. (Press the left arrow button on your remote to see all of these section options.)

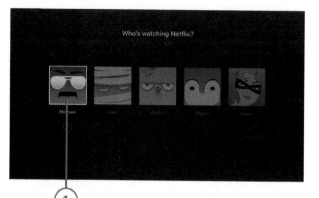

1. Netflix lets you create multiple users for a single account; this way everyone in your home can have their own unique viewing profile. When you first log into Netflix, you're prompted to select a user.

2. Select the Home tab to view programming by type—TV Shows, Trending Now, and so forth. Scroll to the Continue Watching row to view programs you've recently watched.

3. Select TV Shows to view episodes of available television shows.

4 If you selected a television program, select the season and episode you want to watch.

5 Select Movies to view available movies.

6 Select My List to view shows and movies you've selected to watch in the future.

7) Select New to view the newest programs and movies on Netflix.

8) Select Search to search for specific shows and movies.

>>>Go Further

YOUTUBE

There's one more service worth discussing, although it's not a direct competitor to Amazon Prime Video, Hulu, or Netflix. YouTube is technically a streaming video service, because it streams the hundreds of millions of videos on its site, although that's neither how it bills itself or how most viewers see it. Instead, YouTube is a video-sharing community, where its legion of users upload and view all manner of videos on all manner of devices.

Anyone can upload a video to YouTube, and at times it seems like practically everyone has. There are tons of how-to and self-improvement videos on YouTube, as well as pranks and stunts, funny animals and funny humans, videogame play-throughs, product reviews, you name it. There are also tons of old television programs uploaded by users and studios, as well as old and new music videos, movie trailers, and the like. And, best of all, YouTube is all free, no monthly subscription required.

Many people like to watch YouTube videos on the big living room screen, and there are YouTube apps for most Smart TVs and all major streaming media players—*except* Amazon Fire TV devices. (It's that old Amazon/Google war again; Google happens to own YouTube.) So while there are workarounds for watching YouTube on Fire TV devices, if you're serious about your YouTube videos, you're better off sticking to Apple TV, Google Chromecast, or Roku devices.

By the way, there are a couple of variations of YouTube that may be of interest. YouTube Premium (formerly called YouTube Red) is the standard shared-video YouTube without advertisements; it runs $11.99 USD per month. YouTube with Live TV is a totally different service that offers live streaming of broadcast and cable/satellite channels, for $40 USD per month. (Learn more about YouTube with Live TV in Chapter 10.)

Comparing the Big Three

Comparing the offerings and pricing of Amazon, Hulu, and Netflix—which is (or are) best for you?

Table 7.5 compares some of the key features of the Big Three streaming services.

Table 7.5 Comparing Major Streaming Services

	Amazon Prime Video	**Hulu**	**Netflix**
Monthly subscription price	$8.99 USD (or free with $119 per year Prime subscription)	$5.99–$11.99 USD	$8.99–$15.99 USD
Commercial-free	Yes	$11.99 per month plan only	Yes
HD content	Yes	Yes	Yes
4K Ultra HD with HDR content	Yes, no extra charge	No	Yes, $15.99 per month plan only

	Amazon Prime Video	**Hulu**	**Netflix**
Dolby Digital surround sound	Yes, 5.1	Yes, 5.1 (on Amazon Fire TV and Google Chromecast devices)	Yes, 5.1 and 7.1
Dolby Atmos sound	Yes	No	Yes
TV series	Yes	Yes	Yes
Movies	Yes	Yes	Yes
Original content	Yes	Yes	Yes
Available on Amazon Fire TV	Yes	Yes	Yes
Available on Apple TV	Yes	Yes	Yes
Available on Google Chromecast	No	Yes	Yes
Available on Roku	Yes	Yes	Yes
Stream on multiple devices simultaneously	Yes, 2	No	Yes (2 on Standard plan, 4 on Premium plan)

The reality is that many households subscribe to more than one of these services. There are pluses and minuses to each of them, but the big deciding factor is which has the programming that you want. In my household, we like Netflix's original and children's programming, but also play catch-up with recent episodes of our favorite TV shows on Hulu; that's two subscriptions right there. You may find that to watch all your favorites you need two or even three monthly subscriptions.

>>>Go Further

AMAZON, HULU, AND NETFLIX IN CANADA AND THE UK

The big three streaming services become the big two when you leave the United States. That's because Hulu is a U.S.-only service; there is no Hulu in Canada or the UK.

Amazon Prime Video is similar outside the United States to its U.S. counterpart. In Canada you'll pay $79 CAD per year for Amazon Prime membership (including Prime Video), and get a similar selection of movies, TV shows, and original programming. Prime Video is also similar in the UK, costing £79 per year.

Netflix is also available in Canada and the UK, but with noticeably different content. (That's due to different licensing restrictions for different countries.) For example, Netflix Canada only offers about half as many programs as does Netflix in the United States; although Netflix Canada does have rights to *Star Trek: Discovery*, which in the United States is a CBS All Access exclusive. Canadian pricing for Netflix runs from $13.99 to $16.99 CAD per month; UK pricing runs from £5.99 to £9.99 per month.

In this chapter, you learn about streaming services featuring some of your favorite premium network programming.

→ Watching Acorn TV, Britbox, CBS All Access, DC Universe, HBO Now, Showtime, and Starz
→ Comparing Premium Network Streaming Apps
→ Watching Other Network Streaming Services

Watching Premium Network Streaming Services

Individually or combined, Amazon Prime Video, Hulu, and Netflix deliver a ton of quality programming from a variety of sources. But they're not the only streaming services around; many premium networks have streaming apps and services you can use to watch their proprietary programming.

This chapter covers a range of these services, including British programming from Acorn TV and BritBox; original programming from paid cable networks such as HBO Now, Showtime, and Starz; and *Star Trek* and superhero shows from CBS All Access and DC Universe. For just a few dollars more per month, you can watch the specific programming that fits your particular taste.

Acorn TV

We'll start by an examination of British TV, as delivered by two separate but similar streaming services to the U.S. market: Acorn TV and BritBox. They both offer new and classic shows from across the pond, but each has its own unique program libraries.

What's Available

Acorn TV features classic and current programming from a variety of British networks, including BBC Worldwide, Channel 4, and ITV. It also offers a number of original series. The most popular shows include *Agatha Christie's Poirot, Delicious, Detectorists, Doc Martin, Foyle's War, Janet King, Keeping Faith, Loch Ness, Men Behaving Badly, Midsomer Murders, Mystery Road, Partners in Crime, Reilly Ace of Spies,* and *Vera*.

Acorn TV is more than just British television, however. The service also offers some of the best television programming from Australia, Canada, Ireland, New Zealand, and various European countries, including *A Place to Call Home, Bang, The Brokenwood Mysteries, Finding Joy, Jack Taylor, Miss Fisher's Murder Mysteries, Murdoch Mysteries,* and *Republic of Doyle*.

Where You Can Watch It

The Acorn TV app is available for all major streaming media players—Amazon Fire TV, Apple TV, Google Chromecast, and Roku. It is not available as a separate app on most Smart TVs, although it is available as a channel in the Amazon Prime Video app.

What It Costs

A subscription to Acorn TV runs $4.99 USD per month. An annual subscription is available for $49.99 USD.

Free Trial

Most streaming services offer some sort of free trial, which enables you to check out the service for a limited period without having to commit to a paid subscription.

Watching Acorn TV

The Acorn TV app lets you browse or search for the programming you want to watch.

(1) Select New & Featured to view the Acorn TV home page.

(2) Scroll down to view different categories of programming: Most Popular, Staff Picks, Only on Acorn TV, and more.

(3) Select My Acorn TV to view shows you've recently watched.

(4) Select Schedule to view titles recently added and coming soon.

(5) Select Search to search for specific shows.

(6) Select Browse All to view programs by category.

(7) Select the show you want to watch.

(8) Click Resume to continue watching a show you've previously viewed.

(9) Scroll down to view episodes within each series, then select an episode to watch it.

BritBox

The second streaming service for British television programming is BritBox, which offers a variety of current and classic shows from the BBC and ITV.

What's Available

BritBox offers comedies, dramas, mysteries, and more from across the pond. You may be familiar with many of these shows, including classic comedies such as *A Bit of Frye & Laurie, Absolutely Fabulous, Are You Being Served, As Time Goes By, Blackadder, Cold Feet, Dirk Gently, Fawlty Towers, Last of the Summer Wine, Red Dwarf, Yes Minister,* and the original British version of *The Office;* dramas such as *Brideshead Revisited, Broken, Coronation Street, EastEnders, Emmerdale, Kavanaugh Q.C., Life on Mars, Merlin, Poldark, Pride and Prejudice,* and *Upstairs Downstairs;* and mysteries such as *A Touch of Frost, Campion, Cracker, Inspector Morse, The Last Detective, Miss Marple,* and *Prime Suspect.*

(My wife and I really like John Cleese's comedy, *Hold the Sunset,* about two retired neighbors trying to start a new life together, with complications.)

In addition, BritBox lets you watch *Good Morning Britain* and other current BBC programming. It's also the home for all classic (pre-revival) episodes of *Doctor Who,* which alone might make BritBox worth subscribing to.

Where You Can Watch It

The BritBox app is available for Apple TV, Google Chromecast, and Roku devices. If you have an Amazon Fire TV device (or Fire TV Edition television), Smart TV, or game console, you can watch BritBox as a separate channel in the Amazon Prime Video app.

What It Costs

A BritBox subscription runs a little more than one for Acorn TV, $6.99 USD per month. If you opt for a one-year subscription, it's just $69.99 USD.

Watching BritBox

BritBox offers a variety of programming of various types.

(1) Select Home to view the BritBox home page.

(2) Scroll down to view available categories.

(3) Select New to view the latest additions to the service.

(4) Select All to view all available titles in alphabetical order.

(5) Select Search to search for a specific program.

(6) Select a category to view programming in that category.

(7) Within a category, select the series you want to view.

(8) Select the season you want to watch.

(9) Select an episode to begin viewing.

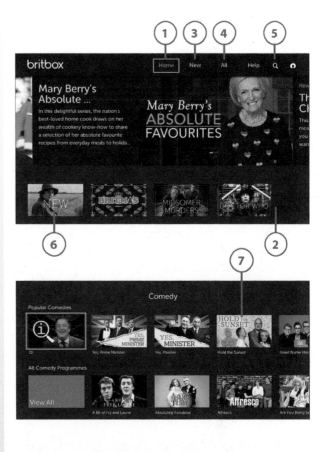

>>>Go Further

ACORN TV VERSUS BRITBOX

If you're a fan of British television, which service should you subscribe to, Acorn TV or BritBox? The answer is, maybe both.

First, know that there is very little overlap between the two services. You won't find many of the same shows on both Acorn TV and BritBox. To get the full range of British television programming, you need access to both services.

For casual viewers, BritBox, with its direct BBC connection, offers the more familiar shows. BritBox is where you'll find *Absolutely Fabulous* and *Are You Being Served?*, *EastEnders* and *Upstairs Downstairs*, *Inspector Morse* and *Prime Suspect*. Plus classic *Doctor Who* and current BBC programming, of course.

Acorn TV is more for diehard Anglophiles, with shows that may be lesser known to U.S. viewers. (It's also not limited to UK content; it's a great place to catch programming from Australia, Ireland, and New Zealand.) The programming on Acorn TV is top-notch, much of it classic, but it hasn't been as widely available here in the States.

So if you want the best-known British shows, go with BritBox. If you want to delve deeper into UK television or expand into programming from other countries, add Acorn TV to the mix. There's lots of good stuff on both services; together, the two subscriptions cost about the same as a single Netflix subscription.

CBS All Access

CBS was the first major U.S. broadcast network to launch its own premium streaming service. It's notable for being the home for all things *Star Trek*, including the current *Star Trek: Discovery* series.

What's Available

What's available on CBS All Access? For starters, every show that's in CBS' current primetime lineup, which makes it a good place to catch up on your favorite network programming, from *Criminal Minds* and *NCIS* to *Mom* and *Survivor*. You can also watch the latest episodes of *Late Show with Stephen Colbert* and *The Late Late Show with James Corden*, as well as *60 Minutes, The Price is Right,* and *The Talk.*

More notably, CBS All Access is the exclusive home (in the U.S. anyway) for *Star Trek: Discovery* and the upcoming *Star Trek: Picard* series. All the other *Star Trek* series are here, as well, including the original series, *Star Trek: Deep Space Nine, Star Trek: Enterprise, Star Trek: The Next Generation,* and *Star Trek: Voyager.*

CBS All Access offers other original series, including *The Good Fight, No Activity, One Dollar,* and *Strange Angel.* The service also has a random spattering of movies.

In addition, you can use the CBS All Access app to watch your local CBS station live in real time. You also can watch feeds from CBS Sports HQ and the otherwise little-known CBSN news network.

Star Trek: Discovery in Canada

Due to some sort of weird licensing deal, in Canada *Star Trek: Discovery* is not available on CBS All Access. Instead, you can find the show on the Netflix Canada service.

Where You Can Watch It

The CBS All Access app is available for all major streaming media players— Amazon Fire TV, Apple TV, Google Chromecast, and Roku. It's also available on Samsung and Vizio Smart TVs, as well as PlayStation and Xbox game consoles. It's also available as a paid channel within the Amazon Prime Video app.

What It Costs

CBS offers two All Access plans. The Limited Commercials plan (which, as the name implies, allows you to suffer through what it deems a limited number of advertisements) runs $5.99 USD per month or $59.99 USD per year. If you'd rather excise advertisements entirely, go with the No Commercials plan for $9.99 USD per month or $99.99 USD per year.

Watching CBS All Access

As you might suspect, CBS All Access offers programming found on the CBS television network, as well as original shows produced especially for the CBS All Access service.

1. Select Home to view the CBS All Access Home page.

2. Scroll down to view different types of programming: Continue Watching, Shows You Watch, Latest Episodes, CBS All Access Originals, and the like.

3. Select Live TV to view live programming.

4. Select your local station to view what's currently being broadcast.

5. Select CBSN to view live national news.

6. Select CBS Sports HQ to view live sports news.

7. Select ET Live to view entertainment news.

8. Select Shows to view shows by category.

9. Select a category to view shows of that type.

10. Select the show you want to watch

DC Universe

If you're a superhero fan (at least a DC superhero fan), you're going to love DC Universe. This relatively new streaming service is all about DC superheroes, in movie, television series, and comic book form.

What's Available

First, DC Universe is the home to all manner of television series and movies featuring DC superheroes, in both live-action and animated form. You'll find classic series animated such as *Batman: The Animated Series, Justice League, Super Friends, Superman: The Animated Series,* and *Young Justice*; classic TV series like *Adventures of Superman, Constantine,* the 1990s *The Flash, Lois & Clark: The New Adventures of Superman,* and *Wonder Woman*; live action movies like *Batman, Supergirl,* and *Superman*; and various animated movies, including *Batman: Gotham by Gaslight, Batman: Year One, The Death of Superman, Justice League: The Flashpoint Paradox,* and *Justice League: The New Frontier.*

DC Universe also offers several original superhero series. First off the block was *Titans,* featuring DC's Teen Titans team. Future series are set to include *Doom Patrol, Star Girl,* and *Swamp Thing.* The service also offers *DC Daily,* a daily news show about DC comics and characters.

Unique to DC Universe are comic books, in digital format. The service offers a rotating selection of DC comics that you can read on your TV screen. (Although, to be honest, they're easier to read on a computer or tablet than on a TV.)

There's not a single Marvel movie or series to be found, but if you're a DC fan, this is the streaming service for you.

Where You Can Watch It

As of early 2019, the DC Universe app is available for Amazon Fire TV, Apple TV, Google Chromecast, and Roku devices, and for Sony Smart TVs. It is *not* available (yet) on most Smart TVs and game consoles. (DC says they're working on compatibility with other devices and TVs.)

What It Costs

A DC Universe subscription runs $7.99 USD per month or $74.99 USD per year.

Watching DC Universe

At present DC Universe's content is somewhat limited, but DC continues to add more programming on a regular basis.

1. The home page displays featured content at the top.

2. Select Search to search for specific programming.

3. Scroll down to view programming by category.

4. Select the series or movie you want to watch.

5. For any television series, select the desired season.

6. Select an episode to begin viewing.

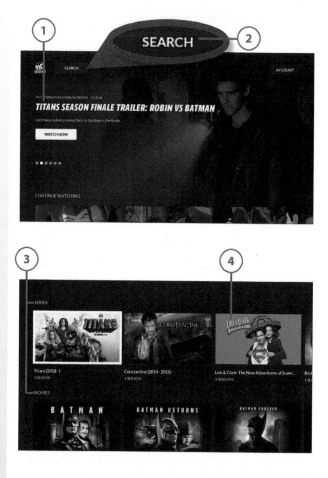

7. If you select a comic book, select Start Reading.

8. Use the right and left arrows on your streaming device's remote control to progress forward or backward through the comic's pages.

HBO Now

HBO Now is essentially HBO without the cable. It's where you find HBO's original and licensed content for playback on your streaming media player or Smart TV.

What's Available

Just about every movie currently playing on HBO is available on HBO Now. It's also the home for all of HBO's original series and movies, both current and classic, including *Barry, Camping, Curb Your Enthusiasm, Deadwood, Entourage, Game of Thrones, The Leftovers, My Brilliant Friend, The Newsroom, Silicon Valley, The Sopranos, True Detective,* and *Westworld*. It's also the place to watch recent episodes of *Last Week with John Oliver* and *Real Time with Bill Maher*.

Where You Can Watch It

The HBO Now app is available for Amazon Fire TV, Apple TV, Google Chromecast, and Roku devices. It's also available on Smart TVs from Samsung, Sharp, and Sony, as well as PlayStation and Xbox game consoles.

What It Costs

HBO Now runs $14.99 USD per month.

Watching HBO Now

HBO Now has a surprisingly large amount of programming from throughout HBO's history.

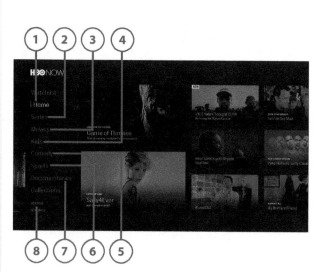

1. Select Home to view HBO Now's Home page.

2. Select Series to view original series.

3. Select Movies to view movies currently showing on HBO.

4. Select Kids to view children's programming, including Sesame Street.

5. Select Comedy to view original comedy programs.

6. Select Sports to view sports programming.

7. Select Documentaries to view documentary programming.

8. Select Search to search for a specific program.

9. Enter the first few letters of what you're looking for.

10. Select the program you want to watch.

(11) If you selected a series, select the season you want to watch.

(12) Scroll right and left to view the episodes in this season.

(13) Select the Play icon to begin watching this episode.

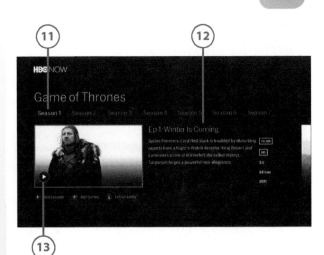

Showtime

Showtime is HBO's chief competitor on cable, and it offers a similar streaming service for its original programming.

What's Available

Like HBO Now, Showtime's streaming service offers all the movies it has available for cable viewing. It also offers Showtime's original programming, including *The Affair, Californication, Dexter, Enemies, Escape at Dannemora, Homeland, The L Word, Queer as Folk, Ray Donovan, Secret Diary,* and *The Tudors.*

Where You Can Watch It

The Showtime streaming app is available on Amazon Fire TV, Apple TV, Google Chromecast, and Roku streaming media players. It's also available on LG, Samsung, and Sony Smart TVs, as well as Xbox game consoles.

What It Costs

Showtime's streaming service costs $10.99 USD per month.

Watching Showtime

Showtime's main menu displays on the left of any given screen when you press the left arrow button on your device's remote control.

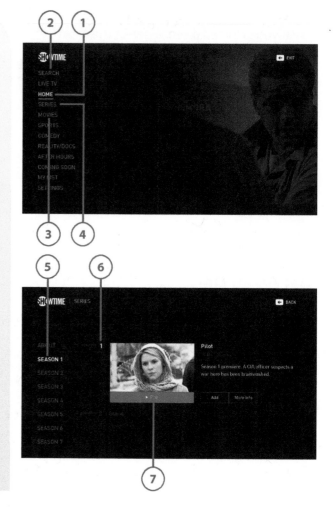

1. Select Home to view the Home screen.

2. Select Search to search for specific programs.

3. Select Movies to view films currently playing on the Showtime service.

4. Select Series to view Showtime original series.

5. Select the season you want to watch.

6. Scroll down to view all episodes in that season.

7. Select Play to watch the selected episode.

Starz

Starz offers a number of cable/satellite networks with a variety of licensed and original programming. If you want to watch Starz content, you can do so via the Starz streaming app.

What's Available

Pretty much everything that's showing on a Starz cable or satellite network, movies and classic TV series alike, is available on the Starz streaming app. There are also some original series available, including *American Gods, Black Sails, Camelot, Counterpart, Outlander, Power, Vida, Warriors of Liberty City,* and *The White Queen.*

Where You Can Watch It

The Starz app is available on Amazon Fire TV, Apple TV, Google Chromecast, and Roku devices. It's also available on select LG, Samsung, and Sony Smart TVs, as well as Xbox game consoles.

What It Costs

The freestanding Starz streaming service costs $8.99 USD per month.

Watching Starz

Starz offers movies, classic television shows, and original programming.

1. Select Home or Featured to view featured content.

2. Select Search to search for specific content.

3. Select Series to view original and classic television series.

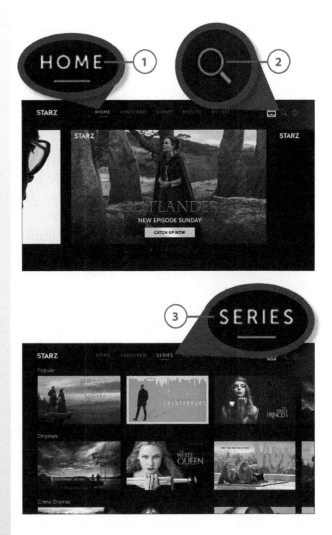

4. Select Movies to view films currently playing on the various Starz services.

5. Select an item to begin viewing.

Comparing Premium Network Streaming Apps

Looking at the seven premium network streaming services discussed in this chapter, it becomes apparent that you could end up spending a lot of money if you decide to subscribe to all of them. At anywhere from $5 to $15 USD per month, the cost of subscribing to multiple premium services quickly adds up. Add in the obligatory Amazon Prime Video, Hulu, and Netflix, and you could end up spending close to $100 a month—which very well might rival your old cable or satellite bill.

When it comes to deciding which premium streaming services to subscribe to, you need to first ask which services are supported by your streaming media device. Fortunately, the major streaming media players support almost all these premium services.

You also might want to weed out the most expensive services. Some services, such as Acorn TV and CBS All Access, are actually quite affordable on their own, and they're relatively painless to add to your monthly budget. Others, such as HBO Now and Showtime, are fairly pricey, and they might not be worth the price. Table 8.1 outlines the monthly subscription price for each of these major services.

Table 8.1   Monthly Subscription Pricing for Premium Streaming Network Services

	Monthly Subscription Price (USD)
Acorn TV	$4.99
BritBox	$6.99
CBS All Access	$5.99 ($9.99 for No Commercials plan)
DC Universe	$7.99
HBO Now	$14.99
Showtime	$10.99
Starz	$8.99

Beyond this, you need to determine what types of programming you're most likely to watch, and then choose the services that best fit your viewing patterns. You might find, for example, that you don't need both HBO Now and Showtime, or that you don't care about the original programming on CBS All Access, or that you simply don't watch the types of superhero shows available on DC Universe. Weed out those services you're least likely to watch, and you should end up with a handful of premium services that collectively won't break the bank.

>>>*Go Further*

AWAITING NEW PREMIUM STREAMING SERVICES

The success of Netflix and similar services has not gone unnoticed. Instead of licensing their content to other streaming services, major production studios/content owners are making plans to create their own premium streaming services, featuring their own content, and thus keeping their own revenues and profits.

One such studio-owned streaming service in the works is coming from Disney. The new service, said to be dubbed Disney+, is due to launch in late 2019. This will be a big one because the Disney Company owns all the Disney movies and TV shows plus programming from 21st Century Fox, the ABC television network, ESPN, Lucasfilm, Marvel, Pixar, Touchstone Pictures, and more. Lucasfilm brings the *Star Wars* franchise, and Marvel brings all the films and TV shows from the Marvel Cinematic Universe, including the *Avengers* movies. When the Disney+ service launches, it's likely that Disney will pull all or most of its movies and television programs from other streaming services and make them exclusive to its own service. For many, this will make Disney+ a must-have streaming service.

Disney isn't the only big media company launching its own streaming service. NBCUniversal, owned by Comcast (which also owns the Sky service in the UK) plans to launch a streaming service sometime in 2020. The company plans a free, ad-supported version of the service for NBC TV subscribers, as well as an ad-free version for $12.99 USD per month. The service will supposedly be available to Comcast and Sky subscribers outside the United States, as well.

WarnerMedia (owned by AT&T) is also set to launch a streaming service, in late 2019. This yet-to-be-named service will feature content from Warner's various properties, including HBO. It's possible that this service will include classic films previously available on the now-defunct FilmStruck service. It is not known how DC Universe (also owned by AT&T/Warner) will fit into these plans.

Speaking of FilmStruck, the Criterion Collection, whose films were distributed as part of the FilmStruck service, is launching its own service in the spring of 2019. Designed for lovers of classic and foreign movies (and Criterion's curated and annotated presentations of such), The Criterion Channel will be the new home for the company's vast collection of important films. Subscription pricing will be $10.99 USD per month, or $100 USD per year.

On the surface, these new streaming services appear to offer additional choices to viewers, which should be a good thing. However, with more services to subscribe to, it's likely that your monthly entertainment bill will balloon to not-before-seen levels. You'll no longer be able to get your entertainment fix by subscribing to Netflix and one or two other services; you'll need Netflix, Amazon, Hulu, CBS All Access, Disney+, The Criterion Channel, and the new offerings from NBCUniversal and Warner—plus whatever else comes along in the meantime. A bill that was $10 to $20 USD suddenly is closer to $100 USD in total. That is not a good thing.

In addition, having to deal with programming across multiple streaming services complicates life for the average viewer. One show you like is on one service, another show on another, and another favorite is on a third service. Figuring out what's where becomes a chore, as does installing and switching between and navigating all those different services. Dealing with a single service, such as Netflix, made viewing simple; dealing with multiple services just confuses things again.

Watching Other Network Streaming Services

Not all network streaming services are premium in nature. Many are available for free, no paid subscription necessary—if you also have a cable or satellite subscription.

Discovering Free Network Streaming Services

Many broadcast and cable/satellite networks offer streaming apps that let you stream their programming, on-demand, to your streaming media player. These apps, such as DisneyNOW and HGTV Anywhere, install on your streaming media device and provide a library of that network's most popular shows. Just browse or search for a show, pick the episode you want, and start streaming.

The caveat is that you have access to that channel as part of your existing cable or satellite plan. If you don't have cable or satellite service, or if this particular channel isn't part of your plan, you either won't be able to watch it, or you'll have access only to a limited selection of programming. This restriction is intended to make sure that you don't bypass available television providers to get the channel's programming for free, but it effectively puts the kibosh on watching that channel if you're a true cord cutter.

Some Let You Watch for Free

While most networks require you to have a cable or satellite subscription to watch their streaming apps, not all do. Try installing and then viewing the app; if you're not asked to provide your cable or satellite provider, you're good to go!

Which networks offer free streaming apps to cable and satellite subscribers? Table 8.2 provides an (undoubtedly incomplete) list.

Table 8.2 Free Network Streaming Apps

Network	Streaming App
A&E	A&E
ABC	ABC
ABC News	ABC News
AMC	AMC
BBC America	BBC America
BET	BET
Boomerang	Boomerang
Bravo	Bravo Now
Cartoon Network	Cartoon Network
CBS News	CBS News
CNN	CNNgo
Comedy Central	Comedy Central
Comet TV	Comet TV
Cooking Channel	Cooking Channel
Destination America	Destination America GO
Disney Channel	DisneyNOW
Disney Junior	DisneyNOW
DIY Network	DIY Network
E!	E!
ePIX	ePIX
Food Network	Food Network
Fox	FOX NOW
Fox News Channel	Fox News
FX	FXNOW
Hallmark Channel	Hallmark Channel Everywhere
Hallmark Movies	Hallmark Movies Now
HGTV	HGTV Anywhere

Network	Streaming App
History Channel	HISTORY
Lifetime	Lifetime
MTV	MTV
NBC	NBC
NBC News	NBC News
Nick Jr.	Nick Jr.
Nickelodeon	NICK
Paramount Network	Paramount Network
PBS	PBS
PBS Kids	PBS Kids
QVC	QVC
Smithsonian Channel	Smithsonian Channel
Sundance Channel	Sundance Now
SyFy	SYFY
TBS	Watch TBS
TCM	Watch TCM
Telemundo	Telemundo
The CW	The CW *and* CW Seed
TLC	TLC GO
TNT	Watch TNT
truTV	truTV
Univision	Univision Now
USA Network	USA
VH1	VH1
VICE	VICELAND
WE tv	WE tv

Discovering Other Free Streaming Services

There are other apps available for your streaming media player that offer a variety of free programming, everything from slightly older movies to much older TV shows. Although the content might not be the freshest around, you don't have to pay a monthly subscription fee to watch it!

Table 8.3 details some of these free streaming services. (Not all apps are available for all streaming media players.)

Table 8.3   Streaming Video Apps with Free Content

App	Content
FilmRise	Movies, '80s and '90s TV shows
IMDb Freedive (Amazon Fire TV devices only)	Older movies and TV shows
Popcornflix	Older movies, reality TV shows, children's programming
Shout Factory TV	Classic and cult TV shows and movies (including *Mystery Science Theater 3000*)
Sony Crackle	Older movies and TV shows from Sony-owned studios
The Roku Channel (Roku devices only)	Older movies and TV shows (including the 1960s *Batman* TV series)
Tubi	Older movies and TV shows, reality TV shows

>>>*Go Further*

NETWORK STREAMING SERVICES IN CANADA AND THE UK

The premium network streaming services discussed in this chapter are U.S.-based services. Some of these services are available in Canada and the UK, sometimes as part of other region-specific services.

Table 8.4 details which of these services are available where.

Table 8.4   Availability of U.S. Premium Network Streaming Services in Canada and the UK

	Canada	UK
Acorn TV	Yes	No
BritBox	Yes	No
CBS All Access	Yes	No
DC Universe	Yes	No
HBO Now	Yes (via Crave)	Yes (via Sky)
Showtime	Yes (via Crave)	Yes (via Sky)
Starz	Yes (via Crave)	Yes (via Prime)

Note that HBO, Showtime, and Starz, while not available separately in Canada, are available via the Crave streaming service. Monthly subscription prices for Crave range from $9.99 to $19.99 CAD. Learn more at www.crave.ca.

In the UK, HBO and Showtime programming can be found on Sky's Now TV streaming service. Starz programming is available on the Amazon Prime Video UK service. BBC content is available as part of the BBC iPlayer streaming service, of course. Original CBS All Access and DC Universe programming is not currently available in the UK—with the notable exception of *Star Trek: Discovery*, which is available on Netflix UK.

In this chapter, you learn how to purchase and rent streaming videos over the Internet.

→ Shopping at Amazon Instant Videos, FandangoNOW, Google Play, iTunes Store, and Vudu
→ Comparing Online Video Retailers

9

Watching Paid and Rented Programs

As you've learned in the previous chapters, some streaming services offer movies and television programming for free; some require a monthly paid subscription. But not everything you want to watch is available from these services.

There's a lot more programming available online than you might find on Hulu or Netflix. Many movies and TV series—especially older or less mainstream fare—is available for purchase or rental on a per-item or per-view basis. There are several online retailers that sell or rent videos through your Smart TV or streaming media player of choice. You'll pay anywhere from $1 to $15 or even $20 USD to watch these programs, and they stream just like the content available from regular streaming services. You just have to pay for them, one at a time.

Shopping at Amazon Instant Videos

Amazon is the largest online retailer today, and for years it has offered physical DVDs and Blu-ray discs for sale on its site. What you might not know is that it also offers movies and TV shows for sale or rental online for your streaming pleasure. And it offers a lot—perhaps the biggest selection online today.

Device Availability

While you can access Amazon's streaming video library from Amazon's traditional website, using your computer, phone or tablet, it's more convenient to shop from your streaming media player, using the Amazon Prime Video app. Unfortunately, not all streaming media players let you purchase or rent videos from the Amazon Prime Video app.

As with all things Amazon, Amazon's streaming video store is not accessible from any Google Chromecast device. That's due to Amazon's continuing feud with competitor Google; the two companies do not play nice together.

As to availability on the Apple TV app, Apple does not allow purchases from other companies within any of its iOS or tvOS apps. You can, however, purchase or rent titles from Amazon from your computer; they'll then be available for viewing within the Amazon Prime Video app on your Apple TV device. It's a work-around, but that's inter-company competition for you.

It's a lot easier to purchase or rent Amazon videos if you have an Amazon Fire TV or Roku streaming media player. Within the Amazon Prime Video app on your device, sale/rental offerings are displayed side-by-side with the content offered for free with a Prime Video subscription. Although you don't have to have a Prime Video subscription to buy or rent from Amazon, you do need an Amazon account.

Most Smart TVs and game consoles also let you purchase from Amazon from within the Prime Video app. For those that don't, you can still purchase or rent from Amazon on your computer or smartphone, and then watch what you bought or rented via the app.

What's Available

Amazon's streaming video store has a huge selection of programming available for purchase and rental. The selection is almost as big as that available on DVD or Blu-ray.

In terms of television shows, there's a huge selection of series from current network fare to classic programs from our youth (and, for some of us, even before!). Most television series are available for purchase only, not rental, and prices run from a buck or three per episode; complete seasons typically are priced from $10 to $30 USD.

Just about every current television series is available for streaming, from *This Is Us* and *Star Trek: Discovery* to *Brother vs. Brother* and *NCIS*. There's a ton of children's shows, from Disney, Nickelodeon, and others. And the variety of vintage television shows is mind-boggling, from *Dragnet* and *Perry Mason* to *Get Smart* and *Leave It to Beaver*. You can typically buy a complete season's worth of episodes, or you can buy just one episode at a time.

If you're looking at current season's fare, you can sign up for what Amazon calls a TV Season Pass. With this you can watch previously aired episodes immediately, and get access to each new episode as it airs.

In terms of movies, Amazon has a ton, and most are available for purchase or short-term rental. As you might suspect, renting costs less than buying; some films can be rented for just a few dollars, while most purchases cost $15 USD or more (especially for more recent films). Amazon is the place to find not only newer and more popular films, but also classic, foreign, and independent fare. In fact, the Amazon streaming video store is the place to buy or rent those obscure movies you just can't find anyplace else. It's like having a quirky neighborhood video store on your streaming media player.

How to Order a Video

Ordering an item for purchase or rental is as simple as searching or browsing for it from within the Amazon Prime Video app, selecting the appropriate button, and entering a payment method.

1. Within the Amazon Prime Video app, scroll to any of the "Rent or Buy" sections.

2. Select the item you want to purchase or rent.

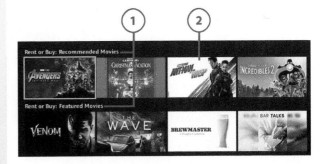

3 To purchase a movie, select one of the Buy Movie options. (You typically have the option of buying in HD or standard definition, which has a slightly lower cost; select More Purchase Options to see all available options.)

4 To rent a movie, select the Rent Movie option.

5 To purchase a television show, select the season you want to watch.

6 Select the episode you want to purchase.

7 Select the Buy Episode option.

8 Confirm your purchase.

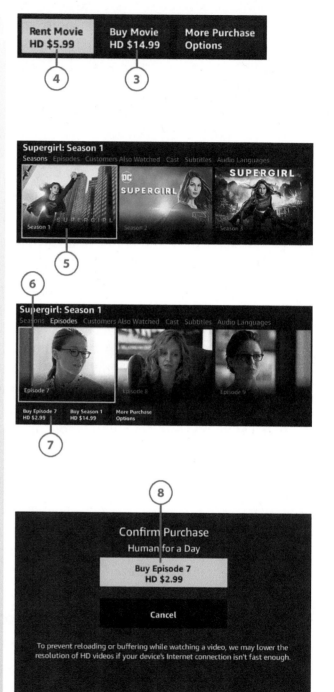

Watch a Purchased or Rented Video

When you purchase or rent a video from Amazon, it's available in your library in the Amazon Prime Video app. When you rent a video, you typically have a set number of days to start watching, and then a few more days to finish. (The precise number of days varies from selection to selection.) You can watch an unlimited number of times after you start, but when the time period is over, the video is removed from your video library. Items you purchase are stored in your library forever, or until Amazon loses the rights to distribute them.

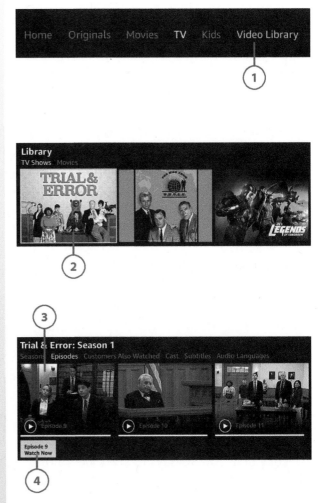

1. From within the Amazon Prime Video app, select the Video Library tab.

2. All the movies and TV shows you've purchased are displayed here. Select the item you want to watch.

3. If you selected a television show, all the episodes you purchased are displayed. Select the one you want to watch.

4. Select Watch Now to begin viewing the item.

Shopping at FandangoNOW

You might know Fandango as a company that sells movie theater tickets over the Internet. They're also in the streaming video business—selling and renting movies and TV shows for streaming over the Internet and on many streaming media players through the FandangoNOW app.

Device Availability

The FandangoNOW app is available only on Roku streaming media players. It is available on both Android and iOS mobile devices, however, that can be streamed to your TV via the Google Chromecast device. The app isn't available for Amazon Fire TV and Apple TV devices—although you can watch videos purchased from your computer or phone through the Movies Anywhere app, which I discuss later in this chapter.

What's Available

FandangoNOW has a much more limited selection than does Amazon, especially in the television category. To be honest, I do not recognize many of the shows available here.

All TV shows are available only for purchase. Some series let you purchase one episode at a time; others only sell complete seasons. Prices vary.

The service does a lot better with movies, with a decent selection of recent and not-so-recent films. Most movies are available for purchase or rental. Rentals typically give you 30 days to start viewing, and then 48 hours to watch it. Rentals run $4 to $6 USD; purchase prices typically run $15 to $25 USD.

How to Order a Video

If you have a Roku device and the Fandango menu options displayed, purchasing or renting a video is relatively easy.

(1) From Roku's main menu, select Movie Store by Fandango to purchase a film. *Or...*

(2) Select TV Store by Fandango to purchase a television show.

(3) Make a selection from the left-hand column to display items of a specific type.

(4) Select the item you want to purchase or rent.

(5) To purchase a movie, select one of the purchase options.

(6) To rent a movie, select one of the rental options.

(7) To purchase a television show, select the desired season of that series.

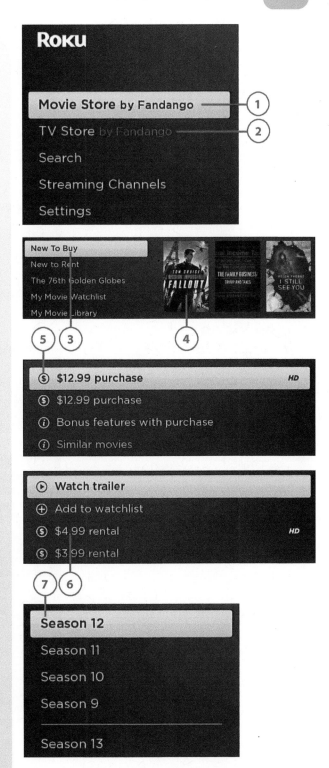

8 Select the episode you want to watch.

9 Select the desired purchase option.

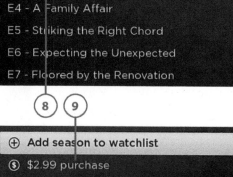

Watch a Purchased or Rented Video

1 From Roku's main menu, select Movie Store by Fandango to view films you've purchased. *Or...*

2 Select TV Store by Fandango to view television shows you've purchased.

3 Select either My Movie Library or My TV Library.

4 Select the item you want to watch.

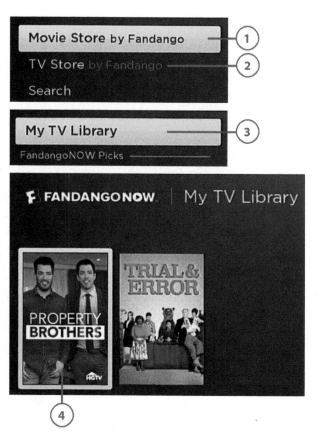

5) If you want to watch an episode from a television show, select that episode.

>>>Go Further

PLAY MOVIES PURCHASED ELSEWHERE WITH THE MOVIES ANYWHERE APP

As you're no doubt starting to realize, not every streaming media player company wants other companies making money by selling or renting videos on their platform. Roku is different, though, with every online store except the iTunes Store being available, but if you have an Amazon, Apple, or Google device, your shopping options are more limited.

Fortunately, many of these companies got together and figured out a way for you to play videos on their devices that you purchased elsewhere. (Typically, on your computer.) The Movies Anywhere app is what they came up with.

The Movies Anywhere app lets you play videos purchased from Amazon Prime Video, FandangoNOW, Google Play, the iTunes Store, Microsoft Movies & TV, Vudu, and Xfinity on Amazon Fire TV, Apple TV, Google Chromecast, and Roku devices. You can use it as a single repository and player for videos you purchase from those multiple sources.

Viewing your video library in the Movies Anywhere app.

The app is free and available in your device's app or channel store. You need to create a Movies Anywhere account and link it to your accounts at those online stores at which you shop. After that, the movies you rent or purchase are available in the Movies Anywhere library, even if you couldn't purchase them otherwise on your streaming media player.

Learn more about Movies Anywhere (and create a free account) at www.moviesanywhere.com.

Shopping at Google Play

The Google Play store is much like Amazon in that it offers a large variety of movies and television series for streaming purchase or rental. It's the store of choice if you have a Google Chromecast device.

Device Availability

As you might expect, the Google Play store is available on Google Chromecast. It's also available on Roku devices. However, you cannot purchase items from Google Play on an Amazon Fire TV or Apple TV device. (Competitors, again.) You can, however, play items purchased from Google Play on any device using the Movies Anywhere app.

What's Available

Like Amazon, Google Play offers tens of thousands of movies and television shows for purchase or rental. I've found Google Play to have fewer foreign, classic, and independent films than Amazon, but the two services have a similar number of recent blockbusters. Google offers most videos in HD format, with selected titles in 4K Ultra HD with HDR.

Movie rentals range from $2.99 to $5.99 USD. Purchase prices range from $9.99 to $19.99 USD. Television episodes are priced from $1.99 to $2.99 USD. (Rentals expire in 30 days or 48 hours after you start watching, whichever comes first.)

How to Order a Video

You need a Google Account (that's linked to a credit card) to purchase or rent from Google Play. After that, it's a simple matter of finding what you want and clicking a few buttons.

(1) From the Google Play app, select the Home tab to view featured items.

(2) Select Search to search for specific movies and shows.

(3) Select TV to view television shows.

(4) Select Genres to view programming by type.

(5) Select a genre.

(6) Select the item you want to purchase or rent.

(7) To purchase a movie, select the Buy button.

(8) To rent a movie, select the Rent button.

(9) To purchase a television show, select the season you want.

(10) Select the episode within that season.

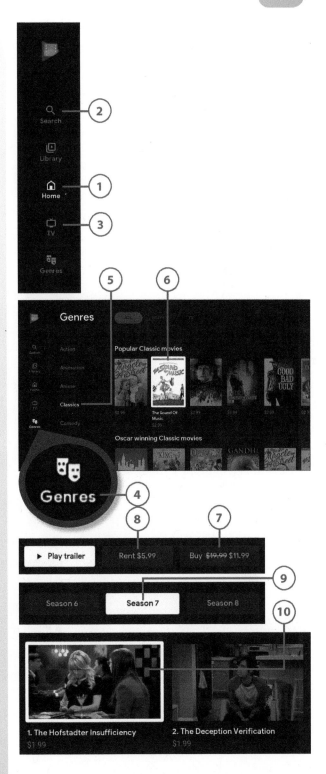

11. Select the SD button to purchase the episode in standard definition.

12. Select the HD button to purchase the episode in high definition (at a slightly higher price).

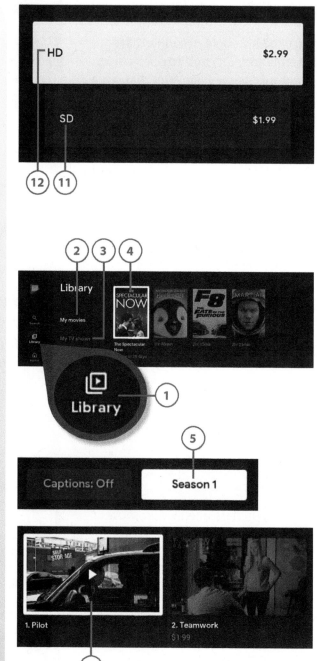

Watch a Purchased or Rented Video

1. Select Library.

2. Select My Movies to view only purchased or rented movies.

3. Select My TV Shows to view only purchased television episodes.

4. Select the item you want to watch.

5. If you selected a TV show, select the desired season.

6. Select an episode to begin watching it.

Shopping at the iTunes Store

The chief competitor for Amazon and Google in the videos-for-purchase market is Apple, in the form of the iTunes Store. If you have an Apple computer, iPhone, or iPad, you're probably already familiar with the iTunes Store; it's where you can buy and download digital music, podcasts, and electronic books for viewing or playback on your device.

The iTunes Store also has a huge selection of movies, television shows, and other videos available for purchase or rental, for downloading or streaming to any Apple device—including Apple TV.

Device Availability

Here's the thing about the iTunes Store—it's an Apple-only thing. So, there is no iTunes Store app available for Amazon Fire TV, Google Chromecast, or Roku streaming media players; the only streaming media player you can use to purchase from the iTunes Store is the Apple TV box. Apple plays well with other Apple devices, but not with anybody else. (Apple recently announced that the iTunes Store is now available on Samsung Smart TVs, so the company culture may be changing a little.)

You can, however, purchase items from the iTunes Store on any computer (or iPhone or iPad), and then play them back on your non-Apple streaming media player. Just use the Movies Anywhere app and service, as described earlier in this chapter.

What's Available

The iTunes Store offers a similar selection of movies and television shows as you find in the Amazon store and somewhat more than in Google Play. We're talking more than 85,000 movies and 300,000 television episodes, from recently released titles to older classics.

Most movies in the iTunes Store are available for both purchase and rental. Purchase prices run from $7.99 to $19.99 USD, depending on the age and popularity of the movie, with HD versions priced more than standard definition (SD) versions. Rental prices run from $2.99 to $5.99 USD; you typically have 30 days to start watching a rental title and 48 hours to finish. Some titles are available in 4K Ultra HD, at no increase in price.

Most TV shows are available for purchase only. Individual episodes are typically priced at $1.99 to $2.99 USD; full-season prices vary depending on the number of episodes included.

How to Order a Video

You need an Apple account to purchase or rent videos from the iTunes Store. Of course, if you have an Apple TV box, you already have an Apple account; just make sure your credit card information is up to date, and you're ready to shop.

(1) From the iTunes Store app on your Apple TV device, select either iTunes Movies (to shop for films) or iTunes TV Shows (to shop for television programming).

(2) Browse or search for the item you want, and then click to select it.

(3) To purchase a television program, select the Seasons button, and choose the season you want to view.

(4) To purchase an individual episode, select that episode, and then select the Episode button.

(5) To purchase the entire season, select the Buy Season button.

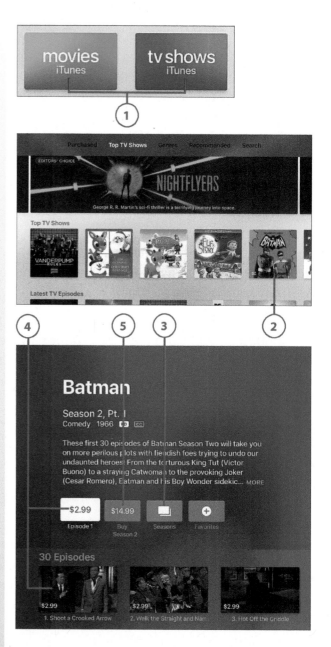

6 To purchase a movie, select the Buy option.

7 To rent a movie, select the Rent option.

8 Confirm your purchase or rental.

Watch a Purchased or Rented Video

After you've confirmed your purchase or rental, that item is available in your iTunes library for future viewing. It's stored in the Apple cloud (not on your Apple TV device), from where you stream it when you want to watch.

1 From the Apple TV home screen, select the Library tab.

2 All your purchased or rented items are displayed. Select TV Shows to display television episodes you've purchased.

3 Select Movies to display films you've purchased or rented.

4 Click to select the item you want to watch.

Shopping at Vudu

The other notable online marketplace for purchasing and renting streaming videos is Vudu, which is owned by Walmart. Vudu isn't nearly as popular as Amazon, Google Play, or the iTunes Store, probably because it doesn't have the same level of visibility.

Device Availability

The Vudu store is available only to Google Chromecast and Roku users. There is a Vudu app for Apple TV, but it's for playback only, not for purchasing. And there's no Vudu app available for Amazon Fire TV devices.

What's Available

Most Vudu videos are available in HD with Dolby Digital 5.1-channel sound. Selected titles are offered in 4K Ultra HD, typically for $5 USD or so more than HD pricing.

Movie rentals run from $.99 to $5.99 USD. Purchases are priced from $4.99 to $24.99 USD. Purchases of television episodes run from $1.99 to $2.99 USD.

Interestingly, Vudu offers a smaller selection of free videos, but these videos include advertising. If you don't mind suffering through the non-fast-forwardable ads, this might have some appeal.

All that said, I've found that Vudu doesn't have quite the selection as its main competitors. Also, its pricing—especially for 4K UHD titles—tends to run a little higher than the other services. If you can find what you want at Vudu for a decent price (or even for free, with ads), go for it. Otherwise, you might be better off shopping at a store with a bigger selection.

How to Order a Video

Vudu operates in much the same fashion as the other online streaming stores. Find what you want to watch, select a purchase option, and click the appropriate buttons.

1. Select Spotlight to view featured and recommended content.

2. Select Movies to view films for purchase or rent.

3. Select TV to view television shows for purchase.

4. Select the item you want to purchase or rent.

5. To purchase or rent a movie, select Rent/Own.

6. Select the desired rental or purchase option. Most films are available for purchase or rental in SD or HD (what Vudu calls HDX); some films are available in Ultra HD (UHD).

7. To purchase a television show, select the episode you want to purchase.

8. Select either the SD or HDX option. (If you're looking at an older show, you'll see only a single Own option, which is in SD.)

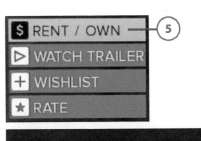

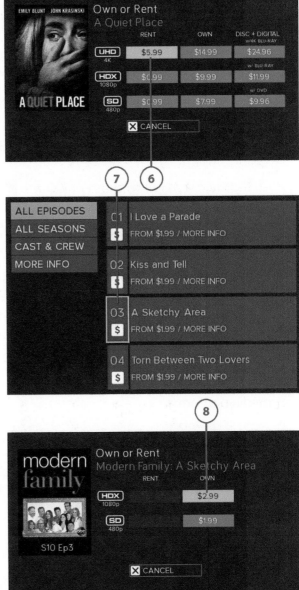

Watch a Purchased or Rented Video

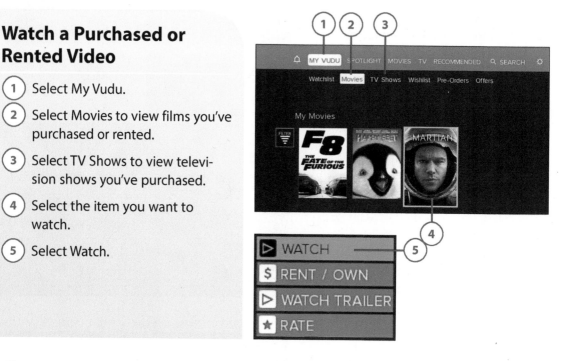

1. Select My Vudu.
2. Select Movies to view films you've purchased or rented.
3. Select TV Shows to view television shows you've purchased.
4. Select the item you want to watch.
5. Select Watch.

Comparing Online Video Retailers

Most of the streaming video retailers discussed in this chapter have similar content available for both purchase and rental. Yes, you'll find some videos in some stores and not in others; that's always going to be the case. The big difference is which stores you can access from your streaming media player or Smart TV.

As mentioned earlier, not all streaming video stores are available on all streaming devices. Table 9.1 details which stores offer videos for sale on which streaming media platforms.

Table 9.1   Streaming Video Store Availability on Major Streaming Media Platforms

	Amazon Fire TV	Apple TV	Google Chromecast	Roku
Amazon Instant Videos	Yes	No	No	Yes
FandangoNOW	No	No	Yes	Yes
Google Play	No	No	Yes	Yes
iTunes Store	No	Yes	No	No
Vudu	No	No	Yes	Yes

Smart TV Availability

The availability of streaming video stores on Smart TVs varies by manufacturer and is constantly changing. You should be able to access the Amazon and Google Play stores on most Smart TVs. FandangoNOW and Vudu are available on LG, Samsung, Sony, and Vizio models. The iTunes Store is currently accessible only from Samsung TVs.

Roku users have the most options when it comes to buying and renting videos, with every store available except the iTunes Store. Amazon Fire TV and Apple TV users have the least number of options; Amazon users can shop at Amazon, and Apple users can shop at the iTunes Store, and that's that. Google Chromecast users are somewhere in the middle, with access to three of the five major stores.

Looking at it another way, if you want to shop at Amazon (which has the largest selection of videos, especially harder-to-find titles), you can do so from Amazon Fire TV and Roku devices, or your computer. If you want to shop at FandangoNOW, Google Play, or Vudu, you can do so from Google Chromecast and Roku devices. If you want to shop at the iTunes Store, you can only do so from Apple TV devices.

>>>*Go Further*

PURCHASING ONLINE VIDEOS IN CANADA AND THE UK

Most of the online video marketplaces discussed in this chapter are global in nature, although pricing and content in other countries may vary from their American cousins. You can find Canadian- and UK-specific versions of the Amazon video store, Google Play, and the iTunes Store.

Other online stores are U.S.-only. Specifically, you cannot access FandangoNOW or Vudu in Canada or the UK.

In this chapter, you learn how to use live streaming services to watch TV in real time over the Internet.

→ Understanding Live Streaming Services
→ Watching AT&T Watch TV, DirecTV Now, fuboTV, Hulu with Live TV, Philo, PlayStation Vue, Sling TV, and YouTube TV
→ Comparing Live Streaming Services

Watching Live Broadcast and Cable TV with Live Streaming Services

Hulu and other similar services are great for catching up on your favorite TV shows, but they don't let you watch those shows live in real time. In the past, if you wanted to watch TV shows live you needed either an over-the-air antenna (which is not always easy or practical) or a cable or satellite subscription (which can be pricey). Now, however, there's another alternative: live TV streaming services, available over the Internet for viewing on your Smart TV or streaming media player of choice.

Understanding Live Streaming Services

A live streaming video service does just what the description implies—it lets you watch live TV in real time, from both local channels and cable/satellite channels, over the Internet. Channels are streamed in real time, as they're broadcast, for playback on your TV, computer, smartphone, or other device.

On-Demand Programming and Cloud Recording

These live TV services typically provide the same sort of grid-like channel guide you're used to from your cable or satellite provider. The guide shows what's currently playing and what's coming up, arranged by channel. Navigate to and select a channel—whatever's being broadcast live is now displayed on your screen.

Most of these services also offer "catch up" services—that is, the ability to watch recent episodes of your favorite shows. These are on-demand programs, the same as what you find with Hulu (regular) and similar services. (Technically, this type of on-demand programming is called *Video On Demand*, or VOD.)

Most live TV services also offer cloud DVR functionality so you can record your favorite live shows for viewing later. Everything you record is saved in the Internet cloud, not locally on your streaming media player.

The functionality and capacity of these DVRs vary from service to service, of course. Some let you save only a limited amount of programming (typically 20 to 50 hours' worth), and often for a limited period of time. Others offer unlimited cloud storage, but keep your recordings for only a month or so. If you record something on these services, it behooves you to watch it quickly.

Over the Top

Live TV streaming services are also called *over the top* or OTT services, because they broadcast "over the top" of the Internet, not over the air or via cable.

Available Channels

Most live streaming services offer the usual suspects of cable and satellite channels, although there are some differences between services. Each live streaming service has to negotiate streaming rights with the various content providers, and they don't always come to an agreement; for this reason, some major channels are missing from some live streaming services.

Then there are the local channels, which is a far trickier proposition. Obviously, each live streaming service wants to provide local broadcast channels to subscribers in every major (and minor) U.S. city, but the thorny issue of streaming rights again comes into play. Bottom line is that not all local stations in the United States are available on every live streaming service. If you live in a large metropolitan area, chances are most of your local stations will be available on most live streaming services, but it isn't guaranteed. There are many cities where one or more local stations simply aren't available on a given live streaming service. This is definitely something you need to check for specifically before you sign up for a service.

Lineups Change

What local channels are available on a given live TV streaming service varies over time, as old agreements expire and new ones are signed. For example, for a time in 2018 Sony-owned PlayStation Vue was forced to drop all the local stations owned by the Sinclair Broadcasting conglomerate, due to a dust-up between Sony and Sinclair. They worked out their differences, however, and the Sinclair-owned stations returned to Vue later in the year.

For those viewers whose local stations aren't available on a given live streaming service, chances are that service offers the national feed of the broadcast network associated with the missing station. So, if your local ABC station, for example, isn't available, you might still be able to watch ABC shows live via the national feed. (You won't have access to any local programming, however—including your local news reports.) And if the national feed isn't available, you might still have access to recent programming from that network, even if it's just on Hulu.

When you're looking for your local stations and broadcast networks, there's one big player missing from all live TV streaming services. PBS does not own streaming rights for all its programming, so you will not find your local PBS station on these services. (At least not yet, anyway.)

Even if your local stations are available on a given live streaming service, don't expect that station's digital subchannels to be available. With only a few exceptions, diginets have rights only for local digital broadcast; they do not have Internet streaming rights. So, you will not find Antenna TV, MeTV, or other popular diginets on these live streaming services; if you want to view them, you'll need an OTA antenna.

Diginets and OTA Antennas

Learn more about diginets, local broadcast stations, and OTA antennas in Chapter 3, "Getting Local and Broadcast Television over the Air."

Pricing

What do these sorts of live TV streaming services cost? They're not free. Expect to spend anywhere from $15 to $100 USD per month, depending on the service and the plan you select. Your cost will be toward the higher end if you want premium channels and sports plans and such. (Yes, live streaming services have different plans with different channel lineups, just like cable and satellite do.) The more channels you want to watch on more devices (TVs in different rooms or mobile devices), the more you'll pay. In fact, depending on your circumstances, you easily can spend the same amount on online streaming services as you do with a cable or satellite plan. You might be cutting the cord, but you won't necessarily be cutting your expenditures!

So, are live streaming services cheaper than cable or satellite? It depends on your cable or satellite bill. If you have a single cable box and a relatively simple plan, it might be a bit of a wash. But if you have multiple cable/satellite boxes in multiple rooms, you'll probably pay anywhere from a little to a lot less for a comparable live streaming service. It's worth checking out if you're thinking of cutting the cord.

Watching AT&T Watch TV

AT&T owns two live streaming services. The first is Watch TV, the budget service from the telecom giant. (The second service is DirecTV Now, the higher-end service.) Watch TV has the lowest pricing of all the major live streaming services.

Available Channels

One of the reasons that Watch TV is so low priced is that it doesn't carry nearly as many channels as competing services. Due to the limited amount of content, Watch TV almost seems like a convenience for AT&T customers rather than a full-blown streaming service. (In my opinion, Watch TV works better on a phone than it does on a living room TV.)

The real limiting factor of Watch TV, however, is its total lack of local channels and broadcast networks. Watch TV does not offer *any* local channels, and it has only a limited selection of other channels. How limited is limited? Just 37, at my last count. All competing services offer a lot more channels. (You can, however, subscribe to HBO, Showtime, Starz, and other premium channels for additional monthly fees.)

Cloud DVR Recording

Concurrent with its low price and limited number of channels, Watch TV has no recording capability. You can watch live and that's that.

Pricing

What Watch TV has going for it is its price. AT&T charges just $15 USD per month for its service, which really can't be beat. It's even better if you're an AT&T cellular customer; if you have one of AT&T's unlimited data plans, you get Watch TV for free.

Using Watch TV

Watch TV works pretty much like all the other live streaming services, but without the availability of local channels.

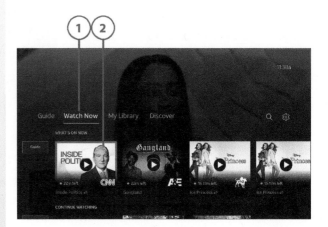

1. The main screen shows the currently selected program playing in the background, and function tabs are available in the foreground. Select Watch Now to view featured programs currently playing.

2. Select to view a live program.

(3) Select Guide to view the program guide. Press the Enter button on your device's remote to view the guide full screen.

(4) Scroll up or down to view all available channels.

(5) Scroll right to view programming at future times.

(6) Select a program to view more about it.

(7) Select Watch Now to view the selected program.

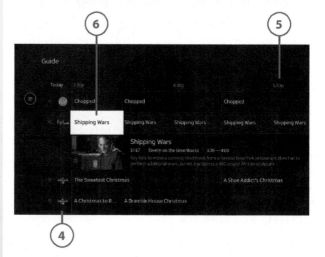

Watching DirecTV Now

AT&T's second live TV streaming service is DirecTV Now. (DirecTV is owned by AT&T.) The DirecTV Now streaming service is pretty much the DirecTV satellite service, but delivered via the Internet. It's a much more extensive (and expensive) service than its stripped-down AT&T Watch TV cousin.

Available Channels

Unlike Watch TV, DirecTV Now carries a full complement of cable and satellite channels, as well as local channels in most major markets. (The latest count is more than 350 local channels nationwide, which is good but not the most out there.) How many channels you get total depends on the specific plan you choose—which I cover in more detail in a minute.

All plans offer local broadcast channels, where available. You also get BBC America, CNN, Disney Channel and Disney Junior, Food Network, Fox News, Lifetime, MSNBC, and TCM at all levels.

Future Plans

As of early 2019, AT&T is rumored to be thinking about both increasing prices and decreasing the number of channels for the DirecTV Now service. As with everything mentioned in this book, check out current pricing and channel availability before signing up to any given service.

Cloud DVR Recording

DirecTV Now offers its True Cloud DVR functionality with all subscription plans. This feature lets you record up to 20 hours of live programming and schedule your recordings up to two weeks in advance. Shows you've recorded are stored for up to 30 days.

Pricing

DirecTV Now offers four basic plans, determined by the number of channels available. Table 10.1 details the four plans:

Table 10.1   DirecTV Now Pricing Plans

Plan	Price (USD per month)	Number of Channels
Live a Little	$40	65+
Just Right	$55	85+
Go Big	$65	105+
Gotta Have It	$75	125+

In addition, DirecTV offers a Spanish-language plan (for $45 USD per month), as well as plans with Brazilian, Korean, and Vietnamese channels. You also can subscribe to Cinemax, HBO, Showtime, or Starz for additional monthly fees.

Using DirecTV Now

DirecTV now displays a menu bar in the middle of most screens. Use this menu bar to navigate to different functions and features.

(1) From the home screen, select Watch Now to view current live programs.

(2) Select a program to view it live.

(3) Select My Library to view programs you've recorded.

(4) Select a recorded program to view it.

5) Select Guide to view a small program guide. Press the Enter button on your device's remote to view the full-screen program guide.

6) Scroll up and down to view all available channels.

7) Scroll right to view future programming.

8) Select a currently playing program to view it live.

9) Select a future program to record it.

10) Select Record to record this program when it airs.

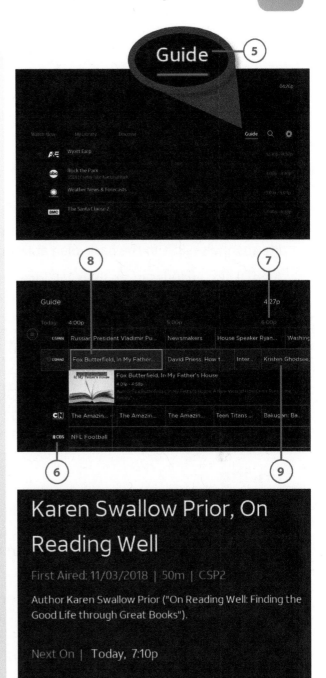

Karen Swallow Prior, On Reading Well

First Aired: 11/03/2018 | 50m | CSP2

Author Karen Swallow Prior ("On Reading Well: Finding the Good Life through Great Books").

Next On | Today, 7:10p

 Record

Watching fuboTV

fuboTV is one of the newest competitors in the live TV streaming space. It started out as a sports-focused streaming service, but recently added a plethora of cable, satellite, and broadcast channels for a full-featured offering.

Available Channels

Today fuboTV is still a "sports first" service, with more sports channels (from all around the globe) than any of its competitors. (Although, unexpectedly, there's no ESPN in its lineup.) But you also get the expected complement of cable/satellite channels—85+ in the basic plan at last count.

fuboTV also includes more than 250 local channels nationwide. That's not as many as Hulu with Live TV, PlayStation Vue, or YouTube TV, but it is on par with DirecTV Now—and substantially more than Sling TV.

Cloud DVR Recording

FuboTV's cloud DVR lets you record up to 30 hours of live programming, including sports games. If you need more storage, the optional Cloud DVR Plus plan ($9.99 per month) lets you store up to 500 hours of recordings.

Pricing

Partly because of its large selection of global sports channels, fuboTV is a little more expensive than some of its competitors. The basic fuboTV package runs $44.99 USD per month; the fubo Extra plan runs five bucks more ($49.99 USD) per month and includes 20 more stations.

In addition, fuboTV offers separate Latino and Portuguese packages. There also are several optional sports packages with even more sports channels, and AMC, FX+, and Showtime (but not HBO or Starz) are available as premium add-ons.

Using fuboTV

You navigate fuboTV from the menu bar at the top of the screen. Press the Up Arrow button on your device's remote to display the menu bar. The fuboTV guide is different from most others in that channels are displayed at the top, from left to right, and future times are on the side, top to bottom.

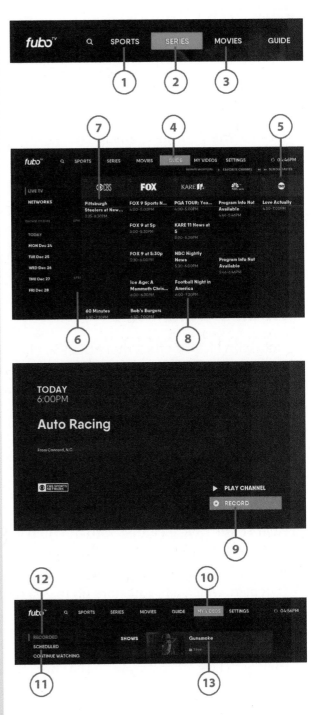

(1) Select Sports to view live and upcoming sports programming.

(2) Select Series to view live and upcoming television series.

(3) Select Movies to view live and upcoming movies.

(4) Select Guide to view the program guide.

(5) Scroll right and left to view all available channels.

(6) Scroll down to view future programming.

(7) Select a current program to view it live.

(8) Select a future program to record it.

(9) Select Record to record the selected program.

(10) Select My Videos to view the DVR.

(11) Select Scheduled to view scheduled recordings.

(12) Select Recorded to view recorded programs.

(13) Select a recorded program to view it.

Watching Hulu with Live TV

You know Hulu as a service that lets you catch up on your viewing of current television shows. It also offers a number of movies and an increasing selection of original programs.

Hulu also offers its own live TV streaming service, imaginatively called Hulu with Live TV. This plan supplements the normal Hulu service with real-time streaming of cable, satellite, and local channels.

Hulu

Learn more about regular Hulu (without live TV) in Chapter 7, "Watching the Big Three Streaming Video Services: Amazon Prime Video, Hulu, and Netflix."

Available Channels

Hulu with Live TV offers more than 50 channels for your live viewing pleasure. That's somewhat fewer than you get with some competing services; noticeably missing are Comedy Central, Nickelodeon, and TCM.

Of course, you do get local channels—and lots of them. According to recent numbers, Hulu with Live TV offers more than 600 local stations nationwide, the most of any live TV streaming service. And they're all part of the basic Live TV plan.

Cloud DVR Recording

Hulu's basic DVR, included with the Hulu with Live TV plan, lets you record up to 50 hours of programming—more than you get with most competitors. If you need more, you can pay a fee of $14.99 USD per month for the Enhanced Cloud DVR plan, which lets you store up to 200 hours of programming.

Pricing

Hulu with Live TV costs $44.99 USD per month. For that price, you get the live TV part of the service as well as Hulu's normal on-demand streaming service, which you can use to catch up on past episodes and original series. Hulu also offers Cinemax, HBO, Showtime, and Starz as premium add-ons.

Using Hulu with Live TV

1. From Hulu's home page, select Live TV. (This option is only available when you subscribe to Hulu with Live TV.) Press the Down Arrow button on your device's remote control to display the program guide.

2. Select All Channels at the top of the guide to view all available channels. (To filter by program type, you can also select News, Sports, Kids, or Movies; you also can select to view only Recent Channels.)

3. Scroll down to view additional channels.

4. Press the Right Arrow button on your device's remote to view What's Up Next on the top selected channel.

5. Select the current channel and then select Watch to watch this channel live.

6. Select the next program on the current channel and select Record to record this program.

7. Press the Back button on your remote until the top-level menu appears, then select My Stuff to view recorded programs.

8. Select a recorded program to view it.

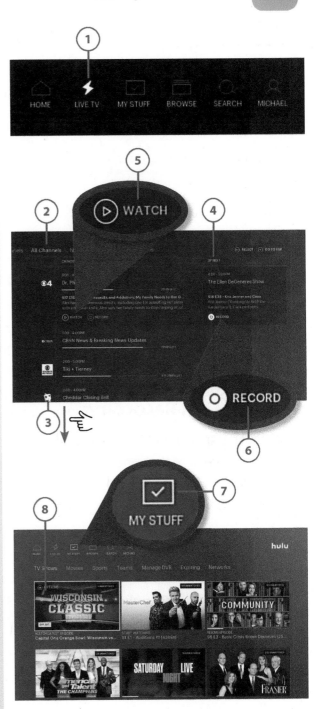

Watching Philo

Next to AT&T Watch TV, Philo is the most affordable live streaming service available today. You pay just $16 USD per month for more than 40 cable/broadcast channels—but you don't get local stations.

Available Channels

Forty channels for 16 bucks a month isn't a bad deal. So, what's missing? First, as noted, there are no local channels or broadcast networks. That's a big minus for many folks.

You also don't get much in the way of news channels; there's no CNN, Fox News, or MSNBC, just BBC World News and Cheddar News. Also, no Disney channels and no TCM, and precious little in the way of sports programming.

That leaves a bevy of the usual suspects, including AMC, BBC America, BET, Comedy Central, Food Network, the Hallmark channels, HGTV, Lifetime, Nickelodeon, and TV Land. It's not a bad selection for the price.

Cloud DVR Recording

For $16 USD a month, you might not expect fancy cloud recording, but Philo gives it to you at that price. Philo's cloud DVR is different from most in that it lets you record an unlimited amount of programming. Anything you record is stored for 30 days.

Pricing

Philo's base plan runs $16 USD per month and includes 40+ channels. For $20 USD per month you get an additional dozen channels, including the Cooking Channel, Discovery Life, and Logo.

Using Philo

Philo's program guide is similar to that of other live streaming services, with channels down the left side and future times across the top.

1. From Philo's home page, press the Up Arrow button on your device's remote control and then select Guide to display the program guide.

2. Scroll down to view all available channels.

3. Scroll to the right to view future programming.

4. Select a program to view it live.

5. Select a future program you want to record.

6. Select Save to record this program.

7. To view recorded programs, select Saved from the top menu.

8. Select a program to view it.

Watching PlayStation Vue

PlayStation Vue is one of the more robust live TV streaming services. It offers the largest selection of local channels nationwide, as well as an impressive lineup of entertainment, news, and sports channels.

Available Channels

One of the chief reasons viewers turn to live TV streaming services is to get their local stations. PS Vue delivers more than 500 local stations for cities across the United States, and is increasing that number monthly.

Vue's basic plan offers 45+ channels, including all available local channels. More expensive plans offer more than 85 total channels, including some robust sports offerings. (Missing in action: Comedy Central, Lifetime, MTV, Nickelodeon, and Starz.)

Cloud DVR Recording

PlayStation Vue's cloud DVR is free with all plans. Unlike competitors that limit the number of hours you can record, Vue's DVR limits the number of *programs* you can record—500 individual recordings, to be exact. Anything you record is stored for 28 days.

Pricing

Sony offers four basic plans plus a smattering of add-on packages. The basic plans are detailed in Table 10.2.

Table 10.2 PlayStation Vue Pricing Plans

Plan	Price (USD per month)	Number of Channels
Access	$44.99	45+
Core	$49.99	60+
Elite	$59.99	85+
Ultra	$79.99	85+ (plus HBO and Showtime)

The Access plan includes more than 45 popular entertainment and news channels. The Core plan adds some more popular entertainment channels, including the Cooking Channel, DIY Network, and TCM, as well as a variety of sports channels. The Elite plan adds even more entertainment and sports channels, for a total of more than 85 channels. And the Ultra plan adds HBO and Showtime to the mix. Vue also offers an optional Sports Pack for $10 USD per month; HBO and Showtime are also available as premium add-ons to the lower-priced plans.

Using PlayStation Vue

The PlayStation Vue guide displays your favorite channels first, then other channels alphabetically. (Vue asks you to select your favorite channels during the initial setup process.)

(1) From the PS Vue home screen, press the Up Arrow button on your device's remote control and select Guide.

(2) Scroll down to view additional channels.

(3) Scroll right to view future programming.

(4) Select a program to view it live.

(5) Select a future program to record.

(6) Select Add to My DVR to record this program.

(7) To view recorded programs, back up to the home screen and select My DVR.

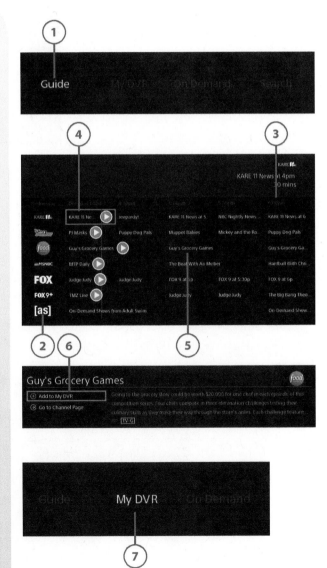

(8) Select a program to view it.

>>>Go Further

PLUTO TV

There's one more live streaming service that isn't quite like the others. Pluto TV offers more than 75 channels of "live" programming, all for free. You probably haven't heard of most of these channels, but they cover a variety of different genres. Plus, they're free. Did I mention that?

The other thing you don't get with Pluto TV is the ability to record the programs you watch. Pluto has no cloud DVR, so there's no recording.

The Pluto TV channel guide.

Nevertheless, you may find something worth watching on Pluto TV, and it won't cost you anything to find out. The Pluto TV app is available for Amazon Fire TV, Apple TV, Google Chromecast, and Roku devices, as well as most Smart TVs. No subscription is necessary; learn more at corporate.pluto.tv.

Watching Sling TV

Sling TV is the granddaddy of live TV streaming services, having been launched by Dish Network way back in the stone age of 2015. (Hey, this is a fast-moving industry!) Sling TV was the first but remains one of the most popular, even with the horde of newer competitors.

Available Channels

Sling TV offers a mix of local stations and popular cable/satellite channels. It offers two distinctly different packages (Orange and Blue) as well as specialty packages and pay channels, such as HBO and Showtime. Note that you might need to subscribe to both Orange and Blue (and maybe a specialty package or two) to get all the channels you want to watch.

Although Sling is competitive with the number of cable/satellite channels offered, it falls short in the availability of local stations. Unlike competing services such as Hulu with Live TV and PlayStation Vue, Sling TV doesn't offer local stations for many cities—currently, fewer than 40 local stations nationwide. So, if you're looking for Sling TV to totally replace your cable or satellite service, you'll probably need to supplement it with an OTA antenna for your local stations.

Cloud DVR Recording

Cloud recording is not included as part of either the Orange or Blue plans. Instead, Sling's Cloud DVR is an add-on to either of these plans; it costs $5 USD per month. With the Cloud DVR you can record up to 50 hours of programming, and you can store those programs indefinitely.

Pricing

Sling isn't the lowest-priced live streaming service, but (depending on the channels you watch) it can be among the most affordable. It all depends on which options you choose.

Sling's two basic plans are dubbed Orange and Blue; they cost $25 USD per month each. The two plans share many channels, but there are a few important channels exclusive to one plan or the other. For example, the Disney Channel and three channels of ESPN are exclusive to the Orange plan; BET, Bravo, Fox, all the Fox sports channels, various NBC sports channels, and USA Network are exclusive to the Blue plan. To get everything you want you may need to subscribe to both plans—which you can do, for a discount price of $40 USD per month.

Even that may not be enough, however. Sling offers a number of "extra" packages that add even more channels to the mix. Unfortunately, to many viewers these "extras" are actually essentials, so adding them can rapidly increase your monthly bill. Table 10.3 details these packages, along with the basic Orange and Blue plans.

Table 10.3   Sling TV Packages

Package	Channels	Price (USD per month)
Sling Orange	A&E, ACC Network Extra, AMC, AXS TV, BBC America, Bloomberg Television, Cartoon Network, Cheddar, Cheddar Big News, CNN, Comedy Central, Disney Channel, ePix Drive-In, ESPN, ESPN2, ESPN3, Food Network, Freeform, Fuse, HGTV, History Channel, ID, IFC, Lifetime, Local Now, MotorTrend, Newsy, TBS, TNT, Travel Channel, Tribeca, Shortlist, Viceland	$25
Sling Blue	A&E, AMC, AXS TV, BBC America, BET, Bloomberg Television, Bravo, Cartoon Network, Cheddar, Cheddar Big News, CNN, Comedy Central, Discovery Network, ePix Drive-In, Food Network, Fox, Fox regional sports networks, Fox Sports 1, Fox Sports 2, Fuse, FX, FXX, HGTV, History Channel, ID, IFC, Lifetime, Local Now, Nat Geo Wild, National Geographic, NBC, NBC regional sports networks, NBC Sports Network, Newsy, NFL Network, Nick Jr., SyFy, TBS, TLC, TNT, Travel Channel, Tribeca Shortlist, truTV, USA, Viceland	$25

Package	Channels	Price (USD per month)
Comedy Extra	CMT, GSN, Logo, MTV, MTV2, Paramount Network, Revolt, truTV, and TV Land	$5
Heartland Extra	Destination America, RFD TV, Ride TV, Outdoor Channel, World Fishing Network, and more	$5
Hollywood Extra	Reelz, Sundance Movies, TCM, and more	$5
Kids Extra	Baby TV, Boomerang, Disney Junior, Disney XD, Nick Jr., Nicktoons, TeenNICK, and more	$5
Lifestyle Extra	Cooking Channel, DIY Network, the Hallmark channels, Lifetime Movies, Oxygen, We TV, and more	$5
News Extra	BBC World News, CNBC, France24, HLN, NewsMax TV, RT Network, Science Channel, TheBlaze, WeatherNation, and more	$5
Sports Extra	Motorsport TV, NBA TV, NHL Network, Pac-12, SEC Network, various ESPN networks, and more	$5 (for Orange subscribers) or $10 (for Blue subscribers)

You can pay extra for Cinemax, ePix, HBO, Showtime, and Starz, if you like. Sling TV also offers Arabic, Brazilian, German, Hindi, French, and various Spanish-language packages.

So that bit about Sling TV being the most affordable live streaming service out there? When you start adding all these "extra" packages, not so much. Determine what specific channels you absolutely need and then add all the packages for the total pricing. Get ready for sticker shock!

Using Sling TV

The channels available in your Sling TV program guide vary depending on which package and extras to which you subscribe.

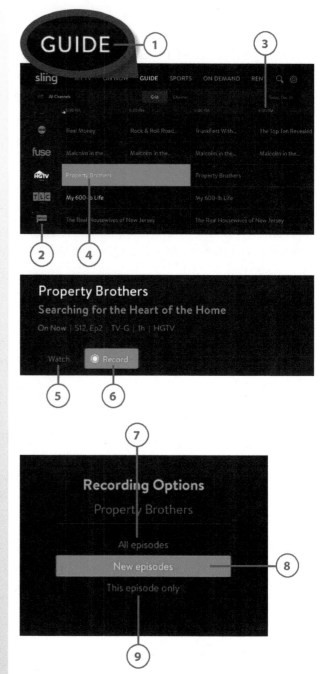

1. From the Sling TV home screen, select Guide to display the program guide.

2. Scroll down to see all available channels.

3. Scroll to the right to view future programming.

4. Select the program you want to watch.

5. Select Watch to watch a currently airing program.

6. Select Record to record the selected current or future program.

7. Select All Episodes to record all episodes of a series.

8. Select New Episodes to record only new episodes (not reruns) of a series.

9. Select This Episode Only to record only the selected episode.

10 Scroll to the top of the screen and select My TV to display all recorded programs.

11 Select a recorded program to view it.

Watching YouTube TV

Our final live streaming service is one of the newest—and one of the more robust. YouTube TV is a streaming service that offers the typical combination of cable, satellite, and local channels, but it has more channels and more DVR capability than its competitors. It also has, in my opinion, the easiest-to-read program guide out there—with larger type and graphics that are great for those of us with less-than-perfect eyesight.

Available Channels

YouTube TV offers more than 500 local stations and the usual selection of cable/satellite channels. Noticeably absent, however, are Comedy Central, Discovery Network, Food Network, HGTV, Nickelodeon, and TLC. Also, there's no Cinemax or HBO.

Cloud DVR Recording

YouTube TV's DVR capability is where this service really shines. You get to record an unlimited amount of programming, and store those recordings for nine months. No other streaming service is this generous.

Pricing

YouTube TV costs $40 USD per month. You can pay extra for AMC, Curiosity Stream, Fox Soccer Plus, NBA League Pass, Showtime, Shudder, Starz, and Sundance Now channels. That's it.

Using YouTube TV

Remember, YouTube TV is above and beyond the free version of YouTube you've probably used before. YouTube TV requires a separate app on your streaming device and provides a program guide for selecting live television programming.

1. From the YouTube TV home screen, select Live to display the program guide.

2. Scroll down to view available channels.

3. Scroll right to view future programming.

4. Select a program to view it live.

5. Select a future program to record it.

6. Select More Info.

7. Select + Add to Library to record this program or future episodes of a series.

8. Select Library to view recorded programs.

9. Select Recordings to display your recordings.

10. Select a recorded program to view it.

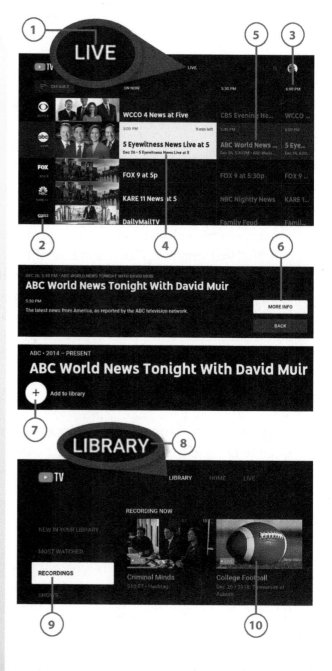

>>>Go Further

WATCH LOCAL NEWS—FOR FREE

One reason that many people decide to cut the cable/satellite cord is to lower their monthly entertainment costs. Subscribing to an expensive live TV streaming service in place of cable or satellite is kind of counterintuitive; you cut one monthly subscription in favor of starting another.

Assuming that receiving local channels via an OTA antenna isn't practical for you, there is a way to receive some or all your local stations for free over the Internet, via your favorite streaming media player or Smart TV.

Many local stations have their own streaming apps that you can add to your streaming media player or Smart TV. These local apps typically are news-focused; they might not provide any local programming except for local newscasts. Some stream live newscasts in real-time; most offer an archive of recent newscasts and individual stories. Go to your streaming device's app or channel store and search for your local stations' call letters to see what's available.

Watching local news from WTHR in Indianapolis from the 13NOW streaming app.

There also are a handful of streaming apps that consolidate local newscasts from hundreds of stations around the country. You can use these apps to view the most recent newscasts from your local stations or from local stations in other cities. (This is a great way to keep up with your hometown news if you're traveling or snowbirding elsewhere for the winter.) The most popular of these apps are Haystack TV and NewsON; look for them in your streaming device's app or channel store.

Local news options from the NewsON app.

If you go either of these routes, you need another option to watch programming from the major broadcast networks. You can try the networks' streaming apps, or play catch-up by watching programs on Hulu (*without* the live TV option).

Comparing Live Streaming Services

Now that you know all about live TV streaming services, which is the best for you?

The first thing you need to check is which services are available for your device. Most services are available on most streaming media players and Smart TVs, but there are some exceptions, as noted in Table 10.4.

Table 10.4   Availability of Live Streaming Services on Major Streaming Media Platforms

	Amazon Fire TV	Apple TV	Google Chromecast	Roku
AT&T Watch TV	Yes	Yes	Yes	No
DirecTV Now	Yes	Yes	Yes	Yes
fuboTV	Yes	Yes	Yes	Yes
Hulu with Live TV	Yes	Yes	Yes	Yes
Philo	Yes	Yes	Yes	Yes
PlayStation Vue	Yes	Yes	Yes	Yes
Sling TV	Yes	Yes	Yes	Yes
YouTube TV	No	Yes	Yes	Yes

You also want to compare pricing. Table 10.5 details the range of pricing for plans from all the major live TV streaming services.

Table 10.5   Live TV Streaming Services Pricing Plans

	Lowest-priced monthly plan (USD)	Website
AT&T Watch TV	$15.00	www.attwatchtv.com
DirecTV Now	$40.00	www.directvnow.com
fuboTV	$44.99	www.fubo.tv
Hulu with Live TV	$44.99	www.hulu.com/live-tv
Philo	$16.00	www.philo.com
PlayStation Vue	$44.99	www.playstation.com/network/vue/
Sling TV	$25.00	www.sling.com
YouTube TV	$40.00	tv.youtube.com

You should also compare other features of the services, such as cloud DVR capability, number of devices you can stream to, and such. See Table 10.6 for that.

Table 10.6   Key Features of Live TV Streaming Services

	Local Channels	On-Demand Programming	Cloud DVR	Streaming on Multiple Devices
AT&T Watch TV	No	Yes	No	No
DirecTV Now	350+	Yes	Yes, 20 hours	Yes, 2 devices
fuboTV	250+	Yes	Yes, 30 hours	Yes, 2 devices
Hulu with Live TV	600+	Yes	Yes, 50 hours	Yes, 2 devices
Philo	No	Yes	Yes, unlimited	Yes, 3 devices
PlayStation Vue	500+	Yes	Yes, 500 episodes	Yes, 5 devices
Sling TV	25+	Yes	Yes, 50 hours ($5 extra per month)	Yes, 3 devices (Sling Blue plan; 1 device on Sling Orange plan)
YouTube TV	500+	Yes	Yes, unlimited	Yes, 3 devices

Finally, and perhaps most importantly, is the availability of your local channels. A given live TV streaming service might look ideal in terms of features and pricing, but it might not have all your local stations—which could make it next to worthless to you.

You can look at the total number of local channels offered nationwide (and gravitate toward those services with the largest numbers, such as Hulu with Live TV, PlayStation Vue, and YouTube TV), but that's not a guarantee that a given service has the channels you watch in your city. Unfortunately, there's no way in this book to list all the local stations for all the different cities and regions in the U.S., and besides, the list of what's available where is constantly changing. You'll need to check with each individual live streaming service to see which of your local channels are currently available.

So, which plan is best for you? Even though they're more expensive than some of the others, I like PlayStation Vue and YouTube TV because of the large number of channels they offer. They also have the largest number of local channels in the most places. Sling TV also is good and more affordable at the basic level, although it gets more expensive when you start adding more channels.

You may also find that no single service fills all your needs. In our household, we use a combination of YouTube TV and Philo. YouTube TV is great for almost everything, including local channels, but lacks Food Network, HGTV, and the Nickelodeon channels, all of which we watch a lot. Philo offers all those channels missing from YouTube TV, and at a low cost. Combined, we spend $56 per month USD for both these services, which is not a bad deal, and the two services complement each other well.

Bottom line, you have to consider those features most important to you, the availability of the channels you want to watch (including your local channels), and the total price with all the add-ons included. Then you can make an informed decision based on your viewing habits and budget.

>>>*Go Further*

LIVE STREAMING SERVICES IN CANADA AND THE UK

As popular as live streaming services are in the UK, they've yet to become practical in other countries. For example, none of the U.S.-based live streaming services are available in Canada or the UK.

In fact, most Canadians don't have access to *any* live streaming services—at least not yet. Bell Canada Internet customers in Ontario and Quebec are the exception; they can subscribe to Bell's Alt TV service. Alt TV works on any connected computer or smartphone, and it also works on Amazon Fire TV and Apple TV devices. (But it *doesn't* work on Roku players!) The basic Alt TV service costs $14.95 CDN per month and offers 30 live channels, including ABC, CBC Television, CBS, Citytv, Crave, CTV, CTV2, Fox, Global, NBC, Omni, PBS, TV1, and more. The $29.95 CDN per month Alt TV Premium service adds a few more entertainment channels and a lot of Canadian sports channels.

In the UK, viewers can watch live TV over the Internet with the TVPlayer service and app. The TVPlayer app is available for Amazon Fire TV, Apple TV, Google Chromecast, and Roku devices. There are several different plans available. TVPlayer Basic includes free OTA channels only, including BBC, C4, Five, and more, but it's free. TVPlayer Premium includes 80 additional channels and a cloud-based DVR, and runs £6.99/mo. TVPlayer Premium+ adds 90 more channels, and runs £9.99/mo.

In this chapter, you learn the best ways to watch live sports on your Smart TV or streaming media player.

→ Watching Sports on Live Streaming Services
→ Watching Specific Sports Apps

11

Watching Streaming Sports— Live!

If you're a sports fan, one of the great things about cable or satellite television is all the live sports available. Chances are you already subscribe to NFL Sunday Ticket or a similar package for your favorite sport.

Watching live sporting events without cable or satellite is slightly more challenging. You can watch sports from the major broadcast networks over the air, of course, but that leaves out ESPN and tons of other national and regional sports networks. Streaming sports over the Internet isn't much better because all the major sports channels and leagues require some sort of paid television subscription to access their streaming content. That means either keeping your cable/satellite subscription or subscribing to a live streaming TV service. Either option lets you access most channels' and leagues' main channels, as well as special streaming apps, on your Smart TV or streaming media player.

Watching Sports on Live Streaming Services

If you don't have cable or satellite, the best way to watch sports on your Smart TV or streaming media player is by subscribing to a live streaming service. These services offer a mix of local channels (with broadcast network sports), dedicated sports channels, and, in some cases, special sports packages. Let's look at what's offered by the major live streaming services.

Live Streaming Services

Learn more about live streaming services in Chapter 10, "Watching Broadcast and Cable TV with Live Streaming Services."

Sports on DirecTV Now

DirecTV's satellite service is one of the best places to watch all sorts of live sports. Not surprisingly, the DirecTV Now streaming service is equally appealing for all manner of live sports.

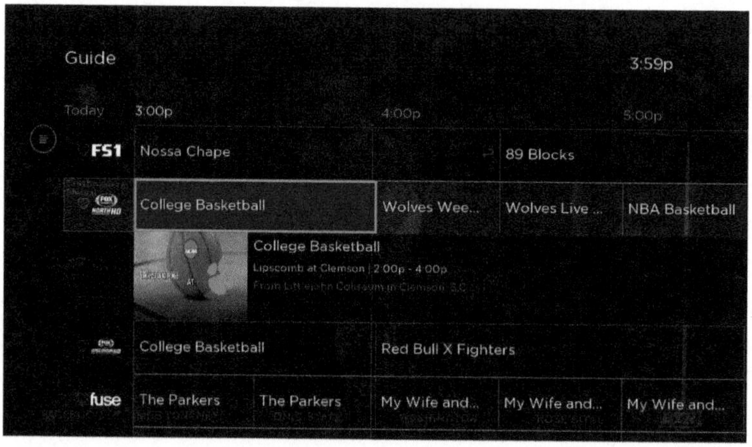

Sports programming on DirecTV Now.

What you get, sports-wise, depends on the plan you sign up for. Table 11.1 details the sports offerings for each plan.

Table 11.1   Sports Programming on DirecTV Now

Plan	Price per month (USD)	Sports Networks
Live a Little	$40	ABC, CBS, ESPN, ESPN2, Fox, Fox Sports 1, NBC, NBCSN, TBS, TNT, Velocity
Just Right	$55	Same as the Live a Little plan *plus* Big Ten Network, ESPNews, ESPNU, MLB Network, NFL Network, SEC Network, Tennis Channel
Go Big	$65	Same as the Just Right plan *plus* CBS Sports Network, Fox Sports 2, Golf Channel, NBA TV, NHL Network, Olympic Channel, Sportsman Channel
Gotta Have It	$75	Same sports channels as the Go Big plan

Sports on fuboTV

fuboTV is a live streaming service that offers a variety of sports programming from all around the world. As I mentioned in Chapter 10, fuboTV started out as a sports-forward service that gradually added other live broadcast, cable, and satellite channels. As such, it's competitive with any live streaming service, but with a heavier emphasis on sports from around the globe.

Sports programming on fuboTV.

In fact, fuboTV is the only place you'll find sports networks such as beIN Sports, Eleven Sports, FNTSY Sports Network, GOLTV, and TyC Sports. This makes fuboTV the go-to streaming service for fans of international football (soccer) and other sports popular outside the United States. It also offers several Stadium channels, which are devoted to college sports across the United States, and the Vegas Stats & Information Network (VSiN), with sports gambling news and data.

fuboTV offers two key plans: fubo ($44.99 USD per month) and fubo Extra ($49.99 USD per month). Table 11.2 details the sports channels available on each.

Table 11.2   Sports Programming on fuboTV

Plan	Price per month (USD)	Sports Networks
fubo	$44.99	Big Ten Network, CBS, CBS Sports Network, Eleven Sports, Fox, Fox Sports 1, Fox Sports 2, Fox Sports regional channels, Golf Channel, NBA TV, NBC, NBCSN, NFL Network, Olympic Channel, Pac-12 Networks, TBS, TNT, and multiple beIN Sports channels
fubo Extra	$49.99	Same as basic fubo plan *plus* four Stadium college sports channels

In addition, fuboTV offers several add-on sports packages, including

- **Adventure Plus** ($4.99 USD per month), with Motorsports Network, Outdoor Channel, Outside TV, Sportsman Channel, and World Fishing Network.

- **International Sports Plus** ($5.99 USD per month), with Fox Soccer Plus, fubo TV Soccer, GOLTV English, GOLTV Spanish, and TyC Sports.

- **fubo Cycling** ($11.99 USD per month), with fubo Cycling, Fox Soccer Plus, fubo TV Soccer, GOLTV English, GOLTV Spanish, and TyC Sports.

- **Sports Plus** ($8.99 USD per month), with Fight Network, FNTSY Sports Network, GOLTV English, GOLTV Spanish, NFL RedZone, Sports Illustrated TV, TyC Sports, VSiN, four Stadium channels, six Pac-12 channels, and three Fox College Sports channels.

fuboTV also offers NBA League Pass, with 30 channels of team coverage for $28.99 USD per month.

The one major hole in fuboTV's sports coverage is the absence of all ESPN-related networks. (All Disney/ABC-owned properties are unavailable on fuboTV.) That leaves out a big chunk of U.S.-based sports coverage, but it's made up for by the abundance of coverage of sports from elsewhere around the world.

Sports on Hulu with Live TV

At $44.99 USD per month, Hulu with Live TV is a good bargain for the casual sports fan. You get all broadcast and cable/satellite sports channels—but not any league-specific channels. (That means no MLB, NBA, NFL, or NHL, other than those games broadcast on ESPN or the broadcast networks.)

Sports programming on Hulu with Live TV.

Table 11.3 details the sports-related channels available on Hulu with Live TV.

Table 11.3   Sports Programming on Hulu with Live TV

Plan	Price per month (USD)	Sports Networks
Hulu with Live TV	$44.99	ABC, Big Ten Network, CBS, CBS Sports Network, ESPN, ESPN2, ESPNews, ESPNU, ESPN Bases Loaded, ESPN College Extra, Fox, Fox Sports 1, Fox Sports 2, Fox Regional Sports networks, Golf Channel, MotorTrend, NBC, NBCSN, Olympic Channel, SEC Network, TBS, TNT

Hulu lets you personalize your experience by picking your favorite teams, leagues, and sports. You then see recommended games for you to watch right on your home page.

Sports on PlayStation Vue

PlayStation Vue is one of the most popular live streaming services, in part because of the large number of local channels it offers. Those local channels bring you live sporting events from all the major broadcast networks, which is a good thing. PlayStation Vue also offers a variety of ESPN channels, Fox regional sports networks, and channels for the MLB, NBA, and NFL.

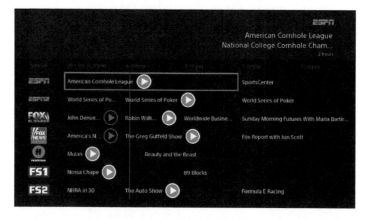

Sports programming on PlayStation Vue.

Exactly what sports channels you get depends on the plan you sign up for. For most sports lovers, that means at least the Core plan, as detailed in Table 11.4.

Table 11.4   Sports Programming on PlayStation Vue

Plan	Price per month (USD)	Sports Networks
Access	$44.99	ABC, CBS, ESPN, ESPN2, Fox, Fox Sports 1, Fox Sports 2, NBC, NBCSN, TBS, TNT
Core	$49.99	Same as Access plan *plus* Big Ten Network, CBS Sports Network, ESPNews, ESPNU, ESPN College Extra, Fox Regional Sports networks, Golf Channel, MLB Network, NBA TV, NFL Network, Olympic Channel, SEC Network

Plan	Price per month (USD)	Sports Networks
Elite	$59.99	Same as Core plan *plus* ESPN Deportes, GiNX eSports TV, MotorTrend
Ultra	$79.99	Same as Elite plan

PlayStation Vue also offers an add-on Sports Pack for $10 USD per month. This package includes Eleven Sports Network, ESPN Bases Loaded, ESPN Classic, ESPN Goal Line, Longhorn Network, MLB Strike Zone, NESN National, NFL RedZone, Outside TV, three Stadium college sports channels, and various NBC regional sports networks.

Fox Soccer Plus is also available as a $14.99 USD per month standalone channel.

Sports on Sling TV

Sling TV is a decent service for live sports, if you can get past the fact that it doesn't offer local channels (and their broadcast network affiliates) in most areas of the country. So, if you can make do with ESPN and Fox regional sports, along with the major league sports services, you'll be okay.

Sports programming on Sling TV.

Know, however, that Sling TV splits its major sports offerings between its Orange and Blue plans. As you can see in Table 11.5, Orange is where you'll find the ESPN channels; Blue is where you find everything else (Fox, NBC, and NFL). That means you'll probably need to pop for both Orange and Blue—and the add-on Sports Extra package, too.

Table 11.5   Sports Programming on Sling TV

Plan	Price per month (USD)	Sports Networks
Sling Orange	$25	ACC Network Extra, ESPN, ESPN2, ESPN3, MotorTrend, TBS, TNT
Sling Blue	$25	Fox, Fox Regional Sports networks, Fox Sports 1, Fox Sports 2, NBC, NBCSN, NBC regional sports networks, NFL Network, TBS, TNT

Sling also offers the Sports Extra add-on package, for $5 USD per month (with the Orange plan) or $10 USD per month (with the Blue plan). This package includes beIN Sports, Golf Channel, NBA TV, NFL RedZone, NHL Network, Motorsport TV, Olympic Channel, Outside Television, Pac-12 Network, and Stadium.

Sports on YouTube TV

YouTube TV gives sports fans a good bang for their buck. There's only a single plan available, and almost all the service's sports-related channels are there.

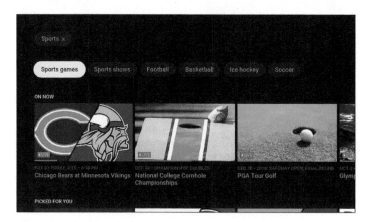

Sports programming on YouTube TV.

As you can see in Table 11.6, YouTube TV's sports offerings are somewhat generous, with a bevy of ESPN, Fox, and NBC sports channels.

Table 11.6   Sports Programming on YouTube TV

Plan	Price per month (USD)	Sports Networks
YouTube TV	$40	ABC, Big Ten Network, CBS, CBS Sports Network, ESPN, ESPN2, ESPNews, ESPNU, Fox, Fox Sports 1, Fox Sports 2, Fox Regional Sports channels, Golf Channel, MLB Network, NBA TV, NBC, NBCSN, NBC Regional Sports channels, New England Sports Network, Olympic Channel, SEC Network, SportsNet New York, TBS, TNT

Add-on sports channels include Fox Soccer Plus ($15 USD per month) and NBA League Pass ($40 USD per month). YouTube TV currently has no NFL packages available.

AT&T Watch TV and Philo

Not all live streaming services offer good options for sports. In particular, AT&T Watch TV does not offer local channels/broadcast networks or ESPN, so there's no live sports to speak of. Same thing with Philo—no broadcast channels or ESPN.

>>>Go Further
LESSER-KNOWN SPORTS CHANNELS

If you're a fan of sports on TV, you're probably already familiar with the various ESPN channels, as well as the offerings from Fox Sports and NBC Sports. Perusing the sports offerings on the various live streaming services, however (especially fuboTV), you're bound to encounter a channel or two (or three or four) with which you are less familiar. These channels include

- beIN Sports (www.beinsports.com), a network of global sports channels operated by Al Jazeera Media Network. Covers French, German, Spanish, and South American football (soccer), as well as major motorcycle road races, professional handball, the Women's Tennis Association, and a variety of U.S. college sports.

- Eleven Sports (www.elevensportsusa.com), offering men's and women's college basketball and football from the Big Sky Conference, Ivy League, and Southland Conference; soccer from the Asian Football Confederation and Belgian Pro League; Can-Am Baseball; NBA G-League basketball; and various European hockey leagues.

- Fight Network (www.fightnetwork.com), covers a variety of combat sports, such as boxing, kickboxing, mixed martial arts, and professional wrestling.

- FNTSY Sports Network (www.fantasysportsnetwork.com), broadcasts sports talk programming related to fantasy sports.

- GOLTV (www.goltv.tv), all about football (soccer) from Mexico, Portugal, Uruguay, Venezuela, and other South American countries.

- Stadium (www.watchstadium.com), offering college sports from the ACC, Big 12, Conference USA, Mountain West Conference, the Patriot League, and the West Coast Conference.

- TyC Sports (www.tycsports.com), broadcasting a variety of Argentinian sporting events.

- VSiN: Vegas Stats & Information Network (www.vsin.com), all about sports betting from Las Vegas, founded and hosted by veteran sportscaster Brent Musburger.

As you can see the world of streaming sports is more than just broadcast games and ESPN. If you're into college sports, soccer, and more, you'll find more options available online than you will from cable or satellite.

Watching Specific Sports Apps

In addition to the major sports networks available on the various live streaming services, a number of individual sports-related services offer even more live games and analysis. These services are available as apps or channels for most Smart TVs and streaming media players.

The only catch to most of these services is that you must subscribe to some sort of paid TV plan to use them. They're not freestanding; they're available only if you subscribe to a cable, satellite, or live streaming media service. When you first install and use one of these apps, you're prompted to enter the name of your television provider, username, and password. If you don't subscribe to a package with the necessary channels, you won't be able to view streaming programming in the app.

>>>Go Further

WHERE TO WATCH GOLF

Whatever your handicap, there's a lot of televised golf to watch these days. In fact, there's an entire channel devoted to the game, NBC's Golf Channel. The Golf Channel carries live coverage of major tournaments as well as historical and instructional programming, all in glorious high definition. (The greens and fairways look especially vivid in HD!)

The Golf Channel is carried by almost all cable and satellite systems. It's also part of the packages offered by most of the live streaming services, including DirecTV Now, fuboTV, Hulu with Live TV, PlayStation Vue, Sling TV, and YouTube TV. You also can watch Golf Channel programming from the NBC Sports streaming app available for most Smart TVs, streaming media players, and mobile devices.

In addition, much of the PGA Tour is carried live on broadcast television. CBS and NBC each carry a handful of PGA tournaments, free with an OTA (over-the-air) antenna or part of most cable, satellite, or live streaming video packages.

Big Ten Network

The BTN2Go app/channel offers live games and on-demand playback of previous games from Big Ten schools. Purchase a (separate) BTN Plus subscription and you get access to non-televised games and events.

The BTN2GO channel on Roku.

CBS Sports HQ

The CBS Sports HQ app and channel offer sports highlights, news, scores, and analysis for professional and college sports. The app and channel also stream selected college games, no subscription required.

CBS Sports HQ on Roku.

ESPN

WatchESPN offers 24/7 streaming coverage of live games and shows from a variety of ESPN networks, including ESPN, ESPN2, ESPN3, ESPNU, ESPNews,

ESPN Desportes, ACC Network Extra, Longhorn Network, SEC Network, and SEC Network+. Subscribers also can watch *Monday Night Football*, NBA regular season and playoff games, Major League Baseball games, the Masters, college basketball and football, Wimbledon and other tennis matches, and thousands of other live sporting events, as well as ESPN's famed pre- and post-game coverage and analysis.

Watching sports on the WatchESPN app.

Fox Sports

Fox is one of the largest sources for live sports worldwide. There are numerous Fox Sports channels—regional channels as well as channels for specific sports. Content from all these channels is available in the Fox Sports app and channel.

Watching the Fox Sports channel on Roku.

The Fox Sports app delivers live sporting events and your favorite shows from the Fox Sports, FS1, FS2, Big Ten Network, Fox College Sports, Fox Soccer Plus, Fox Deportes, and Fox regional sports networks. That includes coverage of MLB, NASCAR, NBA, NFL, NHL, UEFA Champions League soccer, UFC, and college football and basketball games.

MLB

The MLB.TV app and channel is a little different from other sports apps in that you don't need a paid TV subscription to watch. Instead, you subscribe directly with MLB (on its website) to get access to all out-of-market regular season games live (or after the game via on-demand). All games are streamed in HD. Cost for the 2018 season was $115.99 USD; current season pricing should be similar.

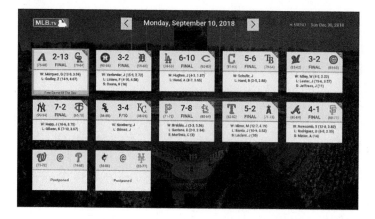

Streaming live and on-demand baseball games via MLB.TV app.

NASCAR DeskSite

If you want to watch racing, turn to the NASCAR DeskSite app and channel. You can watch full races on-demand (but not live), along with post-race recaps, interviews with drivers and coaches, breaking news, and lots of behind-the-scenes footage and exclusive content.

Cars and drivers on the NASCAR DeskSite app.

NBA

There's no live game streaming in the NBA app and channel, but you can watch game highlights, view live score updates, see team and player stat summaries, and view current league standings.

Games and scores on NBA TV.

NBC Sports

NBC Sports is one the of most robust streaming apps and channels available. Assuming you already have a paid television subscription, you can use the NBC

Sports app to live stream thousands of sporting events from NBC, NBCSN, the Golf Channel, and NBC's various regional channels. That includes NFL Sunday Night Football, regular season and playoff NHL games, the PGA Tour, Premier League soccer, NASCAR and IndyCar races, the French Open, the Triple Crown, and select NBA and MLB games.

Featured content in the NBC Sports app.

The NBC Sports app and channel also offers on-demand viewing of game highlights and previews, as well as replays of complete games—some with enhanced views and alternate camera angles. There's a lot to watch here, which makes it one of the key streaming apps for sports lovers.

NFL

The NFL app/channel includes a variety of free and paid content—if you have a paid television subscription, of course. You get around-the-clock news and analysis of NFL games and teams, you can view game highlights, and with an optional NFL Game Pass subscription (an additional $99 USD per season) you can watch replays (but not live streaming) of every league game throughout the regular season.

Games, scores, and news in the NFL app.

NHL

The official NHL app and channel lets you subscribe to NHL.TV ($139.99 USD for the entire season, or $24.99 USD per month), which offers live streaming of every out-of-market regular-season hockey game from across the league. You also can stream games on-demand after they're over, as well as view game highlights, news, and analysis.

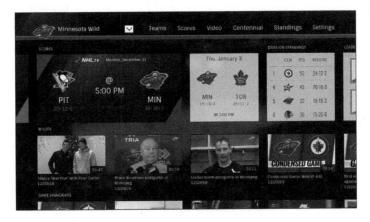

24/7 hockey in the NHL.TV app.

>>>Go Further

LIVE SPORTS IN CANADA AND THE UK

You won't find ESPN or Fox Sports on Canadian TV; they're U.S. networks, not Canadian ones. Instead, there are several Canadian sports networks, all available for streaming on your Smart TV or streaming media player. The two biggest sports networks in Canada are Sportsnet and TSN, both with multiple channels available on streaming devices, cable, and satellite.

It's the same thing in the UK: no ESPN or Fox Sports. There are plenty of football games available on the BBC channels, but for even more in-depth coverage you're going to want both BT Sport and Sky Sports.

In this chapter, you learn how to watch your favorite streaming content on mobile devices and computers.

→ Sharing Accounts Across Multiple Devices
→ Watching Streaming Videos on Your Mobile Device
→ Watching Streaming Videos in Your Computer's Web Browser
→ Mirroring and Casting to Your TV
→ Improving Streaming Performance

Watching Streaming TV on Your Phone, Tablet, or Computer

You're used to watching TV—whether broadcast or cable or satellite or streaming—on your living room or bedroom TV. Now, thanks to streaming video, you can watch your favorite shows from anywhere, home or away, on your mobile device or computer. All you need is your device and an Internet connection to watch TV on the go!

Sharing Accounts Across Multiple Devices

Most streaming video services, free or paid, let you watch their fare on more than just Smart TVs and living room streaming media players. These services offer access to their content from any web browser, via their own websites. Most streaming services also have mobile apps you can use to watch their programming on your smartphone or tablet.

You can watch streaming content on just about any device by sharing a single account with a given service. If you already have an account to watch Hulu or Netflix on your streaming media player, you also can watch Hulu or Netflix on your phone or tablet or computer. All you have to do is sign into your existing account from your new device. At the sign-in screen, just enter the email address (or username) and password you used to set up the account for your streaming device or Smart TV, and you're signed into the same account.

Logging into an existing account from the Hulu mobile app.

Typically, you have the exact same options on your mobile device as you do on your Smart TV or streaming media player. In most instances, you even can resume viewing any video you were watching previously in your home. So, you can start watching a movie in your living room over Hulu or Netflix, keep watching it on your smartphone when you're at your local coffeeshop or restaurant, and finish it up on your laptop computer at the gym. When you start the streaming app on your mobile device or computer, you're typically offered the option of resuming viewing the program that was previously in process; select that option to start up where you left off, or choose another program to watch from scratch.

Again, all this is possible because you log into the streaming service on whichever device using the same account you've always used. You don't have to pay any extra money to do this; it's part of the plan.

Watching Streaming Videos on Your Mobile Device

Although many viewers prefer to watch big-screen entertainment on the big-screen TVs in their living rooms, there's undeniable appeal to watching your favorite shows and movies wherever you are from the convenience of your own smartphone or tablet. It's especially nice when you're traveling; what better way to pass the time than tuning into the latest episode of your favorite television show or that blockbuster movie you've been dying to see?

Find Streaming Apps

You watch most streaming services on your phone or tablet via that service's proprietary streaming app. Whether it's a big service, such as Hulu or Netflix, or something more niche, such as BritBox or DC Universe, chances are there's an app for it.

Where do you find streaming video apps? In your device's app store, of course. If you have an iPhone or iPad, that means the Apple App Store. If you have an Android phone or tablet, that means the Google Play Store. Just search by name for the specific app you want.

Browsing streaming video apps for Android devices in the Google Play Store.

Most, if not all, streaming video apps are free. You might have to pay for the video streaming service, of course, but you don't have to pay for the app.

Watch a Streaming App

As noted, most streaming apps are free. To watch a given app, however, you typically need a subscription to the underlying streaming service. If you already have an account (for your Smart TV or streaming media player), you just enter that account information when you launch the app. If you don't yet have an account, you can typically sign up for a new account from within the app; if a service has subscription fees, you need to enter your payment information when you sign up.

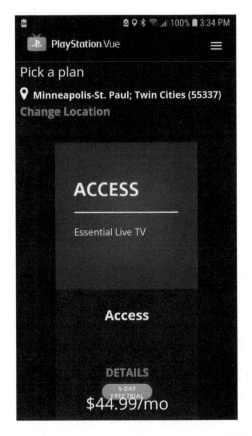

Creating a new account in the PlayStation Vue Mobile app.

Some apps are free to use if you have a paid TV subscription that includes that service. That means you can watch that app if that specific channel is included in your cable, satellite, or live streaming video service package. You're prompted to enter the name of your TV provider and your account information—username or email address and password. If you do not have a paid TV subscription, you won't be able to view content within the app.

Entering information about your paid TV provider into the HGTV app.

Once everything is set up and you're logged in, watching a streaming video is as easy as selecting the program you want to watch. Most apps let you browse or search for specific programs; once you've started viewing, you can pause, fast forward, or rewind the program as you like.

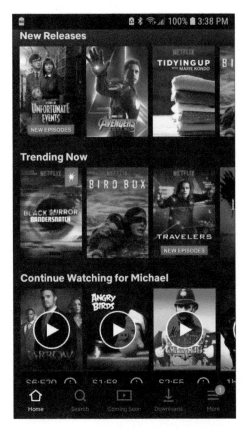

Browsing content in the Netflix mobile app.

>>>Go Further

SCREEN SIZE AND ORIENTATION

Some people love watching movies and TV shows on their smartphones. Others find that the typical smartphone screen is too small for enjoyable viewing. For this reason, many people prefer watching video entertainment on their iPads and other tablets; the larger tablet screen may be just right for watching shows whether you're out and about or lounging in bed.

Whichever kind of device you're using, remember to turn the device sidewise (horizontal) when you're viewing videos. With this orientation, widescreen displays fill up the entire device screen.

Watching Streaming Videos in Your Computer's Web Browser

Most streaming video services let you stream their content over the Internet from any web browser. This is how you watch movies and TV shows on your computer—just open your browser, navigate to the service's website, and click the Play button.

Web Browser on Your Mobile Device

Watching via web browser isn't limited to computers. Although the most convenient way to watch streaming video on your phone or tablet is via that service's streaming app, you also can watch from that service's website via your device's web browser.

Sign In

You can use any web browser to watch streaming video over the Internet—Apple Safari, Google Chrome, Microsoft Edge, whichever browser you prefer. Just make sure you have a good Wi-Fi connection and then navigate to the service's website.

Once there, you need to sign into your existing account or create a new account. If you already have an account, viewing over the Internet is just another perk, there's nothing more you need to pay. If you don't yet have an account, now's the time to sign up.

Signing into DC Universe from Google Chrome.

Some services are limited to those who have a paid television subscription via cable, satellite, or live video streaming service. Enter the requisite information about your paid TV provider and you should be able to watch for free.

Start Watching

Once you're in, the web interface is likely to be similar to that on your Smart TV or streaming media player. You can search or browse for the program you want, then click the Play button to start playback.

Browsing CBS All Access in Google Chrome.

While you're watching a program, you can use your mouse to pause, rewind, or fast forward as necessary. Make sure to click the "full screen" button to view the program full screen on your computer.

Full Screen button

Watching a program in Google Chrome—click the Full Screen button to view full screen.

Mirroring and Casting to Your TV

What do you do when you're watching something on your mobile device or computer and decide it would look a lot better viewed on your big living-room TV? The solution is to send what's displayed on your device's screen to your nearby television screen. There are two ways to do this.

The first approach, called *screen mirroring*, replicates your device's screen on your TV screen; that is, your TV "mirrors" whatever your device is doing. With screen mirroring, you can display virtually any content from your mobile device or computer on your TV screen—not just videos, but photos, documents, and other apps.

The second approach is called *casting*, and it's app specific; that is, when you "cast" an app from your mobile device or computer to your TV, whatever is playing in that app appears on your TV screen. You can't cast just anything, however; it works only with content from compatible apps. For example, you can cast a video from the YouTube app on your phone to your nearby TV and control the playback from the YouTube app.

Mirroring and casting require both your mobile device or computer and your TV to be connected to your home Wi-Fi network. In most instances, once you get everything set up (which involves wirelessly connecting your app to your TV or streaming device, within the app), getting started is as simple as tapping an icon within an app and then watching the selected content appear on your TV screen. You then control playback from the app on your device, from the comfort of your couch or easy chair.

Casting with Google Chromecast

Perhaps the easiest way to cast video content is with a Google Chromecast device. We discussed Chromecast in Chapter 6, "Getting Streaming Media Devices," so turn there for more detail. In general, the Chromecast is a device that plugs into one of your TV's HDMI connections and hangs off the back of your TV. You cast to the Chromecast from any compatible app on your smartphone, tablet, or your computer (via the Chrome web browser). The device is easy to connect and works very well with a wide variety of streaming media apps and services.

Casting to a Roku Device

If you have a Roku streaming box or stick, you can cast directly from selected streaming apps (such as Netflix and YouTube) on your phone or tablet to your TV. The instructions here show how it works with an Android phone, but the steps are similar if you have an iPhone or iPad.

1. Before you cast, you first must connect your phone or tablet to your Roku stick or box. You do this by launching the Roku mobile app on your mobile device and then choosing your Roku player.

2. Launch the mobile streaming app you want to cast from, and then tap the casting icon. (This icon might not appear until you begin playback in some apps.)

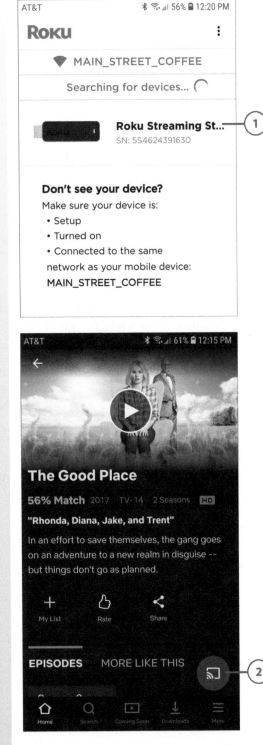

(3) Select your Roku device from the list of available devices. The corresponding channel launches on your Roku device and playback commences.

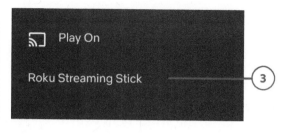

>>>Go Further
CASTING PERSONAL MEDIA FILES TO ROKU

If you want to cast your personal videos, photos, or music stored on your phone, use the Play on Roku feature. This enables you to use the Roku mobile app to cast media files from your mobile device to your TV screen, via your Roku streaming box or stick.

From within the Roku mobile app on your phone or tablet, tap the Photos+ icon in the navigation bar. Tap either Videos, Photos, or Music, and then choose which items you want to share on your TV.

Mirroring to a Smart TV or Streaming Media Player

If you have an Android phone or tablet or a Windows PC, you can use the Miracast technology to mirror your device's screen on an Amazon Fire TV or Roku box or stick. Miracast also is supported by many Smart TVs. (Miracast is *not* supported on Apple TV boxes, iPhones, or iPads.)

The exact steps you take differ a bit from device to device, but in general you should follow these steps.

1. On your Smart TV or streaming media player, enable screen mirroring. For example, on a Fire TV device, select Settings, Display & Sounds, Enable Display Mirroring. (For a Roku device, you first have to launch the Roku app on your mobile app and connect to your Roku.)

2. On your Android device, enable the screen mirroring feature. How you do this (and what they call it) differs from manufacturer to manufacturer; on Samsung phones, for example, pull down from the top of the screen and tap Smart View.

3. Select your Smart TV or streaming media player from the list of available devices.

4. If you see a mirroring request on your Smart TV or streaming player, select Allow.

Amazon Prime Video on Fire TV

Not surprisingly, devices and apps from the same company work together quite well. If you want to cast a video from the Amazon Prime Video app to an Amazon Fire TV device, all you have to do is tap the Watch on Fire TV *Device* button on the video's main screen, where *Device* is your specific Fire TV device.

Casting to an Apple TV

Apple has its own ecosystem for casting content from its mobile devices and computers to an Apple TV box, using the company's proprietary AirPlay technology. This means if you have an iPhone or iPad and an Apple TV device, everything is all set up for you to use.

1. On your iPhone or iPad, swipe in toward the center of the screen from the top-right corner to display the Control Center.

2. Tap Screen Mirroring.

3. From the list of available devices, tap your Apple TV device.

4. The screen of your iOS device appears on your TV. Select a video and start playing it; you see it full-screen on your TV. You can control the playback of the video from your mobile device.

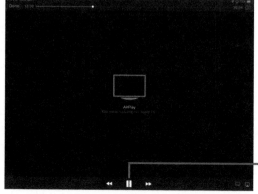

>>>*Go Further*

PHYSICALLY CONNECTING YOUR COMPUTER TO YOUR TV

Wireless casting might work fine for you, but if you have a laptop or desktop computer, you can get faster, more reliable performance by physically connecting your computer to your television set. You do this the same way you connect a standard computer monitor to your PC.

Most computers today, both desktop and laptop models, have HDMI outputs. Connect one end of the HDMI cable to the HDMI connector on your computer and the other end of the cable to an HDMI input on your television. (Some smaller laptops use a mini-HDMI output, which requires an adapter to connect to a full-size HDMI cable.)

Standard-sized HDMI connector on a laptop PC.

Then you need to switch your TV to that HDMI input. What was on your computer screen should now show on your TV. (In Windows, you also might need to right-click the screen, select Display Settings, and then select the external display.)

To view streaming video, launch your computer's web browser, navigate to your favorite streaming site, and start playback. Make sure you select your browser's full-screen option, and you'll be watching movies from your computer on your TV display.

Improving Streaming Performance

Whether you're watching streaming videos in your home or at a Wi-Fi hotspot, there are things you can do to improve the performance of what you're streaming. If your videos pause unexpectedly, stutter, or just won't play, check out these tips to get the show going again.

Connect via Wi-Fi, Not Cellular

It's always better to connect your phone or tablet to the Internet via a Wi-Fi connection, whether that's your home wireless network or a public Wi-Fi hotspot. Most Wi-Fi networks are faster than cellular connections; slower connections can cause your picture to hang up or pixelate. In addition, when you connect via Wi-Fi you're not using your cellular provider's data plan, which can be costly if you go over your monthly allocation.

If you're watching videos on your computer at home, it's even better if you can connect to your router via Ethernet cable instead of wirelessly. Ethernet is even faster than Wi-Fi and not prone to wireless dropouts. (Most computers have Ethernet connections; phones and tablets do not.)

Move to a Different Location

When it comes to making a wireless connection, location is everything. If you're too far away from the wireless router or Wi-Fi hotspot, the signal deteriorates and slows down or drops out entirely. If you're having trouble connecting (which can cause your movie to stutter or stop), move closer to the router.

Similarly, objects in between your device and the router or hotspot can disrupt the signal. Don't put too many walls or doors or big solid objects in the way— and if they are in the way, either move them or your device or router.

Reboot Your Router and/or Modem

If you're having streaming issues at home, the problem might be your wireless router. The quick solution for many such problems is to reboot the router—that is, unplug the router, wait about 15 seconds, and then plug it back in. When it cycles back up, it should be running fine again.

It's also possible that the issue is with the modem supplied by your Internet service provider (ISP). Reboot (unplug and replug) the modem to see if that fixes things.

(If your ISP provides a combination modem and router—called a *gateway*—then reboot this device, instead, also by unplugging and replugging it.)

Close Other Running Apps

Your phone or tablet can get bogged down if too many apps are running either in the foreground or background. Playing a video is an intensive activity, so you need all the processing power at your disposal. Oftentimes you can speed up your video viewing by closing any apps you have running on your device.

The same holds true for watching videos on your computer. Close other applications and browser tabs so that the video you're watching has access to all your computer's power.

Clear Your Browser's Cache

Smartphones and tablets store frequently used pages and data in *temporary files* or a *cache*. When you accumulate too many temporary files, your device can slow down, which can affect the streaming videos you view.

To improve your device's performance, you need to delete these temporary files—what some call clearing the cache. How you do this depends on your device.

On Android devices, tap the Settings button, select Device Maintenance, and then select Storage. On the Storage page, tap Clean Now to clear the cache.

On Apple iOS devices, tap Settings, Safari, and then Clear History and Website Data. When prompted, tap Clear.

On your computer, you can get a similar potential speed boost by clearing your browser's cache. Again, how you clear the cache depends on your specific browser.

In Google Chrome, select the Customize and Control button (the three dots), and then select Settings, Advanced, Clear Browsing Data, Cached Images and Files.

In Microsoft Edge, select Settings and More (the three dots), and then select Settings; in the Clear Browsing Data section, click Choose What to Clear. Select Cached Data and Files and then click Clear.

>>>*Go Further*

ENTERTAINING YOUNGER VIEWERS

If you have younger kids or grandkids, you're familiar with the cry of "I'm bored!" Fortunately, in today's world of streaming video, you can alleviate the situation and entertain the youngsters by handing them your phone and pulling up a kid-friendly video app.

In my household, the kids' app of choice is DisneyNOW, which is available for both Android and iOS phones and tablets. (It's also for Amazon Fire TV, Apple TV, Google Chromecast, and Roku streaming media players. Refer to Chapter 6, "Getting Streaming Media Devices.") The DisneyNOW app is great because it consolidates programming from all of Disney's channels—the main Disney Channel, Disney Junior, and Disney XD—along with music from Radio Disney.

That means there's plenty of entertainment for kids of all ages. For my four-year-old grandson, it's *PJ Masks* and *Puppy Dog Pals* from Disney Junior. For my fifth- and sixth-grade grandkids, it's family-oriented comedies like *Bunk'd* and *Liv and Maddie* from the Disney Channel. There's something for everyone, and that's great.

Not surprisingly, all the other kids' networks have streaming apps, as well. Check your device's app store for Cartoon Network, Nick, Nick Jr., PBS Kids Video, and other similar apps—including the DisneyNOW app, of course. And to help your children and grandchildren make smart media choices, check out Common Sense Media (www.commonsensemedia.org), a website that reviews and recommends kids' apps, games, movies, and more.

A

What's Playing Where

The following table is a guide to the best services offering various types of programming. (All programming is subject to change, of course.)

	Local Channels	Local Diginets	Broadcast Networks	Cable/ Satellite Networks	Cable/ Satellite On-Demand	Streaming Services	DVD/ Blu-ray
British Television			**Yes** PBS	**Yes** BBC America	**Yes**	**Yes** Acorn TV BritBox	**Yes**
Children's Programs	**Yes**	**Yes** PBS Kids Qubo	**Yes** (Saturday mornings)	**Yes** Boomerang Cartoon Network Disney channels Nickelodeon	**Yes**	**Yes** Boomerang Cartoon Network Disney Nickelodeon Other apps	**Yes**
Classic Movies		**Yes** Charge! Comet GetTV Grit Movies! This TV		**Yes** AMC Retroplex TCM		**Yes** Fandor WatchTCM	**Yes**
Classic TV Programs		**Yes** Antenna TV Bounce TV Charge! Comet Cozi TV Decades GetTV Grit Heroes & Icons Laff MeTV Retro TV This TV		**Yes** (various)		**Yes** Amazon Crackle Hulu Netflix Shout TV	**Yes**

	Local Channels	Local Diginets	Broadcast Networks	Cable/ Satellite Networks	Cable/ Satellite On-Demand	Streaming Services	DVD/ Blu-ray
Current Movies				Yes Cinemax HBO Showtime Starz The Movie Channel	Yes	Yes Amazon Hulu Netflix	Yes
Current TV Programs			Yes	Yes (various)	Yes	Yes Amazon CBS All Access Hulu Netflix	
Documentaries	Yes World	Yes PBS	Yes	Yes HBO	Yes	Yes Amazon Fandor Netflix	Yes
Foreign and Independent Movies				Yes TCM		Yes Amazon Fandor IndieFlix MUBI Netflix	Yes
Game Shows	Yes	Yes Bounce TV Buzzr	Yes	Yes GSN		Yes Amazon Hulu	
How-To Programs	Yes Create Ion Life YouToo America	Yes PBS	Yes	Yes Cooking Channel DIY Food Network HGTV	Yes	Yes Amazon YouTube	Yes
Local Programs	Yes						

	Local Channels	Local Diginets	Broadcast Networks	Cable/Satellite Networks	Cable/Satellite On-Demand	Streaming Services	DVD/Blu-ray
News and Weather	Yes	Yes WeatherNation	Yes	Yes CNN FNC MSNBC Weather Channel		Yes ABC News CBS News CNNgo FNC Haystack TV NBC News NewsON Newsy WeatherNation	
Reality and Competition Programs		Yes YouToo America	Yes	Yes (various)	Yes		
Science, Nature, and History Programs				Yes Animal Planet Discovery Channel History Channel Science Channel	Yes	Yes Animal Planet Go Discovery GO History SciGo	Yes
Sports	Yes	Yes Rev'n Stadium	Yes	Yes ESPN FSN regional sports networks major league packages	Yes	Yes beIN Sports CBS Sports HQ Fox Sports fuboTV NBC Sports Stadium regional sports networks major league packages	

Glossary

1080i A form of high-definition (HD) television with a resolution of 1,080 horizontal lines displayed in an interlaced fashion.

1080p A form of high-definition (HD) television with a resolution of 1,080 horizontal lines displayed progressively. Also known as *full HD*.

16:9 The widescreen aspect ratio (16 units wide by 9 units high) used in broadcast HD television.

4:3 The squarish aspect ratio (4 units wide by 3 units high) used in standard-definition (SD) television.

4K A form of *Ultra HD* with a resolution of 3,840 × 2,160 pixels.

720p A form of high-definition (HD) television with a resolution of 720 horizontal lines displayed progressively. Also known as *HD ready*.

8K A form of *Ultra HD* with a resolution of 7,680 × 4,320 pixels.

A/V receiver See *audio/video receiver*

Amazon Fire TV Amazon's line of streaming media players and Smart TVs.

Amazon Prime Video Amazon's streaming video service.

analog television   Pre-HD television, the original technology used to broadcast television signals over the air.

Android   Google's mobile operating system, used in phones and tablets.

Android TV   Google's operating system for Smart TVs.

Apple TV   Apple's streaming media player.

aspect ratio   The ratio of the width to the height of a screen or picture.

audio/video receiver   A component in a home theater system that routes, decodes, and amplifies both audio and video signals.

basic cable   The selection of channels included in the standard subscription packages offered by cable television providers.

Blu-ray   A DVD format designed for high-definition programming.

broadcast television   One of the major television networks—ABC, CBS, CW, Fox, and NBC—that broadcast their programming via local television stations.

cable television   Television that is transmitted via physical cable, not over the air.

cast   See *screen casting*

closed captions   Subtitles for a program, displayed onscreen.

DBS   Short for *direct broadcast satellite*, a technology that enables the transmission of television signals from an orbiting satellite to a small receiving dish.

diginet   Short for *digital network*, a television network broadcast over local digital subchannels.

digital network   See *diginet*

digital television   The current form of television transmission, where all signals are digital in nature.

digital video recorder   See *DVR*.

direct broadcast satellite   See *DBS*

DirecTV   One of two companies offering satellite television services in the United States.

DISH Network   One of two companies offering satellite television services in the United States.

Dolby Atmos   A new type of surround sound that adds "height" to the audio experience.

Dolby Digital   One of the current standards for surround sound, with 5.1-channel surround.

Dolby Vision   Dolby's proprietary HDR technology.

DTS   One of the current standards for surround sound, with 5.1-channel surround.

DTS:X   A new type of surround sound that adds "height" to the audio experience.

DVD   A digital optical disc typically used to store movies and other video content in standard-definition format.

DVR   Short for *digital video recorder*, a device or service that records OTA, cable, satellite, or streaming television programming.

edge lighting   Lighting in an LCD display that uses LEDs along the edge of the display for backlighting.

elevation speaker   In a Dolby Atmos or DTS:X audio system, speakers firing upward or downward to provide the illusion of height.

Ethernet   The cabling used to physically connect devices in a network.

e-waste   Short for *electronic waste*, old electronics devices that cannot be recycled in a traditional fashion.

FALD   Short for *full-array local dimming*, a display with full-array backlighting and local dimming.

fiber optic service   See *FIOS*

FIOS   Short for *fiber optic service*, a type of cable system where content is transmitted over fiber optic cable instead of traditional copper cable.

full HD   Another term for *1080p* high-definition television.

full-array backlighting   An LCD display that uses LED backlighting with local dimming.

gateway   A device, typically provided by an Internet service provider, that functions as both a modem and router.

Google Chromecast   Google's streaming media player.

HD   Short for *high definition*, a video signal or display with significantly higher resolution than standard definition television. HD may be either 720p, 1080i, or 1080p resolution.

HD ready   Another term for *720p* high definition.

HDMI   Short for *high-definition multimedia interface*, an interface for transmitting digital audio/video content. Most electronics devices today are connected via HDMI cables.

HDMI ARC   An HDMI connection that also can function as an audio output for sound bars and audio/video receivers. (ARC stands for *audio return channel*.)

HDR   Short for *high dynamic range*, a technology that produces a brighter picture with higher contrast levels.

HDR10   A popular HDR technology.

Hulu   A popular online streaming video service.

Internet service provider   See *ISP*

iOS   Apple's operating system for mobile devices, used in iPhones and iPads.

ISP   Short for *Internet service provider*, a company that delivers Internet service to homes and businesses.

LCD display   A flat-screen television or computer display that uses liquid crystal technology.

LED display   A type of LCD display that incorporates LED backlighting.

letterbox   A technique for presenting widescreen movies on less-wide displays; the original aspect ratio is preserved by surrounding the picture by black bars at the top and bottom of the screen.

LFE   Short for *low-frequency effects*, an audio channel devoted to deep, low bass sounds, typically played through a separate subwoofer.

live streaming service   An online service that streams live programming from broadcast, cable, and satellite networks.

local dimming   A type of LCD display that uses LEDs behind the screen for backlighting.

mirror   See *screen mirroring*.

modem   A device that translates signals from an Internet service provider for use with a computer or router.

Netflix   A popular online streaming video service.

OLED   Short for *organic light-emitting diode*, a type of display in which a film made from an organic compound emits light in response to electric current. OLED displays produce blacker blacks and brighter colors than competing LCD displays.

on-demand   A service that offers video programming whenever you choose, not on a predetermined broadcast schedule.

OTA   Short for *over the air*, referring to television signals broadcast from a local station to nearby households.

OTA antenna   A passive device used to receive over-the-air television transmissions from local channels.

OTT   Short for *over the top*, a live TV streaming service that broadcasts "over the top" of the Internet, not via airwaves or cable.

pay cable   Those individual channels offered by cable television providers that require an additional paid subscription.

pillarbox   A technique for presenting standard aspect ratio content on widescreen displays; the original aspect ratio is preserved by sandwiching the picture with black bars on either side.

pixel   Short for "picture element," a single point on a television or computer display.

premium cable   The selection of channels included in enhanced subscription packages offered by cable television providers.

QLED   Short for *quantum dot LED*, an LCD display technology that uses small filters ("quantum dots") to produce deeper black levels and an enhanced color range.

resolution   The number of pixels that compose the picture on a television or computer display. The higher the resolution, the sharper the picture.

Roku   A popular streaming media player.

router   A device that distributes a network signal to multiple devices.

satellite television   Television that is transmitted via orbiting satellites to ground-based receiving dishes.

screen casting   Playing the content from a mobile device on a television.

screen mirroring   Replicating the entire content of a mobile device's screen on a television display.

SD   Short for *standard definition*, the older television standard with 640 × 480 pixel resolution.

Smart TV   A television set that can receive and play streaming video from the Internet.

sound bar   An array of two or more speakers in a single enclosure, typically positioned underneath a television screen.

streaming media player   A device that connects to a television set to receive and play streaming video over the Internet.

streaming video   Video content that is transmitted over the Internet for playback in real time.

subchannel   A separate digital channel transmitted from a local broadcaster on the same radio frequency as its main channel.

subwoofer   A powered speaker that reproduces low-frequency signals.

surround sound   A method of surrounding the listener with audio from multiple sides, using multiple speakers.

tvOS   The operating system used in Apple TV devices.

Ultra HD (UHD)   Short for *Ultra High Definition*, a video signal or display with a minimum resolution of 3,840 × 2,160 pixels. Ultra HD is currently available in both 4K and 8K resolution.

upscaling   The technique of converting a lower-resolution video signal into a higher-resolution version.

VOD   Short for *Video on Demand*, any existing (non-live) programming available for streaming at the viewer's request.

widescreen   A display in which the width is significantly larger than its height.

Wi-Fi   A networking technology for transmitting data wirelessly.

Index

B

U

V

W